FOR THE
LIFE OF
YOUR DOG

Also by Greg Louganis
Breaking the Surface (with Eric Marcus)

Also by Betsy Sikora Siino
You Want a What for a Pet?!
Dogs on the Web (with Audrey Pavia)
The Siberian Husky: An Owner's Guide to a Happy Healthy Pet
Alaskan Malamutes: A Complete Pet Owner's Manual
Samoyeds: A Complete Pet Owner's Manual
The Complete Idiot's Guide to Choosing a Pet
The Hamster: An Owner's Guide to a Happy Healthy Pet
Arabian Spirit
Thoroughbred Spirit
Quarter Horse Spirit
American Eskimos
Paws for Fun (with Virginia Parker)
Lippizaner Spirit
Clydesdale Spirit

FOR THE LIFE OF YOUR DOG

A COMPLETE GUIDE
TO HAVING A DOG IN YOUR LIFE,
FROM ADOPTION AND BIRTH
THROUGH SICKNESS AND HEALTH

GREG LOUGANIS
AND BETSY SIKORA SIINO

POCKET BOOKS
NEW YORK LONDON TORONTO SYDNEY TOKYO SINGAPORE

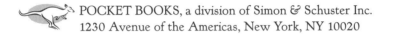 POCKET BOOKS, a division of Simon & Schuster Inc.
1230 Avenue of the Americas, New York, NY 10020

ISBN: 0-671-02450-7

First Pocket Books hardcover printing February 1999

10 9 8 7 6 5 4 3 2 1

POCKET and colophon are registered trademarks of
Simon & Schuster Inc.

All photographs by Greg Louganis (or in his collection with control of rights)
unless otherwise indicated.

Designed by Joseph Rutt

Printed in the U.S.A.

✖/RRDH

To my four-legged family:
Donna and Ryan, who taught me so much in their lives and
their deaths, along with Freeway and Nipper, who are
continuing to teach me.
And to Finnegan, without whom
this book never would have happened.

CONTENTS

THE DOGS IN MY LIFE

In 1995, I published *Breaking the Surface,* a book about my life: my family, my career as an Olympic diver, my identity as a gay man, and my struggles with HIV. Also revealed in that book was my love of dogs. Now I am expanding on this theme, devoting, as I have always dreamed of doing, an entire book inspired by my family of dogs, a book devoted to the care of dogs, from birth to old age.

I owe this book to my dogs and to dogs everywhere. Dogs have always been important players in my life. Sometimes I think I may even owe them my life. Living with HIV, I have come to know personally and intimately the exquisite power of the human/animal bond. I don't need scientific research studies to tell me that when you share a special relationship with animals—in my case dogs—your outlook improves, you enjoy a more fulfilling life, and most significantly, you are better equipped to heal and to fight off disease. There seems to be a direct link between the human/animal bond and the human immune system, and I have been a beneficiary of that link.

There have been times when I wanted to give up, but my dogs have always been there for me, cheering me on, giving me a reason for getting out of bed in the morning. I can honestly say that at times these animals, my lifelines and my protectors, have saved my life just as profoundly, just as miraculously, as the medications I take every day. I couldn't have made it without them.

I am honored to have the opportunity to introduce you to the wonderful animals that have done so much for me: the dogs in my life. What follows is a list of my kids, dogs I have both owned and co-owned.

Because my extended canine family is rather large, here they are, with their awards, dates of birth, and where applicable, dates of death.

FIRST, THE DANES:

FREEWAY: my first harlequin Great Dane, whelped March 9, 1989, and still hanging in with me.

RYAN LUKE: Freeway's half brother, my deaf gentle giant, a white Great Dane, March 9, 1990–March 1998.

LEILANI: a Boston-marked Great Dane, June 3, 1989–October 1995.

THEN THREE FROM THE SAME LITTER:

DONNA: a harlequin Great Dane, Canadian Champion, owner-handled, December 11, 1991–March 11, 1996.

BRUTUS: Donna's brother, a harlequin Great Dane, whelped December 11, 1991.

HEIDI: Donna's sister, a harlequin Great Dane, whelped December 11, 1991.

JOHN-JOHN: Heidi's son, a Boston-marked Great Dane, whelped June 24, 1996.

LAMBCHOP: a harlequin Great Dane, American Champion, whelped June 15, 1991.

JASMINE: a Boston-marked Great Dane, whelped October 21, 1995.

MURPHY: a harlequin Great Dane, whelped July 7, 1995.

AND MY OTHER WONDERFUL DOGS:

TEXAS: a tricolored Pembroke Welsh Corgi (co-owned), American and Canadian Champion, a Best in Show winner, who ranked as high as third in the nation, Award of Merit winner at the Westminster Kennel Club Dog Show, whelped September 13, 1991. (Photo copyright Ashbey Photography)

TREV'R: a sable Pembroke Welsh Corgi (co-owned), American and Canadian Champion, whelped October 1991. (Photo courtesy of Kathleen and Rick Mallery)

TURBO: a Rhodesian Ridgeback (co-owned), American Champion, who ranked as high as third in the nation and won Best of Breed at the Westminster Kennel Club Dog Show, whelped April 6, 1994.

AND MY BABIES:

NIPPER: a black-and-white Jack Russell Terrier, whelped June 15, 1997, who is aspiring to agility and obedience competition.

SPEEDO: a Bouvier des Flandres, who is aspiring to obedience competition and conformation showing, whelped July 7, 1997.

MIKEY: my Border Terrier, whelped May 27, 1997.

Now that you have met the dogs in my life, I invite you to read on in hopes that my experiences with them—and their profound effects on me—will offer some valuable insight for you, and for the life of your dog.

Greg Louganis

FOREWORD

On the first day that Greg Louganis and I began working on this book, we drove down Pacific Coast Highway near his home in Malibu, California. It was a cool February afternoon, a clear and sunny break in the legendary El Niño storms of 1998. We were discussing our favorite subject—dogs—when suddenly Greg's radar kicked in. Almost unconsciously, his gaze zoomed in on a small dog standing dazed and disoriented in the middle of the highway. In an equally involuntary reaction, and despite considerable traffic, Greg pulled the car over to the side of the road, jumped out, and swept the frightened little creature up into his arms and out of danger.

When not cooing to the small dog, who had responded to him as if she had known him since she was a puppy, Greg growled about whoever it was that had allowed her to wander into that life-threatening situation. Thanks to a collar and tag, he located that individual—a merchant in a shop along PCH—but before handing the precious package over, he made it abundantly clear to the owner that inattention, negligence, and jeopardizing your dog's life are patently unacceptable. I had a feeling that the man would never let his dog out of his sight again.

That event gave me a clear and, as I would discover, accurate glimpse of the person with whom I was launching a canine book project. I took it as a sign: saving a dog's life—that's a pretty good omen. I had seen the man in action, and I knew then and there that this book would blossom into the labor of love that Greg had always dreamed of. Many months—and several Greg Louganis dog rescues—later, with finished product in hand, I see that my premonition has come true, that the sign was on the mark.

I suspected this would be a special project even before we crossed paths with that little dog. For more than a decade I have written professionally about animals: more than a dozen books and hundreds of articles for the likes of *Dog Fancy, Dogs USA, Pet Health News, AKC Gazette,* and *Horse Illustrated* magazines. Considering the dog my most inspiring muse, I was honored to be invited to collaborate with Greg on a book about living with dogs from puppyhood to old age. Greg is an Olympic gold medalist and author of a *New York Times* best-seller, but what he is most proud of are his accomplishments in the arena of dog care and communication.

As a veteran of what is referred to as the dog world, I have long been aware of Greg's involvement with dogs and his genuine affection for the species. What I have learned from Greg since our collaboration has happily validated what I had always suspected about him. The entire planet knows Greg for his diving and his gold medals, but what readers will discover from this book is that his first love, his highest calling, is the care and understanding of dogs—his and everyone else's.

Greg's all-encompassing embrace of the canine species, and the sensitivity he has developed from managing a house full of dogs he regards as family, have made him quite an expert through the years. Approaching the challenges and joys of living with dogs with a determination equal to that which propelled him to Olympic greatness, Greg has emerged fluent in the canine language, with a holistic body of knowledge of great value to others who share his passion for the dogs.

This book is the manifestation of that passion. In addition, it's an enjoyable read, populated by the dogs in Greg's life, past and present, and his often humorous, often heartbreaking, always heartfelt experiences. Regarding living with dogs as a privilege, Greg seeks to understand the unique way in which dogs view the world and their place in it. This admirable trait is evident in his care of his own dogs, in his insight into the dogs he meets on the street, and in his unabashed concern and affection for the dog family at large. Given his pure intentions, I am pleased to be a part of this book, and I believe that dogs will be better off for its having been written—and for having Greg Louganis in their corner.

Betsy Sikora Siino

MY LIFE WITH DOGS

I will always be grateful to a dog named Dolly. She was a Great Dane. But more than that, she embodied the word *mother* and the heart of what makes a great dog.

I met Dolly one afternoon when I was looking for a harlequin Great Dane puppy. I had retired from diving and was ready to take on the full-time responsibility of dog ownership that was impossible while I was competing. Previous experience with Danes had led me back to this elegant, sweet-tempered breed—and to Dolly.

There she was, surrounded by her brood of adorable pups. You could see in her eyes that they were her prides, her joys, her reasons for living. She invited me in to meet her family, and she seemed to know innately that my intentions were honorable. She captured my heart, and because of that, so did her puppies.

I suspected that Dolly's puppies would not only genetically inherit a beautiful disposition from their mother, but also reap the benefits of her incredible mothering skills. One of those puppies ended up coming to live with me—Freeway—a dog that is still with me as of this writing and is pictured on the cover of this book. Blessed with the signature temperament of his family line, Freeway has made his mother proud throughout his life, teaching her lessons to me and to all the dogs who have since come to share our household.

I remain inspired by the vision of Dolly taking such tender loving care of her puppies, while at the same time inviting a complete stranger in to enjoy them. It was then that all the most important tenets of dog ownership dovetailed and became a reality for me. It was then that I

Here I am lounging around with, from left, Ryan, Brutus, and Donna, when I was inducted into the Swimming Hall of Fame in Ft. Lauderdale, Florida. My guys came along with me on the five-day drive from Southern California to Florida. It's good to have family around during the special moments of your life, even if they are the ones who attract all the attention.

acknowledged my place in the canine circle of life—a circle of tradition and mutual affection that spans back through generations and generations of dogs and the people who have loved them. I wanted to make Dolly proud.

Although that day made it official, my love and understanding of dogs began years before my fateful meeting with Dolly—it's always been as natural to me as breathing. Even when my experiences with dogs have been negative, I have tried to use them to increase my understanding of this wonderful species.

When I was twelve years old, I was visiting a friend who had two dogs: a big German Shepherd and a tiny Poodle. If there were dogs around, then that was where I wanted to be, so the first thing I wanted to do was go out into my friend's backyard to see his pets.

Well, on this particular day, my plan didn't work out so well. When I got out there, the little dog started barking, apparently more interested in protecting her domain than her larger friend was. But when the

Shepherd heard the barking, he got interested fast. He came running, and unfortunately for me, his reaction was to bite first, ask questions later. He bit me in the stomach and the back of my leg.

I hobbled home, bleeding and hurt and panicked—but not for myself. I was panicked for the dog. What would happen to him? My sister helped clean me up, and I begged her not to tell our mom what had happened. I would be fine. I just didn't want to get the dog in trouble. My sister did tell Mom, of course, and the dog did get in trouble—quarantine and all that—even though I tried and tried to tell everyone that it wasn't the dog's fault. I was in his territory, and I knew it. He was just protecting his buddy.

It may seem strange that I look back and smile now when I think about my one and only serious dog-bite incident. It might have put a lot of people off dogs for the rest of their life. I also still feel the twinge of worry about that big Shepherd and the guilt about my role in his incarceration. Like Dr. Doolittle, I have always had a deep love for animals, all animals. When I was growing up, I always wanted to have a dolphin in my pool or a horse in my backyard. I wanted to sit and talk with all the

Nipper—trendsetter, seasoned traveler, and party animal—got decked out in Dog Chic to judge "Skate, Rattle and Roll," a professional figure-skating competition in North Carolina (with a little help and input from me).

Freeway came along to help me collect money at the telethon for the Children's Hospital of Los Angeles. Philanthropist that he is, he uses his charms to their best fund-raising advantage whenever he gets the chance. How could anyone resist that face?

dogs, cats, lizards, and birds I saw when I walked to school every day.

Now when I think back to those days, I realize that I *did* talk to the animals. I took the time to listen to them, and they taught me to understand them—especially the dogs.

I remember one dog I saw in the yard of a house I passed by on the way to the junior-high-school bus stop every day. He was a white German Shepherd who was trained as a guard dog. Most of the kids were afraid of him, and some would sometimes tease him through the fence, and the dog could be pretty frightening when enraged. But that didn't stop me. Every day for a couple of months, I would sit at the corner of the chain-link fence and talk quietly to this territorial, aggressive dog, who I imagined was also lonely.

At first the big Shepherd viewed me as another intruder. He let me know with his growling and barking that trouble was in store for me if I didn't leave him alone. But I kept at it, and in time I earned his trust. I felt a great sense of accomplishment knowing he might be a little less lonely because of my attention. He began to greet me. He would run along the fence as I'd walk by, wagging his tail. I'd scratch him behind the ears, rub his nose, and know I had made a friend.

Incidents like this helped me learn to see the world through a dog's eyes, a skill that I am still striving to master today, both with my own dogs and the many, many other dogs I meet in my everyday life. Through the years, I have faced the stress of international diving competitions, the ups and downs of an acting career, the physical and emotional toll of HIV, the deaths and illnesses of family members and friends, and the strain of less-than-perfect personal relationships. My dogs have always

Here is Donna assisting me at a book signing for Breaking the Surface *in San Diego. Don't let that shy, innocent look fool you. She was always on alert—the best bodyguard I ever had.*

been there for me with unconditional love and protection. That's what dogs do. Making us feel safe, loved, and healthy is what they were born to do. It's their job. In return for their unswaying loyalty, it's our job to make sure they receive the finest care possible.

I've written this book to help you give your dog that kind of care. My writing a book about dogs may surprise some people. Most people know me for my diving, but my greatest passion is my dogs. They have always been. I grew up with a series of loving mixed-breed pets, and as most kids know, there isn't a more soothing and supportive confidant than a gentle, even-tempered mutt. I got to know plenty of other dogs along the way, too, some belonging to friends, some strays or dogs I would meet on the street, most of which I just couldn't resist introducing myself to.

Then, for my twenty-first birthday, I was given a black, female Great

Freeway may not be a natural show dog, but he does enjoy informal events like this one for Speedo, where he feels comfortable playing the ham. He has always been more popular than me; you have to admit he has "cute" down to a science.

Trying to keep up with all the latest developments in the dog world, Freeway visits the booths at the Long Beach Kennel Club Dog Show. He has always preferred being a spectator at shows to being a competitor.

Dane puppy, who I named Maile. She was the first dog that I was solely responsible for. Maile was my protector and my guardian angel. She is gone now, but my life was never the same after she came to live with me. Inspired by Maile's presence in my life, and the experiences of living with her, I became even more deeply involved in the world of purebred dogs a decade ago when I began showing and breeding.

Freeway, the patriarch of my canine family, launched my journey into conformation and obedience dog showing, a world even more competitive—and humbling—than Olympic diving. Just ask the Danes, the Corgis, the Doberman, the Labrador Retriever, the Pug, the Dalmatian, and the Samoyed who have so generously agreed to work with me in the show ring.

Throughout this journey, I've tried to learn all I can about breed standards, conformation, structure and movement, breeding and whelping, training and behavior, newborn-puppy care, and athletic conditioning. My instructors have been my extended family of Great Danes, gentle giants who have included Freeway, Brutus, Leilani, Donna, and my

A show dog should be both healthy and beautiful. Trev'r exhibited this when he took Winners Dog honors at the Kern County Kennel Club Show in 1994— and that's something! I was a very proud dad.

beloved Ryan, who taught me how to communicate with a dog who cannot hear. Even my newest additions, my Jack Russell Terrier, Nipper, my Bouvier des Flandres puppy, Speedo, and my sweet little Border Terrier, Mikey, are enjoying their opportunities to expand my canine education.

With these wonderful animals, I have experienced everything that living with dogs has to offer, from delivering and playing mom to newborn pups, to agonizing over the inevitable euthanasia decision, and everything in between. Through it all, my dogs have been not only fun-loving, nonjudgmental companions and confidants, but also the finest teachers and the most encouraging coaches I have ever known.

Each of my dogs is unique, and I share a special relationship with each one. I feel safe with my dogs around, and I've worked hard at being as protective of my dogs as they are of me, and at understanding them just as they try to understand me. It's a good mutual arrangement. In every sense of the word, my dogs are my family. I am proud to say that I think they view me in the same way. Sometimes they are my reason for getting up in the morning. Some of the medical treatments I've been through can be rather depressing and debilitating, and sometimes I've gotten out of bed just because I knew I had to get the dogs fed. Having a dog around really helps to motivate and ground you.

I'm never far from my dogs. We've worked on movies and commercials together, and we've traveled across the country for dog shows, television appearances, theater performances, and speaking engagements. I rarely leave the house without a dog, and if at all possible I try to bring at least one dog along on my travels—not always easy when your canine traveling companion stands three feet at the shoulder and weighs 160 pounds. But I do what I can to accommodate them, because life is just nicer with them around. Home is where my dogs are.

Sadly, too many people take dogs and their care for granted. All you have to do is throw them some kibble from time to time, make sure the water bowl is full, and maybe take them out for walks once in a while, right? People have done this for centuries. Why alter the game plan now? Well, altering that game plan is just what I intend to do.

I've always been a goal-oriented person, and my goal with this book is to educate and inspire dogs and their owners just as my dogs have always educated and inspired me, by sharing my own adventures in dog care—as well as my own victories and mistakes.

Caring for dogs properly takes a lot of work, time, and energy—even more than is required to train for a gold medal. No two dogs are alike, and no one trainer or veterinarian has all the answers. Getting to know who your dog is, is the first thing you have to do. Then, to care for your pet right—and in my mind, every dog deserves an owner who does it right—you have to be willing to commit to viewing the animal as a full-fledged, card-carrying family member. From there, you will be better equipped to be sensitive to your pet's point of view; to have a more realistic expectation of what this relationship can be; and to be open to a variety of possibilities whether they be for grooming, training, or health care. I hope this book will help.

This isn't a training book. It isn't a how-to. It's a look at caring for dogs from puppyhood to old age. You see this little puppy and you say, "Oh, how cute." But that puppy isn't going to stay a puppy and you need to be prepared to deal with the different stages he will go through during his life. We will be traveling through all of these stages in this book, and the journey will be guided by someone who has taken on the monumental, some would call nightmarish, responsibility of managing a rather large multidog household. By sharing my experiences, I hope to help you see the world through your dog's eyes. Do that, and everybody—dogs, their people, everybody—is going to be happier.

As for my own progress in this mission, it's an ongoing thing. I'm still learning, always, always. When I was diving, the ultimate goal was winning a gold medal, but the ultimate goal of becoming the perfect dog owner is unattainable. We'll never completely understand our dogs. As someone who loves dogs, I'll always keep working to do that. But trust me—join me in this, make that commitment, make that effort, and we will all discover one of the greatest treasures the world has to offer: the love of a dog.

PART ONE

A
LIFETIME
COMMITMENT

ONE

A MEMBER OF THE FAMILY

People used to accuse me of hiding behind my dogs. There was probably some truth in that. When I'm standing next to a harlequin or white Great Dane—they're pretty impressive animals—people don't notice me so much.

The first dog I remember was my grandparents' farm dog, a mutt named Curly, whom I met when I was around three years old. I would hang out with him, and even at that young age I realized I was more comfortable with Curly than with the adults. Then when I was about four or five, my family adopted Hercules, another little mutt. I felt more comfortable around him, too, because by the age of three, I was already performing onstage. In a sense, I was a trained seal having to perform, and it was nice being with someone, a quiet, friendly dog, who didn't demand that from me. My dogs have never thought of me as a performer, and I love them for that, among many other things.

Despite the fact that much of my life has been played out in the spotlight, I am by nature pretty shy. Through my work I go to a lot of social events, and I'm usually pretty nervous about them. I worry about what I'll talk about and what I'll have in common with the people there. Everyone asks what I'm up to, but I'm tired of talking about myself. I love to turn the conversation in the direction of dogs. Other people's dogs and my own. When that happens, I'm immediately more comfortable. Dogs are the perfect icebreaker, and I am most comfortable with them around—or just talking about them.

I always refer to my dogs as "the kids." It's not unusual for people to want to talk on and on about their kids, and I'm no different with mine.

The idea of dogs as surrogate kids is controversial. People will say, "Only people who don't have kids dote on their dogs so much." Well, all that counts in life is that you feel love and you give love. That's what my mom taught me, and she's proud of how I treat my kids. "When I come back in my next life," she always says, "I want to be one of Greg's dogs."

I also know what it feels like to be really proud of my "kids," and not for the reasons most people might think. When I was showing my dogs regularly, I was always so flattered when I was around the show ring and everybody would say, "Oh, your dogs are so well-behaved." As far as my dogs' conformation and my handling skills, well, they may have been saying something else about that, but it was the comments about my dogs' good manners that meant the most to me. I worked long and hard to get them into that condition. That's the highest compliment someone can give me. Compliment my dogs and you're complimenting my family.

The highest compliment my dogs can give me is to let me know that they consider me to be their family, too. Dogs know when someone in the family is hurting. I often think of when I was taking care of my dad during the last weeks of his life during his struggle with cancer. One day, I took him for a walk in his wheelchair with my Great Dane, Freeway. Freeway stayed with my dad, not at my side as he usually would. He stayed at my dad's side. When we stopped, he sat down and put his head over my father's arm, which is the dog equivalent of putting a hand on your shoulder. He knew my dad needed him. My dad reached out and petted him and said, "I wish I was more mobile so I could have a dog." I said, "Dad, we're here. He's *our* dog." Freeway knew we were all family. He knew he was comforting my father.

Anyone who has had a dog as a companion knows moments like that. It's all part of the human/animal bond, which is one of the most wonderful connections we can have. My bond with dogs has definitely had a thera-peutic effect on me. Some of the treatments I've had to go through are pretty harsh. When I feel most scared and insecure, my dogs have been there for me. They sense this and stay closer to me. When my treatments or their side effects are most debilitating, we stay in, snuggle into bed, and watch TV, and the dogs don't leave my side. Tell me dogs aren't family.

Me and my crew: Ryan with his signature T-shirt, Donna looking back to monitor the driveway entrance (always the protector), Barron (a guest—we always have canine guests around) and Pembroke Welsh Corgi Trev'r trying to make a break for it and find something to herd.

Dogs are family to millions of people around the world, but this amazing relationship doesn't happen by magic. We have to work at it. We have to learn the canine language and develop the sensitivity to think and anticipate so that we can keep ourselves and our dogs out of trouble. We have to learn to be consistent when we communicate with our dogs, and we have to help them learn their manners. There's nothing better—and I'm sure veterinarians appreciate this, as well—than a well-mannered dog.

In the pages that follow, you will meet my family, the dogs I live with now, the dogs I have lived with in the past, the dogs I've met through friends, the dogs I've met during my periodic visits to the animal shelter, and the dogs I've rescued off the street. They all have a special

It was a joyous day when I brought Ryan home to join the family. That rather large handful of puppy is only seven weeks old here, where he enjoys a warm welcome from Leilani (the sweet maternal soul on the left) and his older brother Freeway (on the right).

place in my heart. They are all part of the family. Each and every one of them has helped to make me a better companion to the canine species, as well as a better person.

A BIG DECISION

A successful relationship between your dog and you begins before you purchase or adopt your new dog. You have to get educated. Read books. Talk to breeders and shelter workers and veterinarians. You have to know what you're doing when you're choosing this new member of your family. You have to prepare yourself and know what you're getting into. It's only fair to the dog, and it's the only way that you can make sure that this relationship will last.

My situation is complicated because I choose to live with several dogs at the same time and is further complicated because I am actually allergic to some dogs. Too many people learn the hard way that having several dogs is not necessarily the best option for everyone. They ignore the research and forethought and just keep adding more dogs. They end up in a house with a bunch of dogs, and it's a disaster.

More is not necessarily merrier. It's more expensive, it's more challenging, and it can be unfair to both the new dog and to the dogs that already live with you. Someone who takes in too many dogs is called a collector, which is not a good thing to be. Many dogs out there need homes—and many need *better* homes. I see homeless and lost dogs every day. I've picked up dogs running loose along Pacific Coast Highway or in the hills near my house. I've even had them show up at my doorstep. When I find lost dogs—or they find me—I bring them home, get them fed and cleaned up, and then either take them to the shelter or track down their owners myself.

Even though I always have several dogs living in my house at a time, a lot of thought and planning goes into choosing each one and managing the place once they're there. For the most part, it's a situation that works for me. I have the time and the resources to invest, and I know how to rely on my dogs' help and input. We all work together to figure things out.

ONE DOG OR MORE?

A multidog household can be tough to deal with—not something I recommend for everyone. For most people, one dog is plenty. There is nothing better than having that one buddy to devote your time to—for you and for your dog.

When I was diving, I used to visualize each new dive in my mind before I'd try it. Now I do the same thing with my dogs. First I visualize what the situation will be like if this particular dog comes to live with us, how I will manage the whole thing, feeding, training, exercise, play, and all that. Then I try to see the situation through the eyes of each of my existing dogs. They're all individuals, and each one will have a different take on the situation.

Freeway, the old patriarch, would just as soon be an only dog. He'll tolerate the others, and he has for years. He'll just hang back patiently, knowing that eventually he'll get the attention. As for Ryan, he's gone now, but he was always accepting of anything and anyone so that nothing new really bothered him—unless, of course, it was a dog with aggression on his mind. Some of my other dogs, though, haven't been so flexible. Males usually fight over food and females in heat and then get over it. But females can fight over something as simple as a toy, and it can be permanent. That's how it was for two of my female Danes, Lambchop and Leilani. They got into it over a rawhide toy and that was it. From then on they both held a grudge and I had to keep them separated.

When I first brought home my Jack Russell Terrier, Nipper, she wreaked havoc with my two older boys, my Danes Ryan and Freeway. She would jump up in their faces and bite them as an invitation to play. But the boys, so much larger and wiser, nipped Nipper's antics in the bud right away just with a grumble and a growl—and sometimes a set of Dane jaws wrapped ever so gently around Nipper's tiny head. My dogs have always been much better trainers than I am, whether it was Ryan teaching me how to discipline puppies effectively, or Freeway getting the message through my thick skull with his hurt feelings that the traditional "jerk the chain" training method was much too harsh, and even insulting, for his very willing, cooperative nature.

EVALUATING YOUR LIFESTYLE

The first dog I had by myself was Maile, the sweet Great Dane I received as a gift when I was in college. Unfortunately, my experience with her taught me the hard lesson that college is not always the right time to get a dog. I was traveling a lot then and it just wasn't fair to her. I also didn't know as much then about canine behavior as I do now, so when I made the excuse to my college professors that the dog ate my homework, she really *did* eat my homework—as well as the couch and my shoes and a few books. Let's just say I've come a long way in my canine education since then.

But people go ahead and get dogs in college all the time. They think, "Oh, I'm away by myself, I'm on my own, I can do whatever I want—I'll get a dog." They don't think about what happens after college when they get jobs and no longer have the time to spend with the dog. They don't

Here is Freeway at his first puppy match. Even at the tender age of three months, you can see in his eyes that this whole gig just wasn't for him. It took me a while, but I finally got the message.

think about where they are going to live (wherever it is, it probably won't allow dogs). What happens to the dog then? Go visit the animal shelter in a college town. You'll see what happens.

For me, it wasn't until after I retired from diving that I got serious and decided that I now had the time and energy to take care of dogs the right way. I figured I was going through a major change in my life and I wouldn't be on the road so much. So that's when I got Freeway. He was my first great teacher. I chose him wisely and he set the stage for all the dogs that would follow.

I learned from my sad experience with Maile and my great success with Freeway that smart choices begin with the would-be owners' own soul-searching. It's important to evaluate the health and temperament of a potential pet, but it's also important to evaluate yourself and your lifestyle and what you can offer a dog in terms of exercise, attention, and health care. You have to realize that as soon as you get a dog, he will determine where and how you live from then on, for the rest of your lives together.

My dogs have even influenced what kind of cars I drive. I always want to make sure that my car or truck is big enough for all my dogs to fit into—and easy for my older dogs to get in and out of. Living in Malibu, California, I even have a disaster plan in case of an earthquake or fire. At one time I kept a fully stocked recreational vehicle in my driveway all the time in case we ever had to evacuate. You have to think ahead. If I ever had to get out quick, I wouldn't question for a minute what I would bring: the dogs. Everything else is just things, and things can be replaced—even my gold medals. But the dogs can't be replaced.

Your household decorating is another thing to consider—and your landscaping. I once made the mistake of installing natural Berber-wool carpeting in my house. It was a beautiful carpet—for about a week. If you want to live with dogs, you have to make concessions. There's no way around it. Throwing a dog out in the backyard is not the answer. Dogs want and need to be *indoors* with their human companions at least part of the time—even big dogs like Great Danes. Some home furnishings and materials are more resistant to the effects of dog hair and chewing than others, so think about this before you get a dog—and before you redecorate your house.

Dogs need to be outdoors, too, and yes, many dogs love to dig. One of my Danes, Murphy, would uproot plants just by running across the yard. Barking, too, can be a problem, and your neighbors may not be as tolerant as you are of your dog's sweet voice. But all of these natural behaviors that we call problems can be controlled. Controlling behaviors requires time, patience, and attention. We just have to be willing to deal with them in a positive way.

You also have to think about who will take care of the dog. Kids will promise forever that they will take care of the new puppy. I know how that is. I did it myself when my family adopted our little pound puppy Hercules. Even though I loved that little dog, it was my mom of course who really took care of him. A dog can be a great buddy to hang out with, but his care is a big responsibility for a little kid. My mom understood from the beginning that this was how it was going to be. And that's what parents have to do. Let the kids help out so they can learn, but remember that this is an adult responsibility.

Families with young children, military people, businesspeople who travel a lot—all of these people may want dogs, but not all of them may be able to take care of them properly. Certain dogs fit in better with certain lifestyles. You have to be honest about evaluating that to make sure you make a successful match. It's tough to give a young puppy the attention she needs if you have a newborn baby in the house. And if you have to move every two years with the military, you should avoid the temptation to get a large dog. Something like a small Poodle-mix will be a better, more convenient choice than a Great Pyrenees or a Lab-mix.

HONEST EVALUATIONS

The breed or mix of breeds you choose will make a big difference in how a dog fits into your life. If you're really active and really sports-oriented and you want a companion to jog with, then look at a Labrador Retriever or a Doberman or maybe a Shepherd-mix—that kind of dog. But you can't go into it saying, "Well, I'd like to be walking a mile a day, and that's the reason I'm getting a dog." If you're not doing it now, chances are you're not going to do it after you get a dog either.

One of my most recent additions to my canine family is a Bouvier des Flandres show puppy named Speedo. I spent a year researching her breed before I took the plunge. I was intrigued by the intelligence of the breed, which is used for police and protection work in Europe, and thought it might be a good candidate for competition obedience work. But I was worried about the grooming. A Bouv is eye-catching, but it takes a lot of work and time to keep her looking that way. I had to make sure that I would be able to keep up with the grooming. That's something else to consider for anyone who is choosing a new dog or puppy. Even short-haired dogs need regular grooming.

AVOIDING THE IMPULSE

I know how hard it is to resist a puppy, but a puppy doesn't stay a puppy forever. You have to work hard to make sure that the adult dog is healthy and well-mannered. You're not likely to be ready to do that if you purchase or adopt a dog on impulse.

When you consider getting a dog, you should expect to be together for the life of that dog. But no one is immune from the impulse. Even though I know the right way to choose a dog, I struggle with the temptation constantly. I torture myself by reading the pet classified ads every day, and I visit the animal shelter all the time, just to see who's there. I'm often so tempted to make them part of my family, and that happens with dogs I rescue, too. "Oh, she's so sweet," I say. "No one will ever adopt her. Maybe I should just take her." Then my common sense kicks in. It's hard, but you can't save the whole world. You can only give a good home to so many.

My only impulse dog was Ryan, my deaf Great Dane whom I named in honor of my dear friend Ryan White. In his case, I admit I was a sucker, feeling sorry for the poor little deaf pup, but the breeder knew we were meant to be and she knew how to push my buttons. She kept telling me to come over and see the litter. When I finally did, she picked up this little white puppy and put him in my lap. "He's deaf," she told me, "and I really don't want to put him down. I've seen you working with Freeway and I know you've done such good work. I think you'd be wonderful in taking care of this very special dog." Do I have *sucker* written on my forehead or what? Well, I took Ryan and devoted the next year of my life to working with him and training him and understanding his special needs, and I was never sorry about it for a moment of his long and happy life.

Ryan may have been an impulse, but he was not a mistake. He and I became soul mates. Being deaf, he gave me a new insight into canine body language and sharpened my sensitivity to all dogs. He passed on during the writing of this book after a long illness, and I miss him terribly, but I will always be grateful to him for what he taught me about dogs.

I'm not saying it's okay to choose a dog because you feel sorry for him. People do that all the time, and sometimes it can work out, but more often it doesn't. Ryan was no mistake, but he would have been for someone who was not prepared or willing to take care of him in the right way.

You also have to be careful not to jump in and get yourself a dog just because it's the hot new breed of the moment, the way Rottweilers or Dalmatians were a few years ago—or the way my new little girl's breed, the Jack Russell Terrier, has become.

Nipper was not an impulse buy. She came to me after months and months of research, which is now being followed by months and months of training. People come up to me to say, "Oh, she's so sweet," and, "I want a dog like that, too." "No, you don't, I tell them. No, you *don't*. You have no *idea* what you'd be getting yourself into."

When I used to go to dog shows with my Danes, people wouldn't automatically want one of their own, even though my dogs were well-behaved and wonderful. Their sheer size is a limitation. But when people see a well-behaved smaller dog whose breed they see starring in *Frasier, The Mask,* and *Wishbone,* they don't see the limitations. They don't know that Nipper almost ended up going back to her breeder, which often happens with these tenacious little dogs. They don't know how hard I worked to prevent that, how seriously I took her training. They don't see how difficult it is to get a Jack Russell to the "well-behaved" point. Most people aren't willing or able to do what it takes.

The popularity of a breed can also lead to overbreeding, which can lead to health and temperament problems. Rottweilers are one example. These were meant to be wonderful, even-tempered, stable, family-oriented dogs. I've met plenty of Rotties like that. But many inexperienced backyard breeders are breeding Rottweilers because they're popular, and I often find myself asking, "If that's a Rottweiler, why does it look like a Doberman?" You don't want to deal with the temperaments of poorly bred dogs. That's a problem with any popular breed—just ask some Dalmatian people. Now that we're seeing so many Jack Russells, I'm worried about them, too. JRTs aren't the easiest things to live with, and chances are, most of them will end up outsmarting their owners. When that happens, it's the dogs who end up the losers.

So be realistic in what you expect from a particular breed or dog. Be careful in your choice, and don't take on more than you can handle. Too many people are clueless, such as one guy with a Mastiff in one of my conformation handling classes. The dog decided to attack Freeway. My adrenaline started pumping—I would have done anything to protect my dog—and I lifted Freeway up and blocked the giant animal that was coming after him. The Mastiff clipped me in the leg instead. The dog's owner had no idea what he was doing, he had no control of the dog, and he had no business having a big, bull-headed Mastiff in the first place.

When you live with dogs, you learn quickly that the biggest danger comes from other people, people who don't pay enough attention to training and manners. My friends have pointed out that I can be pretty rude to oblivious dog owners. Call it rudeness if you want, but I have lit-tle patience for inconsiderate, insensitive humans.

WHEN YOU CAN'T HAVE A DOG

Some people just love dogs but are wise enough to know that because of their circumstances, they can't have one at present. I admire people like that, who can wait to satisfy that desire until they are better able to take care of a dog with the necessary emotion, time, and money. There are many ways you can still spend time with dogs—to get your puppy fix, as I call it.

Sometimes when I'm on the road away from my dogs, I stop in pet shops to see the puppies. (We'll discuss the sad plight of the pet-shop puppy in chapter 3.) This is an activity safest to do when I'm out of town, when I know I can't bring a puppy home. The pet-shop puppy fix can also be depressing. Some shops carry too many puppies, and you can't help but wonder about their fate. It's sad to see them marked down because they're getting too big and not selling.

Volunteering can also satisfy the need for a puppy fix. I became a volunteer for an organization called Pets are Wonderful Support (PAWS), which helps people with HIV care for their pets. Volunteering for an organization like PAWS—or one that helps older people with their pets, an animal shelter, or any group that helps animals and their people—is a great way to get a puppy fix in a positive way.

With a lot of these organizations, you have to be serious about your intentions to help. When I first contacted PAWS, I said, "Okay! Put me to work!" But I had to prove myself. Being a dog walker, for example, required being available every day, which was more of a time commit-ment than I could handle, so I decided to do grooming. I loved being a mobile grooming unit. I would show up with my brushes, my combs, my shampoos, and my nail trimmers. Usually the only problems I had were with dogs who didn't care to have their nails trimmed.

Freeway looking noble—outshining a spectacular sunrise. We're early risers at our house. My dogs have learned, as all dogs have to learn, to adapt to the rhythms and schedules of the human members of the household. In return, I make sure they always have a daily routine they can depend on.

I liked going into the people's houses to do the grooming because I could make sure the places were clean and the people were able to keep up and take care of themselves and their dogs. At the volunteer orientation, they pointed out how important it was to take a look at the person's environment—not just for the dog's well-being, but for the person's, too. It wasn't unusual to see situations where the dog was fine, but the owner needed some help. That was always how I imagined myself. It would be easier for me to ask for help for my dogs than for myself.

Another option is to get a job as a pet-sitter or even at a veterinarian's office. I had one sitter who was working toward becoming a veterinarian. Even though she wanted a dog, she knew that with all her hard work, it wasn't the right time for her to have one, so my dogs provided her puppy fix. They loved her and she loved them. Also, lots of kids want a dog but their moms and dads say no. These kids can get a great puppy fix by volunteering, maybe as dog walkers or bathers at the local shelter or animal hospital—or even in their own neighborhoods. It becomes a win-win situation all around.

TWO

A RESPONSIBLE OWNER

One day I was driving along Pacific Coast Highway on my way home, and I spotted a Chow Chow walking nonchalantly into traffic. No owner around. Just the dog. "That dog is not going to survive," I thought. Just as I always do, I stopped and picked the dog up—not necessarily a smart move since Chows can be a little unfriendly at times, but that never stops me.

This dog, unlike so many others I have found in my career as a dog rescuer, wore a collar and a registration tag, but no identification tag. I called animal control, and they said they would have the owner get in touch with me. In the meantime, I looked closely at the dog. He had been pretty from a distance, but his coat hadn't seen soap and water for a long, long time. I decided that I might as well give him a bath. It was risky, I know, because he wasn't real crazy about being in the water, but lots of time and conditioner later, he was clean and untangled again. He ended up being really sweet, and he liked the attention.

Then the dog's owner called. "Why did you take my dog?" he demanded. He was furious. I told him his dog had been walking along PCH. "No," the guy said defensively, "he couldn't have been. He wouldn't have done that. He never goes down there." Now, how was I supposed to answer that? I shrugged. Then, as much as I hated to think of that sweet Chow with this guy, I returned his dog without getting so much as a thank-you. That is the typical attitude of the irresponsible dog owner.

A responsible dog owner would not allow his dog to wander along a busy highway. If by chance the dog ended up there, he would appreciate that someone cared enough to get his pet out of that dangerous situa tion. Being a responsible owner is the cornerstone of the bond between people and their dogs.

Being responsible covers a lot of territory. The responsibilities include basic care—feeding, providing water, preventing your dog from wandering around loose—but also communication. You've got to get to know your dog, what he likes, what he doesn't like, and what he's afraid of. You've got to talk to the animals like Dr. Doolittle, but you've got to listen to them, too.

PREVENTING THE LOST DOG

Even a contented, well-monitored dog can wander away to find a bitch in heat or bolt out of fear of a fireworks display, thunder, or a siren. Once you understand these potential problems and your dog's personality traits and sensitivities, you can take action to prevent your dog from becoming a casualty.

MY PET PEEVES

There are too many examples of irresponsible dog ownership out there, and from them has come my own collection of pet peeves: things people do to and with their dogs that just drive me crazy.

Not controlling your dog. Live with a dog for a while, and one day you realize that you're always on the lookout. You look at the sidewalk when you're walking your dog to make sure there's nothing in your path that might hurt your pet's paws. You survey the landscape to see what other dogs, people, and kids might be approaching, and you examine their body language to see if their intentions are friendly. Usually you don't even realize you are doing this. Then, every once in a while, you spot trouble. In my case, that trouble is usually another dog. I guess because most of my dogs have always been so big, they bring out the Napoleon complex in smaller dogs.

One morning I was eating at a little outdoor café when a guy came around a corner with his dog—a Chow—on one of those twenty-six-foot extensible leashes. My Great Dane Freeway was on a leash in a down-stay at my feet, and he was, as usual, obeying beautifully. The guy holding the Chow's leash wasn't paying any attention at all—he was on a cell phone—and the dog charged up to Freeway with aggression obviously on his mind. He was ready to strike.

"Control your dog!" I yelled as I leaped out of my chair. The friend I was with was a little shocked at how "rude" I was about it. But is it rude to protect your dog? I don't think so. I never even thought twice about it. I didn't know the temperament of that dog. All I had to go by was his aggressive behavior and his owner's lack of control and attention. I couldn't just sit back and expect Freeway to deal with it on his own. We depend on each other. And I know that just because I am in control of my dog, I can't expect that everyone else out there will be in control of his.

ATTENTION, ATTENTION

I respect an owner who is out training and socializing a dog amid public distractions and noise, which can be frustrating and embarrassing at times. But when you are out in public training your dog, you've got to pay close attention to your dog and to all the other dogs, people, and vehicles around you. Anticipate and avert problems before they happen.

Dogs running amok. As you can probably tell from my incident with the Chow on Pacific Coast Highway, I'm not a big fan of dogs running loose in public. It's dangerous for the dogs and it can be devastating to the people they come into contact with—especially if that contact involves a car. A loose dog is a prime target for a driver who doesn't see him, and the violent result can be devastating. If your dog is hit by a car, it impacts not only the dog, but also the person who hits the dog and the passengers in that car. It's horrible to do that to somebody just because you're not paying attention.

Other safety issues are also involved. A loose dog can be stolen. In my area, a loose dog is prey for coyotes. We also have hawks, a definite danger to little dogs who are allowed to wander around without super-

Freeway consented to join me in a professional photo shoot when he was a ten-month-old adolescent. He's looking perfectly angelic here, but as soon as we were through he was off getting Leilani in trouble, conveniently forgetting all the commands he had learned and wreaking typical teenage havoc. (Photo copyright © David Cherkis)

vision. And a loose dog can result in unplanned puppies in need of homes, and we don't need any more of those. So it's your responsibility to know where your dog is all the time and to make sure that wherever that is the dog is safely confined or supervised.

A *failure to poop-scoop.* When you share your life with a large family of dogs, you get pretty used to cleaning up dog poop. You also learn quickly just how fast it can accumulate if you don't clean it up. I can never understand why so many dog owners think it's all right for the general public to walk down the street and encounter the calling cards their dogs have left behind.

For the responsible dog owner this goes beyond just the unsanitary, disease-carrying nature of it all and becomes a public relations issue. Every owner who shirks his or her cleanup responsibilities reflects badly on the rest of us who do clean up and who pride ourselves on our responsible dog care. So carry the proper supplies with you *whenever* you're out with your dog and always be a good ambassador for dog ownership.

Age-appropriate exercise. Puppies grow quickly, but we can't let ourselves be fooled by their size. Within a year, a big friendly black Lab, for example, will have reached what will probably be her full size, but she is still a puppy. She still has plenty of growing to do physically and emotionally. This is growing that you might not be able to see—the growth of bones and muscles and the strengthening of joints—all pretty critical to the dog's long-term health. If you get a dog hoping that you can teach her to jog with you or run alongside your bicycle, remember that you can't do this with a six-month-old puppy, dragging her along. Make play your pup's exercise, and let her grow up. Wait until she's physically mature to tackle the more intense stuff.

The same goes for older dogs. Sure, you can get an old dog to run with you even though he's arthritic. He'll do it because he wants to please you, but you have to be fair to the dog. If the dog can't make it through the workout or has difficulty making it, he'll feel like a failure; he'll feel that he's let you down. So exercise your puppy and exercise your older dog, but do it appropriately.

Chaining. Another accepted dog-care practice that just makes my skin crawl is the sight of a dog chained to a tree or a post or something like that. Now I'm not talking about temporary situations, say, when you are out shopping or doing something around the house and you tie the dog off briefly with a lead (assuming he's trained to tolerate that). But if you intend to use a chain daily instead of fencing, then you shouldn't get a dog. So many things can go wrong with that situation: the dog can slip his collar or be strangled by it, or the dog will just be miserable and lonely, which can lead to aggressive behavior.

An alternative is the invisible fencing that employs a special shock or sonar collar that lets a dog know when he's in a "safe zone"—and

Here I am getting sloppy kisses from Pembroke Welsh Corgi Trev'r at the Corgi National Show. Even though a dog show can be a rather intimidating event, I make sure that my dogs always remember that show dogs should be companions too. (Photo copyright © Kathleen and Rick Mallery)

when he's not. Some people find success with this "fencing" method, but there is some training involved. You can't expect your dog to figure it out on his own. Some dogs never "get it." They either can't figure it out or just don't want to. This type of confinement is not right for every dog, and long-term, permanent chaining isn't right for *any* dog.

Dogs as matchmakers. Having a dog and spending time out in public with your dog makes you part of a special club. Dogs are a great way to meet people, through formal dog clubs and activities and just out on the street. Many people are more apt to approach somebody with a dog than not because somehow the dog's being there makes the situation feel safe.

But it drives me crazy when people treat a dog not as a wonderful animal, but as a babe magnet or a guy magnet. Please don't get a dog to attract a romantic partner. That's not what dogs are for, and it's an insult to them to use them that way.

Kids running amok. You have to teach kids how to behave around

*Ch. Castell's Killin' Time—
known to his friends as Texas—
is the consummate show dog.
He loves being in the spotlight,
which was most evident when I
tended to him as kennel help at
the Westminster Dog Show in
New York City. Here at the
Corgi National you can see
where his interests are. He
seems to be telling me, "Hey,
let's go. They're calling my
class."*

dogs. I can't stand it when a kid runs up to my dog yelling and practically pounds her on the head as a way of "petting" her. Dogs hate that, and we would hate that, too. It's natural for a kid who may have met a few friendly dogs that will tolerate that treatment to assume that all dogs are that way, but they're not. Lots of kids learn that the hard way—look at the number who are bitten by dogs every year. It's just as important to teach kids their dog manners as it is to socialize the dogs they're going to be around.

I've been there: I know what it's like to be a kid who loves dogs and wants to meet every single dog he sees, but kids have to be educated. They have to be taught to approach dogs quietly and with respect, and they have to be taught to ask the owner if it's okay for them to pet the dog. They have to learn that sometimes it's not okay. These protocols protect children and make life easier for dogs. A kid who understands how to deal with dogs at the park or on the street is much less likely to become a dog-bite statistic—and less likely to get a dog in trouble.

SAFE AND SANE INTRODUCTIONS

Just as I advise kids to do, when I introduce myself to a new dog, I first ask for the owner's permission. Then I crouch down close to the dog's level and offer an open hand. The dog has the option of accepting the invitation or not. Dogs appreciate a less threatening, less dominating approach. Their owners do, too. Some dogs—terriers come to mind—can get wound up pretty easily, viewing any action as a challenge. This may look "cute" to you, but the person at the other end of the leash has to live with that behavior, and it may not be so cute to them.

LIVING UP TO YOUR DOG'S EXPECTATIONS

Dogs give us unconditional love, but we often put conditions on the love we give back to them. We have high expectations of what and who our dogs should be. We have strict rules, and we expect them to obey perfectly, 100 percent, all the time—even if we don't communicate these rules to them clearly. It can get pretty confusing and upsetting for everyone involved—especially for the dog. Often it ends with the dog being hauled off to the animal shelter, a victim of a lack of communication.

The most important thing for us to understand is that we have to be fair. We have expectations, but what about our dogs' expectations of us?

We have to work to earn our pet's respect. You can't do that by ignoring the dog, throwing him out into the backyard to entertain himself for days on end, treating him in a harsh or cruel way, or failing to communicate with him patiently, sensitively, and consistently. You can't do it by deciding that the formula for owning a dog is no more than food, water, and a backyard. Your dog expects a lot more from you than that.

I always think back to my first experiences training Freeway—and I still feel guilty about it. Freeway taught me that you have to be fair with dogs. I didn't know a lot back then about training and behavior, so I took Freeway to a class that taught the old jerk-the-chain, negative-reinforcement stuff. But every time I gave him a correction, Freeway would pout. He would lower his head, lower his ears, and go through the motions, but he wasn't enjoying it. I was correcting him overly harshly. By doing so, I was essentially betraying the trust he had already placed in me.

The problem was, I just didn't know better. But I listened to Freeway, and just as I did when I finally acknowledged that I was uncomfortable with my first overly harsh diving coach, I began to look around at other handlers. Finally I found a trainer named Karen Price, who approached each dog as an individual and used a more positive, encouraging approach. Her dogs responded beautifully, and unlike Freeway, her dogs were having fun. They *wanted* to work for her. So we began working with her.

Karen made all the difference. I am grateful to her, but I'm also grateful to Freeway for teaching me that some training methods are better for some dogs than others. It took a while for me to get the message, but Freeway never gave up on me. Among other virtues, Freeway taught me patience.

Freeway taught me how to listen to dogs. There's always a reason for their behavior, and you can discover it if you pay attention. People are usually at the root of any dog's problems, and during Freeway's early training, I was the problem. Dogs never lie. People often do. Listen to dogs and you'll find the answers, and you'll become your dog's hero.

Freeway taught me how to listen, but all my dogs taught me to be consistent. You must always strive to be consistent with the commands you use in training, the corrections you give and the situations you give them for, and the rules you set down for the dog. Many people get a new puppy and let the cute little puppy play on the couch. When the puppy grows up, they don't want him on the couch anymore, but the growing puppy doesn't understand why he was allowed there yesterday but not today. This is the quickest way to confuse a dog. If you train yourself to be consistent from day one and resist the temptation to allow unacceptable behaviors, your dog will appreciate it more than he will appreciate coddling.

However, you can also introduce changes gradually. Changes in diet and household routine are not so traumatic if you can see the situation through your dog's eyes and learn your dog's language. One of my favorite things to do is to put myself in my dog's position in a certain situation and try to guess what his or her reaction would be. If you're at all empathic, you can usually figure out what's probably going on in the dog's head.

Finally, dogs expect us to treat them humanely, to try to see their point of view, and to give them attention and affection every day. Often, they are much wiser than we are. They understand what it takes to maintain a relationship, and they struggle daily to understand us. They never give up on us, even when we only make half the effort that they do. If we could love each other the way dogs love us, there would be no divorce. Think about it.

THE BASICS

Food, water, shelter: it's not too hard to meet those basic needs of a dog, but the responsibility does not end there. Attention, exercise, and training are all part of it, too. If you're going to own a dog responsibly, your time will no longer completely be your own. You will have to devote part of each day to your dog, and you will have to make lifestyle decisions based on your pet. My dogs influence my decisions on where I live, what I drive, and even how I schedule my days. Like many dog owners, I like it that way.

When people consider the basic rules of responsible dog care, training should come to mind as naturally as feeding does. You have to do the groundwork with your dog from day one with training and socialization and make sure that the dog is adaptable to all kinds of situations and environments. Moving, kenneling, the arrival of a new family member (canine or human), an emergency evacuation: you never know what might happen down the road. Preparing your dog to tolerate change is like an insurance policy you can give to your pet. Things are going to come up and you'll feel better knowing that both you and your dog can deal with it.

I wish that the need for identification were more widely accepted. I've rescued plenty of dogs who didn't have any identification at all. How do their owners expect them to get home if they get lost? "It will never happen to my dog," they think. These days, animals are being iden-

tified with microchips and tattoos, and that's great, but the plain old collar and tag is still the first place people look when they find a lost dog.
It's the quickest and easiest way to make sure your dog gets home.

Dogs do not make great latchkey kids in the long term. They need
attention and they need to be around the people they love. In my travels,
when I'm doing an event, I try to keep my trips short. I've even declined
doing events altogether because of my dogs. People running an event will
often ask me to stay and go to dinner afterward, but I usually have to tell
them that I have responsibilities at home with my dogs. I always have
someone responsible back home to look after them, but nobody looks
after your dogs the way you do. I speak from experience on this, too—sad
experience. Many dog owners are like me in that respect. Perhaps we
seem antisocial, but we have made our dogs a priority in our lives.

Of course I'm even more comfortable at events when I can bring a
dog along with me. I couldn't always do that with my Danes, but I can
do it with Nipper. I introduced her to airline travel when she was just a
few months old, and now she loves traveling with me. We've had lots of
flights to practice on, and we have it down to a science. She goes right
into her little in-cabin airline carrier and I put her under the seat in front
of me. She can look out a screen and see that I'm right there. I usually
make sure she is asleep before I go to the bathroom; I try to be respectful
of the other passengers, who may not appreciate her barking in my
absence.

Grooming is another area where the responsible owner can shine. I
hear from many groomers who get certain dogs in once a year—usually
before a holiday when the extended family will be there and everyone
wants to make a good impression. These groomers tell horror stories
about the condition of these animals' coats and the intense pain this
annual procedure puts the dogs through. Regular grooming and bathing
lets the world know what a good caretaker you are.

I bathe my dogs probably more than I should, but they love it. It also
gives me a chance to check them over regularly for signs of possible health
problems. We play with the towel, and after I dry them off, I massage them,
and they just love the attention. I love giving them that attention, and sometimes I wonder if I do this more for myself than for the dogs.

Even though Murphy was eventually diagnosed with a heart murmur and had to give up her show career, her good breeding is evident in the way she carries herself. (Photo copyright © Marco Franchina)

Finally, a serious subject that makes many people squirm: spaying and neutering. The answer is clear: if you aren't going to breed your dog—and as we'll discuss, most people *shouldn't* breed their dogs—the dog should be spayed or neutered.

The evidence is also clear: dogs are healthier and more relaxed when they are altered, they are safe from certain cancers, and they enjoy longer, less stressful lives. But bring up the subject, and you won't believe how some people take it so personally. A lot of times it's a guy thing. A guy may be willing to spay a bitch, but "castrate" a male dog? Forget it! "Would you do that to me?" a guy inevitably whimpers as he gingerly crosses his legs. ("Well, yeah, maybe we should.") If you are struggling with feelings like that, push them aside. They're ridiculous and have nothing to do with the well-being of a dog. And everything to do with being a responsible dog owner.

Committing to being a responsible owner is the best way to pay your dog back for all the love and support he brings into your life. It's the first step toward living up to your dog's expectations and making your fair investment in the bond that you share. The rewards are priceless.

THREE

WEIGHING THE OPTIONS
Mutts vs. Purebreds,
Puppies vs. Older Dogs

For me, dogs are dogs. Yes, I love purebred dogs, and all of my dogs right now are purebreds, but I also love mutts. You won't find me looking down my nose at any creature with four legs, a tail, and a bark.

I grew up with mutts, which we now call mixed-breed dogs, and I will always consider them to be some of the greatest dogs anyone could have. But through the years I have also fallen in love with various breeds that for me represent beauty, history, culture, and the deliberate production of canine characteristics tailored for working with humans. They are all members of the dog family, so they are all members of my family.

Different people prefer different dogs for different reasons, and some reasons are better than others. If the only reason you are interested in a particular breed of dog or a particular mix is because of the dog's appearance, well, that's just not a good enough reason. But if you like the dog's looks and *temperament*—like the loving temperament of a herding breed, the protective nature of a working dog, the feisty quality of a terrier, or the sweet spirit of the mutt you find at the shelter—then you're respecting the dog for itself.

You have to consider certain factors when you are looking for *any* kind of dog, and these apply to both purebred and mixed-breed dogs. Consider them all, be honest with yourself, and you will be more likely to find yourself in a happy, healthy relationship with a canine companion. Remember, you are choosing a new family member and making a major commitment. You need to know as much as possible about what you're getting into.

PUREBRED DOGS VERSUS MIXED-BREED DOGS

The first thing people usually think about when they start thinking about getting a dog is whether to get a purebred dog or mixed-breed dog. For many people it's prestigious to have a purebred dog, but lately it's also become kind of politically correct to rescue a mixed-breed dog. Either way, what you really need to think about are the inner qualities of the dog and how you intend to incorporate that dog into your life.

If I were to go into a shelter—and I go to shelters all the time, either looking for dogs for friends or just to tempt myself—I would look for a dog with a personality that matches mine. If the dog was a mixed-breed, I would try to figure out just what mix of breeds it might be and how those breeds might affect the dog's health and disposition. Most of all, I would want to see how I connected with the dog, which is a two-sided thing. That's how I've always tried to place the puppies that I've bred. In the long run, matching personalities matters more than anything else.

Mixed-breed dogs are often loaded with personality, and the combination of different personalities varies widely from dog to dog. Assuming that owners choose their mixed-breed pets wisely and with common sense, these dogs can often be genetically healthier than purebreds, both in terms of physical health and temperament. Don't discount what mixed-breed dogs can bring to a dog/owner relationship. Some of the best pets I've ever known have been mixed-breed dogs.

CHOOSING A MIXED-BREED DOG

If you're thinking of getting a mixed-breed dog:

- Research all the breeds that you suspect might be represented in his pedigree, which should give you an idea of what to expect of his temperament, adult size, and exercise needs.

- Find out as much as you can about the dog's past experiences, where he came from, and who has been caring for him.

- Choose for temperament not appearance; look for a dog that is friendly and outgoing, not one that cowers in the corner, growls at you, or tries to attack you.

- Don't choose a dog out of pity. You can't save them all.

- Mixed-breed dogs are usually very healthy, but for your own peace of mind, have the dog examined by a veterinarian for his or her stamp of approval on the dog's health.

- Choose a friendly, outgoing dog or puppy who likes you, and vice versa.

When choosing a mixed-breed dog, you have to start by looking at what is known about the background of the dog you're looking at. Try to figure out what breeds are in the mix and just who this dog is and what he or she can become. Too many people go to a shelter saying only, "Well, I want a dog this size." You may find the perfect-sized dog that has come from an abusive situation, a dog that doesn't trust men—or women—or *both,* or a dog that growls at your kids. Personality is more important than size.

All this applies to purebred dogs, too—with some extra considerations thrown in. Before you even think about getting a purebred dog, you have lots of research to do. What type of health problems are prevalent in the breed? How is the temperament described? How will that temperament fit into your household? What will the time and energy requirements be in terms of grooming and exercise? This all goes way beyond just liking the way a dog looks.

To gather the necessary information, you should read books and magazines. You should also talk to breeders, owners of the breed, and people involved in the breed's rescue. You can learn so much from good breeders and owners. Since I began showing my dogs, I have learned that other valuable sources of information are handlers and judges who are experts in the breed you're interested in. They can often give you some valuable insight that breeders and owners might not be motivated to discuss: hard, cold facts about temperament and health, as well as both positive and negative trends in the breed. They might tell you, for instance, that the trend to breed a certain large dog larger is taking a toll on movement or structure, or that a particular breed renowned for a levelheaded temperament in the past is suddenly beginning to exhibit some aggression because of sloppy and excess breeding. The more you learn, the better off you'll be.

But remember when you're doing your research that you have to learn to read between the lines. There's an overload of information out there, so you have to learn to recognize what is solid and what is just public relations. Maybe you're considering a breed described in book after book as a "one-person dog," and you get the same description from breeders you meet. "One-person dog" usually translates into "protective," "possessive," and even "aggressive." Do you have the time, experience, and the know-how to sufficiently socialize a dog like that?

Or maybe you like Border Collies, and the breeders and the literature say, "Border Collies need exercise, lots and lots of exercise, every single day." Are you up for that? If not, it is imperative that you consider a different breed despite how beautiful you think Border Collies are. Be warned, too, that "very intelligent," which is another common description of Border Collies, does not translate into "easy to train." These are often the most difficult dogs to train. They have their own ideas about what they should be doing and may be too smart for their own good. If you're not careful, they will most likely end up training you before you even think about training them!

I paid attention to everything I discovered when I was researching Jack Russells, and I came close to scrapping the whole idea. I was a little bit nervous about the whole "terrier" thing, since I knew their personalities would be so different from the canine personalities I was accustomed to. The joke around the show ring is that the Terrier Group is known as the Terrorist Group. Did I really want to introduce a Jack Russell Terrorist into my house?

Every single book and article describes Jack Russells as being "tena-cious." I thought long and hard about what that means. Obviously the dog would try my patience. She would always push and try to get the upper hand. She would always keep me on my toes. Jack Russells don't know when to quit, and they won't hesitate, being all of twelve pounds, to take on a Mastiff or a Great Dane, which was a serious consideration for me. Nevertheless, I just couldn't let go of the idea. I had already expe-rienced herding dogs, sporting dogs, and working dogs, and Nipper would be my first terrier.

Because I knew what a big commitment a Jack Russell would be, I promised myself that I would not have unrealistic expectations about her. I would be ready for a tough new challenge. I prepared for the dive and dove in with my eyes wide open. Nipper and I have certainly had our moments, but I can't imagine my household now without her.

Nipper, my Jack Russell Terrier, came to me as a young puppy, while Bouvier Speedo was almost a year old when she joined our household. Although each came with her own special challenges, we soon became family, and now Nipper and Speedo share common interests like chasing rabbits in the yard and comparing notes about who's better at it when they stop for a breather.

We've been so successful in our partnership that she inspired me to add another terrier to the mix—my Border Terrier, Mikey. As much as I love and admire Nipper, I've also enjoyed living with a Border Terrier, which is by nature one of the mellower members of the terrier family.

CHOOSING A PUREBRED DOG

If you're thinking about getting a purebred dog:

- Do ample research on your breed of choice by reading, attending dog shows, talking to owners and breeders, and meeting as many dogs as possible.

- Choose a breed whose physical and temperamental characteristics mesh with your personality and lifestyle. There's more to a canine companion than just appearance.

- Work with an ethical show breeder, who is concerned with health and temperament as well as appearance, and who genetically screens his or her dogs for such conditions as hip dysplasia and eye problems.

- Try to meet the dog's mother (and, if possible, her father) to see what type of temperament she may have inherited from her parents.

- Choose a friendly, outgoing dog or puppy who likes you, and vice versa.

PUPPY PROS AND CONS

Everybody loves a puppy, and why not? Puppies are wonderful, warm, squirmy, soft, and sweet smelling. But a puppy is a young canine who doesn't know yet how to be a dog. You have to teach a puppy to be a dog so it doesn't become a monster. Remember: Once you take that puppy away from its mom, the responsibility for teaching becomes yours. Ask yourself if you are really up for that. A lot of people think they are, but as soon as they realize the true magnitude of the responsibility, they run away, leaving the poor confused puppy behind them, wondering, "Where's my mommy? What do I do now?"

I've had plenty of puppies in and out of my house, my own puppies and puppies that belonged to friends and family members. And though there's nothing more wonderful, I will be the first one to admit that a puppy can be a pain. Puppies are demanding and loud and messy—and destructive. They keep you up at night, they break your eardrums with their squeals, they can do incredible damage with their needle-sharp teeth, and they have an innate instinct for risking their lives and getting themselves into trouble.

There's so much that puppies need to learn, and so much that we need to teach them. They're blank slates ready to be filled with a great deal of knowledge that they need to know in order to be well-mannered dogs and to cohabitate peacefully with humans. To instruct them in this, you have to be patient, consistent, and understanding. You also have to have eyes in the back of your head. Puppies need to be watched constantly to make sure they don't destroy your carpet, chew up your shoes, electrocute themselves, or decide to teethe on the legs of your antique furniture.

That cute little Shepherd-mix offered "free to a good home" looks a little different in this light, doesn't she?

Don't get me wrong. I've said it before and I'll say it again: I love puppies. But I also love taking on the responsibility of raising them. Being Dad to a puppy is a rewarding experience, but only if you have the time and the desire to do it right. The rewards and the experiences and the memories I have gotten from doing this are priceless. I wouldn't trade them for anything.

When I raise a dog from a puppy, I personally know every experience he has ever had. The puppy and I have no secrets, and I can anticipate almost every one of his moves. I know what he's going to do and how he's going to react in almost any situation. If something's a potential problem, I usually know how to prevent it from escalating. When you raise a dog from a puppy, you have an enormous sense of pride, knowing

After living for so many years with a houseful of dignified Danes, the terrier world was something entirely new and different for me, as Jack Russell Terrier Nipper (on the left) can testify. Nipper and I have worked hard to make it a go, and I'm happy to say we have succeeded. Here in a rare moment of inactivity, Nipper suns herself by the pool with a guest, terrier-mix Spike.

that you helped mold this dog into who he is. You have wonderful puppy memories and the wonderful ability to say, "Remember when . . ." But puppy raising is not the only way of getting to that special relationship. Older dogs can take us there, too.

OLDER-DOG PROS AND CONS

You don't have to be ashamed if you'd rather not take on the responsibility of raising a puppy. That doesn't mean you don't like dogs or that you shouldn't have a dog as a pet. That's just being honest, and the dog you eventually bring into your life will be better off for your honesty. Millions of older dogs in need of homes will benefit from it, too. You just need to exercise a different type of care when choosing an older dog for a pet.

Go to the animal shelter and look around and you'll probably see lots of dogs, medium to large in size, who are all about one year old or so. These are the dogs who outgrew the puppy cuteness and whose impulsive owners decided to "get rid of" the dog because it was "too much of a hassle." Most of them are perfectly good dogs who just need an owner with a better understanding of commitment and consistency, and the patience to set rules, stick to them, and discourage any bad habits the dogs have developed in the hands of their former owners.

In many ways these dogs are the great unknown, which is the major "con" about adopting an older dog. You don't really know where the dog has been, or at least you weren't there with him when he was there. You don't know if he was abused or if he has been sick or if he was ever injured. That doesn't mean the dog is damaged goods, but you have to be careful.

OLDER DOG OPTIONS

If you'd rather get an older, more settled dog for a pet, consider a retired show dog or even a dog who was destined to be a service dog—a guide dog for the blind or a wheelchair-assistance dog—but who didn't make the cut. This reduces the risk in choosing an older dog, because these dogs are usually well-bred, well-trained, even-tempered animals that can make wonderful companions.

I'm the last person in the world who should go through the newspaper classified ads each morning looking for dogs in need of homes, but I can't resist. I've been tempted by everything from an Otterhound-mix to a blind Chihuahua. I remember a Shepherd named Omar, who was "obedience trained." He was two and a half years old. What happened that they would give up Omar? Was it a military family who had to move? Was it a divorce? Was it an elderly owner who passed away? As sad as his story probably was, he sounded like the kind of dog that had the potential for making someone a wonderful pet. What happened to Omar? What happens to all those other Omars out there?

If I were adopting an older dog, I'd look for some indication that someone cared about the dog so that I'd know the dog was a little more stable. There are lots of stories of abused animals, and lots of them have been rescued and need homes. But the care and rehabilitation of mistreated dogs like that is beyond most people's expertise. Dogs can sometimes be more like a loaded gun than a loving companion. Do your research and find a dog that is right for your life and your circumstances.

A lot of people have big ambitions that they're going to rescue a pathetic little creature and turn her into Lassie or Old Yeller. Common sense dictates that temperament should be the first consideration on your list, not cuteness or a history that makes you cry. Trust your intuition: when you're choosing an older dog, you can usually tell that, yes, this one will work out, or, no, this one takes too long to warm up to you. Don't ever think, "Oh, I can change this dog." You may be able to correct a habit such as imperfect housetraining, but you probably won't be able to cure fear biting or other types of aggression. Most people don't have the time or the skill for that kind of behavioral rehabilitation.

A friend of mine recently learned this the hard way with a Poodle he adopted from a rescue group. The dog's background was relatively unclear, but it quickly became evident that it probably hadn't been pretty—I even sustained an unprovoked bite to prove it. As time wore on, the little dog's fear-biting tendency and his all-around mistrust of humans escalated. Finally, the Poodle had to go back to the rescue group. His well-meaning adoptive owner had no choice. He realized that he just didn't have the time or the know-how to deal with this poor little creature's serious problems. My friend entered the relationship with noble intentions and lots of love to give, but that just wasn't enough to counteract whatever abuse this dog had experienced.

You can't assume, though, that every older dog looking for a new home is an abused dog. You have to be aware that even though an older dog may eventually be a more settled, relaxed animal, reaching that point can take a little time. You'll need to work together and get to know each other. You will almost undoubtedly have to attend regular obedience classes together to build a strong foundation to the relationship. Quite often there is a honeymoon period. Even if you look really good to each other and everything's going great, the dog may at some point decide, "Well, I'm comfortable here now, so I can revert to my old habits," habits that came from who-knows-where. You can deal with that positively if you build a strong foundation from the beginning.

After a while, you will realize that it doesn't really matter what happened to the dog before he came to you. You realize that you've been through a lot of experiences together and that now you are family. Your mutual experiences will be all that matter now. You won't be able to remember what life was like without your dog, and he won't remember what life was like without you. All that will matter will be the love you share.

BREEDERS

If it's a purebred dog you've decided you can't live without, then you're wise to look into the breeder option. I'm not talking about the backyard breeder here, the pet owner who happens to own a purebred dog and decides to breed it for whatever reason. I'm talking about a full-time, ethical show breeder who dedicates his or her life to improving a certain breed and striving for perfection. That's the difference: the backyard breeder won't be striving to perfect a family line.

Some people are intimidated at the thought of contacting a purebred-dog breeder, and I'll admit that there can be kind of a snootiness to the whole thing. But some wonderful people out there just love to talk for hours about their breeds and their dogs. If you find one of those, you'll find that the passion is contagious.

You can find breeders in your area by contacting your local kennel club, the American Kennel Club in New York City, or the United Kennel Club in Kalamazoo, Michigan. Take a look at breed listings in all-breed and breed-specific dog magazines; almost every breed now has its own individual publication. Some ethical breeders sometimes advertise in the newspaper—along with some unethical ones. That's how I found Freeway's breeder—in the newspaper—and I sure lucked out with him.

PATIENCE AND THE PUREBRED

If you're seeking a well-bred purebred puppy from a breeder, be patient. It could take six months to a year or more on a breeder's waiting list before you finally find the right pup.

The best way to meet breeders is to attend dog shows. There you'll meet lots of dogs, and you'll learn even more about the breed you're interested in. Just find a dog person and say, "God, that's a beautiful dog!" and he or she will probably start to tell you everything you need to know about the dog and the breed. Spend enough time and you'll learn a lot about temperament, structure, and if you're lucky, some of the health problems they have come up against. This information is vital, whether you're looking for a companion dog or a show dog. The ethical breeder puts equal time and effort into producing both, knowing that both are critical components to the line.

Dog shows are actually a lot like diving. A layperson can go to a diving competition and do pretty well with the judging, based on nothing more than "I like that dive, I don't like that one—I may not know why I like that dive, but it's better than the others." It's the same with dogs. You go to a dog show and you may not know why, but you like one dog over another and you naturally gravitate to that dog.

ANIMAL SHELTERS AND BREED RESCUE GROUPS

Another option is, of course, the animal shelter. It's best to adopt from a shelter if you can go in without being predisposed to what you want the dog to *look* like. Go solely on temperament, how you bond with the dog, how the dog takes to you and how you take to the dog. Just because he's cute doesn't mean he'll be a good pet.

There are no guarantees for any dog you take into your home, but there's a little more risk of experiencing problems with health and temperament with a shelter dog. Nevertheless, you could end up with a great pet. Don't be surprised, either, by all the purebred dogs you're likely to find at the shelter—German Shepherds, Labrador Retrievers,

Poodles, Cocker Spaniels, Rottweilers—don't be dazzled by the pure-bred labels. "Purebred" does not mean healthy or even well-bred. If you're looking for a pet, you're looking for pet qualities, not just a pretty face and a pedigree. Do this smartly, and you'll have a better chance of finding what you're looking for at the shelter.

THE GRACE PERIOD

Whether obtaining a dog or a puppy from a breeder, shelter, or rescue group, ask for a grace period to make sure it's a match—especially if you have other animals. If things don't work out, don't feel like a failure if you have to return the dog. You may just be incompatible, or the dog may simply be more than you are willing or able to deal with.

More and more people these days who are looking for a purebred dog are checking out another option: purebred rescue groups. This is sort of a modified version of the animal shelter. It's usually a network of breed enthusiasts, usually breeders, who try to rescue as many representatives of their breed as they can. They usually find the dogs advertised in newspapers or at animal shelters. They evaluate the dogs and rehabilitate them if that's necessary. Then they keep them in foster homes until an appropriate adopter comes along. The benefit here is that the foster families really get to know the dogs. They get to know what they like and dislike, whether they get along with cats, other dogs, kids, that kind of thing. Serious breed rescuers work hard to make sure that the right dog ends up with the right owner in the right home for the rest of the dog's life.

But as with animal shelters, you can't assume that just because a dog is being placed by one of these organizations, it will have great pet potential. You'll find all kinds of dogs available from both shelters and breed rescue groups, and some of them are from abusive situations. I've had lots of experience helping friends adopt dogs from breed rescue groups and shelters. Some work out great, matches made in heaven. Others . . . well, as we've already seen, they aren't so lucky. It has to be the right match. If it's not, you have to have the courage to return the dog to the rescue group or shelter. You can't feel like a failure if you decide you have to do this. What's important is that you be honest, both for your sake and for the dog's.

When adopting a rescue dog of any kind, whether from a shelter or rescue group, you can't get caught thinking, "If I don't adopt this dog, is she ever going to find a home?" Pity alone is not a valid reason to adopt a dog—or to keep a dog you've adopted if it's not working out. This return business happens a lot.

It's hard to deal with a dog who has already been through one or more other homes. He's already had experiences that may not have been positive. He may be bringing some pretty serious baggage with him. A dog with an abusive background may come into your house, bite anyone who approaches her, and attack, or maybe even kill, your cat. You may or may not be capable of dealing with her behavior. Although you want to save the dog, you have to understand that may simply not be possible. Meanwhile, so many other wonderful dogs are out there without these problems, who may never find homes.

Think of it this way: an aggressive dog with an abusive background will have to go through therapy throughout the rest of her life. That will require a lot of work, a lot of attention, and a lot of intuition. You know the dog has a history, but as much as you want to, you can't take that history away. You can't out of pity or guilt keep a dog who is a mismatch. You have to use your common sense. Adopter beware, and admit defeat when you have to.

PET STORES

Buyer beware is all I can say to the person who decides to get a puppy from a pet store. Choose a cute puppy from a pet store and you're just asking for the risk of health, genetic, and temperament problems. Pet shop puppies typically come from puppy mills, where puppies are bred like products on a factory assembly line. Genetic and general health and temperament of mom, dad, and pups are usually ignored, and puppies, who are usually taken away from their stressed-out puppy-machine mothers before any of them are ready, may not receive much in the way of socialization.

A favorite canine activity in our household has always been hiking in the hills around my house. Ryan and Brutus, here waiting anxiously for me at the top of a hill, needed a good deal of daily exercise—and an owner who was willing to give that to them.

A pet store may promise to take the puppy back if problems occur, but by the time they do, you've already become attached to the poor little guy. Just ask my neighbors who had to surgically correct both of their pet shop puppy's hips before he reached six months of age. It's just been one thing after another with them, and they're not alone. You can't measure the emotional investment that makes it so hard to walk away. It's a heartbreak for you and for the dog. Have I made my case? Okay, then how about this: pet shop puppies are also often more expensive than a healthy, well-bred, properly socialized pet from a legitimate show breeder. Case closed.

One pet store exception would be the pet supply stores that partner with animal welfare organizations and invite them in to adopt out their dogs and puppies from the pet stores. The idea has become popular in recent years and has resulted in win-win situations for everyone. The shelters, still carefully evaluating and educating would-be adopters, get greater public exposure for the animals they are trying to place. Dogs benefit because they have a better chance of landing in decent, permanent homes, and in the bigger picture, because the stores don't sell puppies in the traditional manner, the vicious puppy-mill cycle is completely bypassed. The store profits because often an adopter will from then on choose that store for all his or her pet-supply purchases.

A breeder, shelter, rescue group, or pet store adoption event can all successfully match a dog with an owner. The right dog plus the right owner equals a relationship with the best chance of permanence, from the dog's early years on into old age.

FOUR

THE BIG DECISION
Evaluations and Lifetime Choices

Here's how *not* to buy a puppy: go to the mall, see a puppy in the window at the mall pet store, and say, "Oh, what a cute puppy. What a good idea. I'll take it."

When it comes time to choose your new pet, your new family member, the key is patience. It is essential to wait until the right one comes along. That means being willing to wait for a breeder's next litter or for the right dog to walk through the animal-shelter door. This can be tough, I know, but your decision could affect the next decade or more of your life, so it's definitely worth the wait.

EVALUATING BREEDERS

How do you know which dog is the "right" one? If it's a purebred dog or puppy you're after—show puppy or pet—the breeder could help you through the first step. Good breeders put the same effort into the care and socialization of their pet puppies as they do with their show puppies.

The more breeders you talk to, the more you'll learn and the more accurate picture you'll get of the breed, but all breeders are not created equal. There are good breeders and not-so-good breeders. Even the word *breeder* can be deceiving. Backyard breeders can call themselves breeders, and so can commercial breeders who supply pet stores. Technically they are all breeders. Even so-called reputable show breeders can vary dramatically in their philosophies and their practices. The buyer's job is to try to find a breeder that he or she is most comfortable with because they share the same ideas about what is best for the puppy.

A BREEDER'S SECOND BREED

Sometimes you can hit the jackpot when the breed you're looking for is a particular breeder's second breed. Many people make their mistakes when they're just starting out with their first breed; then with their second breed, they really shine. The second time around, when they're more experienced, they start out with the best dog they can find, make more knowledgeable decisions, and become better breeders.

Ideally, you should be able to look to the breeder as a kind of men-tor. I was a real neophyte when I started out breeding and showing, and it was comforting to be able to rely on people who had been at this for years and made it their life—some for thirty years or more. A good, eth-ical breeder can be a great resource down the line if you have problems. The good ones will also want to know if their puppies get sick or develop a genetic problem, so they can be aware of what is happening in their lines. That's a policy I have tried to stick to with the people who have bought my puppies. If one of the dogs I have bred develops some-thing—dysplasia, bloat, or something like that—I want to know about it.

Genetic health is really important to me because I have dealt with some pretty serious problems in my dogs, and purebreds seem to have quite a few of these. When I first meet breeders, I want to find out their perspectives on this, but I usually bring it up in a nonthreatening way: "Have you ever dealt with such and such?" or "Have you ever heard of this or that?" If they are forthcoming with honest answers, the more cred-ible and ethical they seem and the more I would like to work with them.

You evaluate breeders by the quality of their stock, of course: What do the dogs look like? Are their coats clean and healthy? Are they in good shape? Well socialized? Properly nourished? But it's also important to ask how many litters they have bred. Because of the fear of overbreeding and the problems it can cause, I am more leery of someone who just breeds and breeds and breeds. Someone like that may not be paying enough attention to quality, but I also know for certain that with so many puppies, they can't be getting the intense one-on-one socialization and handling they need from early on. Temperament and health are the most important things of all to me. A dog can be the most beautiful dog in the world, but inside be a time bomb of health and temperament problems.

Pay attention to what a breeder wants from you, too. What questions is she asking you? Is she checking you out to see if you're going to be a good owner for this dog, or is she just interested in taking your money? When I first met the breeder of my Great Dane Freeway, she didn't know who I was. All she knew was that I walked in to buy a show-marked harlequin Great Dane. She asked me some specific questions: Did I have a yard? Where was the dog going to sleep? How was I equipped to take care of the animal? I was impressed with how much she wanted to know about Freeway's potential home.

It's best when a breeder sells his or her puppy with a sales contract. Animal shelters and breed rescue groups increasingly adopt their animals out with adoption contracts. These help to protect the dog and the new owner, so don't be insulted if you are asked to sign one. The breeder contract usually outlines what the breeder guarantees as far as health: eyes, hips, and anything particular to a specific breed—that type of thing. If the breeder addresses health issues in a contract, it's going to give the buyer a lot more confidence. If something does crop up, it increases the chances that the buyer is going to let the breeder know about it. A good breeder wants to know.

The buyer also makes some promises in the sales contract, as does the adopter in an adoption contract. These are usually guarantees of how the dog will be housed and, if the animal is to be a pet, that he or she will be spayed or neutered. With the sale of my puppies, I always include in the contract that if for any reason the buyer can't keep the dog, the dog will come back to me. This is called a return-to-breeder clause. Steer clear of any breeder who doesn't use a sales contract. That breeder may just not be all that interested in the fate of his or her puppies. Do you really want to work with someone who doesn't care?

MEETING MOM AND DAD

It's so difficult when you go to a breeder and you see the puppies. All of the puppies are so cute, so adorable, and you want to bring each and every one of them home. The problem is, they grow up. They go through stages, some of which are pretty hard to live with. Only a strong commitment is going to get you through those tough times, and that has to be built on more than just how cute the puppy is at eight weeks old.

You need to look at the dogs that created that adorable ball of fur in your hands. When people purchase a puppy, they think they're starting with a clean slate, a blank page, but they're not. Certain genetic factors come along with that puppy and help to make her who she is and who she will be. These influences can be just as powerful as the long-term effects of her treatment during her first weeks and months of life.

The mother and the father both pass on genetic traits to their pups that affect their temperament and health, but the mother is the one who teaches them how to be dogs during their first formative weeks of life. If she does a poor job of it, the puppies may never be the loving, well-adjusted, even-tempered animals they are meant to be. When choosing a puppy, if possible, meet the puppy's mom—and dad, too, if you can. This will give you a better idea of who you can expect the puppy to become. It's not a fail-safe way, but it's a good start.

When I chose Freeway, it was because I fell in love with his mother, Dolly. When I went to see the litter, I ended up spending little time with the puppies. They were cute, they were sweet, and I played with them all—but then I met Dolly. I couldn't believe it. She was so much like my first Dane, Maile. She had gentle mannerisms that reminded me of Maile, such as burying her head in my lap and pushing so that I'd scratch her neck—all while I, a complete stranger, was sitting there with her puppies. She was just a big love, happy to show me and her little guys how wonderful it was to be with us.

My decision was easy. I looked at Dolly and then I looked at Freeway. He was healthy and robust and had the classic harlequin markings, which was everything I was looking for, but beyond that—and even more importantly—he seemed to have the same personality and disposition that his mother did. I thought, "This is the dog that I want," and I've never been sorry. Dolly and Freeway proved to me the power of genetics and early maternal care—so much so that I went back after she had had her next litter for another of her puppies. That puppy was my sweet, gentle Ryan Luke. Dolly could be proud of the incredible influence she had on her boys.

I have recently witnessed the same phenomenon with Nipper. While I was exploring the possibility—and challenge—of adding a "tenacious" little Jack Russell Terrier to my family, I came upon Nipper's mother and was pleasantly surprised. She wasn't at all what I expected of this breed. I found her eager to please, accepting, and sweet. I wouldn't have described her as "laid-back" in the classic sense, but for a Jack Russell, I guess she was. I'm now happy to say that Nipper seems to be blossoming into a clone of her mother—and therefore a rather misleading ambassador of her breed.

Of course, the opposite is also true. If you go to see a litter of puppies and the mother stands growling and snarling at you at the front door and refuses to allow you in the house, or she hides shivering in the

Border Terrier Mikey—my second terrier—couldn't be more different from my first terrier, JRT Nipper. This became evident on Mikey's first trip with me. Where Nipper would have reveled in a journey to Florida, Mikey longed to be back home. Instead of trying to mold him into Nipper Jr., I respect his individuality and indulge his desire to remain at home on a soft, cushy pillow, the quintessential homebody.

corner when you enter the room, well, this probably isn't the litter you've been looking for. Consider a mother's fear and anger serious warning signs. Just what kind of dog is this mom teaching her pups to become? Probably not the kind that is fun to have around the house. I've heard plenty of stories from and about people who took a puppy from a mother like this. When the trouble starts weeks or months down the line, they think back to that first meeting and say, "You know, this dog is just like her mother." Take this very seriously. It's the best advice anyone can give you.

TEMPERAMENT, TEMPERAMENT, TEMPERAMENT

I am a stickler for temperament. What drew me to dogs in the first place was the classic bond between dogs and people, and that bond is what I try to achieve with my own dogs. There's just nothing more important than temperament testing when you are choosing a new dog or puppy. These evaluations do not guarantee you will end up with a pet with the kind of disposition you want—the owner plays a big role in that, too—but testing will give you some idea of what you're getting into and what you'll have to work with.

Through the years my skills at evaluating temperament have dramatically improved. The more time you spend with dogs, studying their body language and listening to what they are trying to tell you, the sharper your instincts become in communicating with them and understanding their messages. You also become better equipped to catch the little signals that indicate a possible problem.

On the show circuit, temperament is always a big subject of conversation. You talk about training successes and the personality traits that one dog inherited from another dog. Being around so many dogs at once in such an intense situation, you learn which dogs are dog aggressive, which dogs can only be with females, which dogs have to be separated—show dogs aren't always very even-tempered. You learn to read the signs and anticipate certain behaviors. You can use these skills to evaluate new potential companions and to help you manage them once they join the household.

A QUICK TEST

When evaluating a dog in a shelter, or even an older dog from a breeder, see if the dog can be lured into a sit with a treat held above his nose. Will he play with a ball? Is he curious when you throw a squeaky toy or make unusual noises? The dog who interacts with you in this way is more likely to be on the friendly, outgoing side of the personality spectrum.

Actual temperament testing and what you evaluate depends on what you're getting the dog for. One common exercise is to flip the puppy on his back to see if he struggles or submits peacefully and lies still. You can do this with an older dog, too, but it can be dangerous, especially with a rescue dog that may be feeling scared and insecure. Some dogs just assume the position naturally the moment they meet you, asking immediately for a scratch on the tummy. It's an endearing trait and one that advertises a friendly, trusting nature. This is a vulnerable position for a dog, so essentially, the struggler is considered more dominant, the submitter more submissive.

I like to be more practical with temperament evaluations. Let's say you want a dog who will play Frisbee or do some other type of retrieving, even retrieving lost people in search-and-rescue work, which some owners get involved in these days, first as a weekend hobby with a local search-and-rescue club, and later as a serious volunteer vocation. If a retrieval-related activity is what you're interested in, you want a puppy that early on exhibits a natural *desire* to retrieve, whether he is actually able to do it yet or not. The pup should have an interest in it—say, in chasing a tennis ball across the room—and he should look as if he enjoys it.

Don't try to force a dog into something that he doesn't have a natural interest in doing. I learned that the hard way when I tried to convince Freeway that he was destined for greatness in the conformation show ring. Some dogs are born with showmanship in their blood, and others just aren't. You see it right away when the young puppy who is barely able to waddle across the rug stands beaming with charisma and demands your attention. Freeway wasn't like that. He wanted to be a

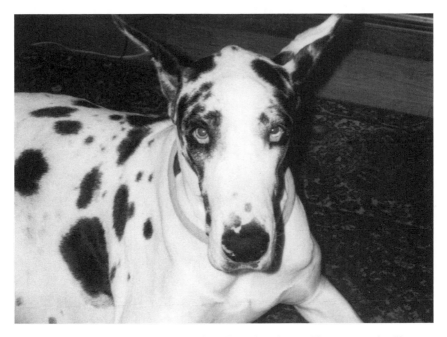

My Great Dane Donna was one of the best dog choices I've ever made. She blossomed into my soul mate and protector, and even though she is now gone, I still feel her presence and regard her as the matriarch of my household.

pet, a companion, not the center of attention in Madison Square Garden.

It's also important to look around and test the temperament of the people taking care of the puppies. Heredity and TLC from Mom are critical, but so are the contributions of the human handlers who are providing a puppy with his first experiences in this big scary world. Pay attention: Are the people gentle and encouraging and positive with the puppies? Do they protect the puppies from harm, either from their environment or visiting neighborhood kids? Have they introduced the pups to various grooming rituals? As puppies begin to grow more adventurous, it's important that they be exposed to a variety of different experiences, sensations, and even rooms around the house. They should also be handled by different people, preferably of all different ages, styles, and demeanors.

I am also a firm believer in early handling—assuming one has a close, trusting relationship with the mother and she will permit it. I did this instinctively with the first litter I bred. I couldn't believe this beautiful litter of ten puppies. I would handle their feet and their tails, hold them gently and securely on their backs, and even take a cotton swab and run it between their toes. At the same time, I would cuddle the puppies, holding them in my hands, amazed that these little things that could fit into the palm of my hand would grow to be 130-some pounds.

It helped, of course, that I had such a wonderful relationship with Leilani, the puppies' mom. She *wanted* me involved. She took such pride in her litter that she wanted everyone to come down and see the pups.

If you're adopting an older dog or a puppy from the animal shelter or from a rescue group, you probably won't have the opportunity to meet her parents or find out much about her early handling and experiences. You can still evaluate her temperament by checking out how she reacts to different people and places, and how she responds to you. Remember: temperament first, looks second. Funny or less-than-classically-beautiful looks can grow on you, but bad temperament can mean success or failure—sometimes life or death.

When you visit a shelter, some dogs are totally engaging, are instantly happy to see you, and practically beg you to take them home. However, some are a little bit shy because of their predicament. They're interested, but a little bit nervous. Then there is the terminally shy and retiring pup, the one shivering in the corner, the one who was either born that way or made that way by a cruel and/or ignorant owner. This is the legendary "one you feel sorry for."

Be careful with this legendary dog. If you take this frightened puppy home, you will have your work cut out for you. Make sure you're up to it, and be realistic. You'll need to commit yourself to a heavy program of socialization and rehabilitation—with no guarantees of the outcome. You could end up with a perfectly good pet, or you could end up with a fear-biter who spends every waking moment of her day hiding behind a chair in the family room. Love cannot always overcome all.

Don't assume, though, that shyness or timidity is a sign that means "stay away from this dog!" Sometimes you just have to give the dog a little time. She may be a little nervous, a little frazzled being in a new situation and all, especially if she's a rescue dog. Her shyness may be just a temporary reaction to all she's been going through. Once she's comfortable and starts to trust you, her calmer, more relaxed nature may begin to shine through. Unfortunately, though, too often it's the shy and nervous behavior that people gravitate to. They believe they can bring the dog out of it, but they end up reinforcing that behavior by pitying the dog and never allowing her to overcome it. What these owners should be doing is strengthening the dog with socialization and confidence-building exercises.

RESISTING THE CODDLE IMPULSE

When dealing with a pup who's on the shy side, don't say, "Oh, how cute. He's so shy," and then cuddle him. This just reinforces the dog's behavior and encourages fear-biting tendencies. Instead, ignore the shy, timid behavior, and let the dog come to you. When he does, praise and treat him for his courage. As his confidence builds, the shyness should subside.

Donna was never big on retrieving, but of course I didn't choose her for her hunting talents. Though she considered carrying the mail or a newspaper to be somewhat beneath her, she would accompany me every now and then to the mailbox. She was good company and a proficient supervisor while I did the retrieving.

Obedience training is a wonderful confidence builder—probably the best there is. I've seen it happen again and again, even in my own home. You bring a dog with behavioral problems home, but once you start going to an obedience class, the dog thrives with the structure and the companionship, and everything falls into place. Shower the dog with the firm gentleness and consistency that tell her you are here for the duration, but that she has to live up to her end of the deal. Dogs thrive on training the way we thrive on new experiences.

I was worried about my Bouvier, Speedo, when I first brought her home. She came to me from a breeder in Michigan, and at first she was shy. I thought that I might have made a mistake, but once we got working on the obedience training and consistent handling that a dog's confidence is made of, I didn't have to worry any longer. Now we all live in harmony. Speedo fits in beautifully, and she is gentle with the littler guys—even when Nipper, all twelve pounds of her, tries to push her around.

Finally, *your* temperament should mesh with the dog's temperament. A good breeder, rescuer, or shelter staff member makes a lot of effort to match personalities. Some puppies and older dogs are just naturally better suited to some people than others. Look for the one you share a rapport with, one who offsets your personality. If a buyer or adopter is a shy and rather quiet type, for example, it wouldn't be wise or kind to match that person up with the most demanding and dominant member of a litter.

HEALTH EVALUATIONS

Would-be buyers and adopters tend to gravitate not only to the shy pups but also to the sickly ones. You could get yourself into big—and expensive—trouble here, too. With all that I've been through with my dogs with health problems, from wobblers to heart murmurs to pyometra, I try to learn as much as I can about canine health. This is one of the most important educational steps an owner can take.

Genetic and overall health are important for any dog, but if you're buying a show puppy, health is a critical factor in the breeding potential

When I first went looking for a Great Dane puppy, I met an incredible creature named Dolly and ended up with two of her kids: first Freeway (in back) and a year later, Ryan. Choose a dog carefully from a reputable source and, if possible, from an excellent mom, and you up the odds that that dog will become the dog of your dreams.

of that animal. We will only conquer genetic health problems in dogs if we refuse to breed affected animals, and screening is the first step.

The most common screening these days is done for hip dysplasia, a presumably hereditary malformation of the hip joints. Good breeders have their dogs x-rayed to determine what their potential might be for developing hip dysplasia. The results are registered with the Orthopedic Foundation for Animals. In my opinion, and the opinion of others in the dog world, only dogs that are OFA Excellent or Good should be bred. The smart puppy buyer, whether he or she is looking for a show puppy or a pet, will look into the OFA status of a puppy's parents to reduce the risk of surprises in the future. This is important for any dog, but it has always been especially important to me with my Danes. They're so big, they don't need the additional stress and trauma of corrective surgery for bad hips.

The eyes can be another problem, and the Canine Eye Registration Foundation keeps track of genetic eye problems in hopes of stopping them. This is another tool breeders and buyers can use to gauge a dog's fitness as a breeding animal. If you are researching a particular breed, you might also find that certain genetic problems are specific to that breed, which you will also need to be aware of. Collies and Siberian Huskies, for example, can have eye problems, Alaskan Malamutes can be affected by dwarfism, and there may even be a genetic link to the incidence of canine bloat, especially in the deep-chested breeds.

Unless you do your research, you won't know about the problems inherent in a specific breed and you won't be prepared to avoid and prevent them. Don't be afraid to ask questions—and don't expect a backyard breeder or a pet-shop employee to be able to answer them. A good breeder should be able to, though, and if the breeder gets insulted by your questions, find another breeder. A good breeder will be open and honest about the problems in his or her breed and in his or her line, and so will an ethical breed rescue person or animal shelter representative.

THE NEARLY PERFECT DOG

I'm not saying you should buy or adopt a dog only if it's perfect—there's no such thing as a perfect dog. There isn't a perfect line either. But you owe it to yourself, to your family and friends, to your dog, and to the whole dog family at large to be informed and prepared about health issues when you bring a new dog into your family. You'll not only be prepared to make a wiser choice, you'll also have a better idea of what to do if things go wrong.

Genetic problems have to be addressed through screening and family history because they probably won't be apparent when you first meet a litter of adorable little puppies or a big strapping shelter dog. Beyond that, you have to do some on-the-spot health evaluating to get an idea of the animal's overall health. First, pay close attention to the skin and coat. They are excellent barometers of what is going on inside. A dull haircoat and dry, crusty skin are danger signals that something is not right internally, anything from disease to parasites to malnutrition. Look, too, for a dog or puppy with bright eyes and an enthusiastic nature, a clean bite, a clear nose, and clean ears.

It's best to do everything you can to choose a healthy dog or puppy, or at least to be aware of potential problems you might face down the line. A lot of sources, from show breeders to pet stores, will "guarantee" the dog, meaning that if the animal gets sick, you can return it "for a full refund or replacement." But think about that: Most people bond quickly to a new dog or puppy. Say you have bonded to your new pet and then he is diagnosed with juvenile cataracts or hip dysplasia before his first birthday. Are you really going to be able to take him back to the store? Some people could do that, and some people *do* do that, but what a nightmare it is for all involved. Many decide to pay the high veterinary bills instead, which could be many thousands of dollars. It's a sad situation, but one that you might be able to prevent by taking health seriously when you are making the important choice of a new dog or puppy.

PART TWO

THE JOYS
AND
PAINS OF
PUPPYHOOD

FIVE

THROUGH A PUPPY'S EYES

A new puppy has come into your life. What a wonderful little animal. But how will he become the incredible dog that every dog is supposed to be? The first step in understanding this adorable little creature who has invaded your household is to try to figure out how he looks at the world. He doesn't see it the same way you do, and don't ever assume that he does.

Think about what it means to raise a human toddler, though, and you might be on the right track. The comparison is not far-fetched. You have to follow the same guidelines of consistency, you have to protect the puppy from hurting himself, and you have to communicate with him clearly and calmly in a way that you can both understand. More than anything, you have to be willing to see yourself, your family, your other pets, this entire new situation, through your puppy's eyes. His brain, like the human toddler's brain, is in development. It's not quite there yet. So be realistic with your expectations.

When Nipper first came into our household, she was immediately on the defensive. It was obvious to me what she was going through. She had come into a house with huge dogs, and she was so small and vulnerable that she really felt that she had to stand her ground. Even at her young age, only a few weeks old, she sensed danger, that it wasn't safe. Once she started to realize that we spoke her language and that those huge dogs weren't going to eat her, she was willing to put her guard down. She was willing to be submissive to them, and she realized that it wasn't going to kill her to do that.

You need to be your puppy's eyes. You need to be alert, always look-

My most rewarding breeding experience was with Leilani, shown here, exhausted but relaxed, with her litter of ten. She was a natural mom, just the kind that the prospective puppy buyer should look for when searching for a new canine member of the family.

ing ahead to prevent trouble. I'm always trying to anticipate how my dogs are viewing a certain situation or person, such as a carpenter carrying lumber up to the house or a stranger in a uniform at the gate. How does that carpenter look to my dogs? Of course he seems threatening. It's my responsibility to get out there and diffuse the situation.

Seeing the world through a dog's eyes has become second nature to me, as it has for many empathic dog owners. Maybe we were dogs in another life. When I try to explain to other people why two dogs are fighting over a treat, or why you can't feed this dog next to this one, or why you can't expect a puppy to understand that he can chew on a rawhide bone but not on an electrical cord, they look at me with that blank look that says, "Don't be ridiculous."

The shelters are filled with puppies, older puppies, whose owners could've tried being a little "ridiculous." They didn't try to see things from their puppies' perspective, and look what happened. "There was something wrong with the dog," they decide. "He just wouldn't do what he was told." But often the puppy never had any idea what his owners expected of him. What a sad waste for the people as well as for the puppies. There's really nothing more rewarding than working together to build communication. That's the ultimate partnership. In the end, you learn more about yourself by working with your dogs, not by forcing them into submission, but by learning to work with them and by earning their respect.

CANINE AS A SECOND LANGUAGE

Dogs have their own language. If you're going to learn to see the world through your puppy's eyes, you have to start learning her language. Let's say you're training a puppy and she makes a mistake. You can't just blame it on the pup. It's a partnership, and you have to take responsibility for it. It's like throwing people into a foreign country and saying, "Okay, deal with it!" The writing, the language . . . they're not going to understand it unless they've studied for years and years and years. This is what our dogs go through every single day of their lives: they're living in a foreign country, and we have to be sensitive to that.

I've spent my life working toward goals. Some of those goals had to do with diving, and some had to do with dogs. Mastering canine communication is one of those goals. I like to believe that every day I become more fluent in my second language—Canine. Both diving and the canine language are rooted in the physical, and both involve observation and timing. Corrections, for example, are all in the timing. You can't scold a puppy three hours after she has chewed up a book you left on the floor and expect her to understand why you are angry. Sure, she'll look sorrowful and (presumably) guilty, but only in response to your anger, not to something she did three hours ago, something she probably can't even remember doing.

When I was teaching theater movement, I learned that it doesn't matter what you say or how you say it, but how it's perceived. Give your puppy clear signals that will help her to understand, to accurately perceive, just what it is you're trying to tell her and what you expect from her.

I became a lot more sensitive to—and fluent in—canine body language through my Great Dane Ryan. Because of his deafness, we learned to communicate silently. We trained with hand signals, which I now consider a must for every dog. He learned to read my body language, and I learned to read his and that of countless other dogs. When I was out with Ryan, I would evaluate the body language of other dogs who were coming toward us or who were meeting Ryan for the first time. I had to make sure no threats were involved. Little by little, I realized that my skills were sharpening.

Without Ryan around during my first months with Nipper, I don't know if Nipper and I would ever have made it. At first we just couldn't seem to figure out how to communicate with each other, and all my fears about living with a Jack Russell Terrorist seemed to be coming true. I would try traditional discipline methods when she got out of control, but she seemed immune to everything, and my feeble attempts to rein her in would just escalate her behavior. Then I noticed that when Ryan was around, she was a perfect angel, so I started to watch him more closely. Maybe he could show me a thing or two about what I could do differently.

I noticed that whenever Nipper would bite at his face as an invitation to play, Ryan would reach out, grasp her gently in his jaws, and with a low growl tell her, "That's enough." And she would listen. She would practically stand at attention and do—or not do—what he asked. Some people might have feared that he was intending to hurt her, but I know my dogs well enough to distinguish between a threatening growl and a grumpy-old-man growl. It was definitely the latter type he was using to put the annoying little sprite in her place. So I tried it. I mastered Ryan's growl, and it worked. I had learned how to get Nipper's attention in her own language.

I carried this a step further by learning to yelp. Nipper and I were playing with a squeaky toy, and as puppies do, she began to spin out of control in a wild-eyed frenzy. She snapped at the toy and got my hand instead. I gave out a sudden high-pitched yell as if I were another dog. She stopped in her tracks, lay down at my feet, and just looked up at me. Obviously the most effective method of reaching her involved communicating with her in a dramatic, doglike manner that she could understand.

Ryan at three months of age. He never seemed to realize that his deafness made him different from other dogs—or at least he never let it bother him. We started training right away, and he caught on to my hand-signal training method pretty quickly. It was a great experience for us both.

SOCIALIZATION: FOSTERING YOUR PUP'S POTENTIAL AS A SOCIAL ANIMAL

Dogs that are well-socialized become dogs who enjoy a greater amount of freedom and a more exciting life, but getting to that point is a big job. The earlier you start socializing a puppy, the better. I started right away with Nipper, as soon as she came into my house, continuing what her breeder had started long before that, and Nipper has since become quite a worldly pup. She is a seasoned airline traveler, and she's always popular at the hotels we stay in. She's been so well socialized to people that I can have hotel staff members take her for walks if I can't be there to do it. If I hadn't paid attention to socializing her, I would never be able to take her with me to the places I do. She would be a monster, and she'd have to stay home all the time.

Socialization can be time-consuming. You must introduce your puppy to as many people, places, and experiences as possible, and to other dogs of all sizes, shapes, and colors. Dogs have to learn to play with other dogs in a civilized way—they don't necessarily come to it instinctively. That's something people don't think about, but socialization can diminish the aggressive tendency of an "only" dog to view other dogs as rivals or pests.

SOUND ADVICE FROM DR. DUNBAR

A puppy should meet a minimum of one hundred people during his first year. So says renowned behavior expert Dr. Ian Dunbar, and I agree!

Be careful when you're out introducing your puppy to the world. See it as your puppy sees it. Imagine how you would feel if all you had known was the protection of your mom and the security of a dog crate. Then you're thrown out into the big scary world of new experiences, new people, and new dogs. As your puppy's protector, you have to arrange to keep the first experiences positive. That's your job.

When I introduce my little guys, Nipper and Mikey, to larger dogs, I kneel down and lift them up so that they can all meet on an equal level and minimize the Napoleon complex. A small dog's unprovoked aggressive attack is usually designed to preempt a first strike from a larger dog. This can mean serious trouble, so I try to be sensitive to one puppy's small size in relation to another's massive build and predatory instincts.

Large or small, I find that if dogs meet on an equal level, there's less apt to be a problem. Nipper has met Rhodesian Ridgebacks and even a two-hundred-pound Mastiff with this method. It has worked out great, even though at first fleeting glance, the larger dogs probably mistake her for prey. She greets them on their same level in a civilized manner, giving the big guys time to realize that she is a dog—one of their own—not a squirrel or a chipmunk. Then, assuming that we get through the introductions without teeth-baring or growls, we move on to the tail-wagging, play bow, and the "I want to play! I want to play!" stage. I put Nipper down and the games begin. With no thought at all to size, they play like long-lost buddies who have just been reunited.

I'm not foolish enough to think that I can do this with a strange dog, though. It has to be dogs I know. I can't assume that a large, aggressive dog was ever taught the protocols of canine introductions. I would never risk my guys with a dog like that. It's a shame we have to think about that so much these days, but large dogs are getting more popular, and many owners haven't kept up with the training and socialization skills necessary to help them become model citizens.

An aggressive dog can be a pain to deal with, especially now that we're all living closer together. A sound socialization program can help prevent the problems associated with aggressive dogs, but only if the owner is willing. I have had people tell me that they don't *want* their dogs to be friendly to everyone—they prefer the protection element of living with dogs. They go for isolation rather than socialization. This is most often a big mistake. Isolation and lack of experience and exposure breed aggression. It's unnecessary to treat a dog like this. I honestly believe that dogs, even the friendliest dogs, have a sixth sense that tells them when someone's a threat, and they will react appropriately. It doesn't make sense to inhibit and suppress a dog's natural friendliness. It's just not logical, and I think it even borders on cruelty.

CHEWING, BARKING, DIGGING, AND OTHER SO-CALLED BEHAVIOR PROBLEMS

"I chew. I bark. I dig. So? What's wrong with that?" This is what your dog might ask you if he were able to ask such a thing. Seen through his eyes, these are natural behaviors he was born wanting—and even needing—to do. It's really cruel not to allow him to follow his instincts, but we do that to dogs every day. A lot of dog owners wish they could extinguish these behaviors completely, and they go to extremes in trying. These are behaviors that go back to the dog's wild roots. They're part of the canine personality. You just have to learn to deal with them in a positive way so that everyone can live happily ever after.

Consider, for example, the puppy who chews. Puppies have to chew, just as babies do. It's part of the teething process. It brings relief to their itchy and irritated gums. It's not the *chewing* that's the problem— it's what's being chewed on. In raising a puppy, your job is to provide distractions and prevent disaster whenever possible. In this case, that means making sure the puppy has the right things to chew on.

Your puppy is chewing on your shoe? Ask yourself, what is your shoe doing where she can get to it? Now, find a diversion—a differ-ent, more acceptable toy for the puppy to use as a teething device, and keep toys like that all over the house. My house has been described as having been decorated in "puppy-toy modern." As soon as one of my puppies gets her sharp, little teeth into something she's not sup-posed to have, I just reach out and make the switch so quickly that she never even knows what happened. By the time she no longer needs to chew to relieve the irritation of teething, she'll know which toys are hers.

CHEWING REMEDIES

Dogs of all ages need to chew. Keep toys for your puppy— and someday for your adult dog—all over the house. A particular favorite of my dogs is a hollow bone or rubber toy filled with cheese spread or peanut butter, but this should be offered only to dogs who don't have weight problems. For teething pups, roll up a washcloth, saturate it with water, and then freeze it; this inexpensive toy satis-fies the chewing impulse and helps numb sore gums at the same time.

Most dogs love to dig. When I take my dogs out to the beach, I can't even describe the expressions on their faces as they dig trenches in the sand. This is also a female nesting trait. When my Great Dane Leilani was pregnant, before I put her whelping box together, she dug a huge crater in the backyard for a nest. I could actually climb in there with her. A lot of people would have gotten angry at her for destroying the land-scaping, but I understood what was going on.

DIGGING MANAGEMENT MADE EASY

Does your dog like to dig? Choose a corner of the yard that you fence off and designate as your pet's own private—and acceptable—digging spot, or make her a sandbox: a sturdy plastic pool filled with clean sandbox sand.

Don't get me wrong: you don't just have to sit back and tolerate your dog's digging and chewing because they're natural behaviors. You have to take on the responsibility of living with a puppy and teaching him how to be a well-mannered dog. You can't be with the puppy twenty-four hours a day, but you don't have to give him free run of the house when you're not home. When the puppy or dog is home alone, confinement to a designated room, dog crate, or exercise pen will save everyone some grief. But if you have a puppy, no matter what you do, sometime, something is going to be destroyed. You shouldn't take this plunge if you're not willing to deal with that. I felt terrible when my dogs got into my teddy-bear collection. I had some rather expensive ones, and those were the ones they got, of course. My dogs have good taste. They tore them up and all I could say was "my fault": they shouldn't have been allowed in the room with the stuffed animals.

Although you should take responsibility for such mishaps, you should not let the behaviors go uncorrected. Try to figure out why the dog is behaving in a certain way. Barking can be disruptive to a neighborhood and put you on a first-name basis with Animal Control. When a dog seems to bark and bark and bark constantly, it's usually caused by separation anxiety. Dogs can have abandonment issues, too, especially if someone in their past really did abandon them. Dogs never forget that kind of treatment, and they carry abandonment wounds with them, just as humans do.

A dog who barks incessantly is usually a lonely dog. For a lonely dog, even the negative attention of being yelled at or told to shut up is good attention. Most dogs just want to please their owners, but if they don't know how to please them, or aren't given the opportunity to try, they will try anything and everything to get the attention they crave. (Again, just like humans.) The constant barker should actually be given

As Leilani's puppies got older, I would take them out on what I called puppy adventures around the house—in this case out to the deck of the pool—to introduce them to the world. At first they'd follow me around like ducklings following their mother, but as they grew, so did their courage and independence, and soon I felt more like a herding dog overseeing a bunch of unruly sheep than a mother duck.

more positive attention, more intimate involvement in her family's daily activities, more exercise and play—more physical and emotional stimula- tion. She also needs to learn that it's okay to bark, but only for a reason—say, when someone is at the door or when a burglar is climbing through a window.

Behavior problems and defiance usually reach their peak during the puppy's adolescence, beginning at about four to six months of age. The dog is getting bigger and stronger and feeling more independent, just like a human teenager. This may leave you red in the face and pulling your hair out, but stay calm and consistent and persistent.

If you handle this stage gracefully and keep up with obedience train- ing, you'll eventually come out of it with a levelheaded dog who respects you and knows you are the boss. If you treat the dog with anger, fear, or indulgence, you'll be asking for trouble. That's how spoiled dogs are made. How you deal with this stage will help to determine just how the relationship will go—and who will be top dog—from here on out. Now is not the time to lighten up on the rules. Keep the pressure on and stick to the routine. The dog must understand that you are the voice of authority, and he isn't.

When my Great Dane Donna hit adolescence, she developed a sudden passion for the "catch-me" game. When I called her to me, she'd take off in the opposite direction. The main thing to remember when working on this common adolescent problem is that you mustn't punish a dog for coming to you. She won't want to come to you again if she knows that punishment or a correction is waiting for her when she does. The dog has to have a positive association with running into your arms, not a negative association that comes from punishment. My trainer and I worked on this by turning the tables on Donna and playing the catch-me game ourselves. The trainer held Donna while I showed her a treat and got excited about it. Then I would run away from her and call her name enthusiastically. Finally the trainer would let her go. Now not only was Donna doing the chasing, she was also learning to come when called—in a fun, positive, rewarding way.

If there's only one rule that you regard as the gospel in addressing behavior challenges, it is that you absolutely have to be consistent. It doesn't matter how old your pet is, puppy or adult, consistency is at the heart of mutual communication. To flip-flop is to confuse the dog.

To deal with the rebellion of adolescence, and with any type of behavior that becomes a problem, you must always remain consistent with the rules, your expectations, and your commands. Keep the puppy confined when you're not home, and make sure he gets plenty of exercise to vent the excess energy—play and walks, things he can do at his own pace. Most of all, be patient. We're always looking for the quick fix, a pill for everything, so of course we assume that a dog can learn through osmosis. But a dog learns only by repetition—consistent repetition.

When you are faced with a behavior problem—and most dog owners are at one time or another—any good behaviorist or trainer will tell you that first you should rule out any medical causes of the problem. It could be a disease, an infection, or even a vitamin deficiency that is to blame. The dog could be in pain. Then look at your routine and your role in your dog's life. Is your pup secure in his position in the family? Are long absences of his human companions causing him a severe case of separation anxiety? Does he need more attention? More exercise? A better method of confinement when you're not home? It's tough, because sometimes a dog may seem as if he's challenging your authority, but in truth he really doesn't understand what you're asking him to do. We always assume, "Oh, he's just testing me," but that's not always the case. Try to look at it from your dog's point of view. There's always a reason.

EARLY EXPERIENCES

Dogs have long memories. That's why it's important to remember that a negative experience during puppyhood can have far-reaching effects. When dogs are at this impressionable puppy age, it's important to try to prevent "bad" things from happening to them. The memories of those "bad" things and the fear can stick, and they can undermine the young animal's potential as a well-adjusted pet. Once it happens, it's much harder to bring the dog back around than it is to avoid negative situations in the first place.

Ryan was a poster puppy for dealing with potentially stressful situations. He had long suffered from a variety of health problems, so he was no stranger to the veterinarian's office or the drill of surgery. But these things never fazed him. His veterinarians would always tell me how nice it was to walk into the recovery room after one of Ryan's surgeries and find Ryan wagging his tail, anxious to let the doctor know how happy he was to see him.

Ryan wasn't always that way, though. When he was younger, I took him to an animal hospital for his vaccinations. Without even asking me about his background or getting to know him or anything, before I knew what was happening, they immediately tackled him, wrestled him to the floor, and muzzled him just to give him the injection. I was horrified. I never went back to that vet again, but the damage was done. For a long time after that, Ryan was terrified of anyone in a white coat. Who could blame him? After all the doctors I've known, I kind of feel the same way. But I recognized his fear and took it seriously. With the help of a much more sensitive veterinarian, I worked with Ryan and convinced him to trust those white coats again.

Now some trainers would disagree with me, but when overcoming negative experiences or introducing positive ones, treats can be a godsend. Many trainers don't believe in bribing a dog with treats, but I say, if bribery works and it doesn't hurt the dog, then go for it. Take nail clipping, for example. Most dogs don't like it. It's scary, and sometimes it hurts. But if the clipping of each nail is followed by a treat—a small healthy treat, of course, that won't interfere with the dog's overall nutrition—then it's much more tolerable. Just take it easy and respect your dog's or puppy's hesitancy. Start out slowly and do only a few nails at a time. You can't expect the puppy to sit and tolerate the clipping of all his nails in one sitting.

NAIL-CLIPPING DISTRACTIONS

In addition to treat bribes, distractions can also help a puppy get through a nail-clipping session. I sometimes put a dab of peanut butter on the roof of a dog's mouth to help keep her mind off what I'm doing to her paws. Do whatever you have to do to keep it all as pleasant as possible. You want nail clipping to be a positive experience, not a battle.

The earlier you introduce a puppy to nail clipping and other grooming procedures, the better—especially if the dog's future is in the show ring. This begins with helping her get accustomed to your touch as early as possible: gentle brushing, combing and bathing, plus introductions to the more sensitive procedures such as ear cleaning and the detested nail clipping. When you're just sitting and relaxing together, play with your puppy's ears and his feet, and lift his lips occasionally for a peek at his teeth. Toothbrushing and show judging are a lot more pleasant with a dog who will willingly open his mouth without biting. Anything you do like this with your puppy in a positive way will have long-term benefits for the dog and for the people who care for him. The veterinarian and the groomer will certainly appreciate your efforts, and you'll feel more confident knowing that your dog isn't going to attack someone poking around in his more sensitive areas during an important examination.

Even though dogs are creatures of habit, and essentially homebodies, every dog will experience some sort of abnormal event in her life, whether that is hospitalization, kenneling at the "pet hotel," a long car trip, or a bath and styling at the grooming shop. Do your pet a favor. Prepare her for the inevitable. Puppyhood is the ideal time to introduce your dog to these experiences in a positive way, even if that means just visiting the veterinarian's office or grooming shop for a treat. Make it positive and keep the treat bribes handy. Even after all that you've done, your dog may still shiver whenever she catches the scent of the veterinarian's office or realizes you've turned into the driveway of the boarding kennel. Don't worry—some of that is for dramatic effect. If she has been properly, positively, and consistently prepared, she'll get through it fine. And so will you.

SIX

THE PUPPY COMES HOME

Imagine you're a puppy. For eight weeks you have lived with your mom and your brothers and your sisters, safe and cozy and warm. Suddenly, a stranger comes into the room, and before you know what has happened, you're in a car. Then you're in a strange new place, filled with strange new sights and sounds and scents. It's kind of traumatic, isn't it?

It takes a while for both owner and puppy to feel that this is a permanent situation. As the new puppy owner, the stranger who caused all of this upheaval in the puppy's life, you need to make your new puppy feel at home. The best way to do that is to think ahead and do all you can to make the necessary arrangements, long before your puppy comes into your house.

PREPARING FOR THE NEW ARRIVAL

When you decide to bring a new puppy into your life, it's important to think everything out ahead of time: how the puppy will be cared for, where he will sleep, when, what, and where he'll be fed. Too many people make it up as they go along. If you do that, you're going to be frustrated, the puppy is going to be frustrated, and it will probably be a disaster. You'll end up allowing the dog to make it up as he goes along, too, and that is always a mistake. A dog, especially a young puppy in a new home, needs structure. Only a structured existence can give him a sense of security in his new environment.

So call a family meeting of everyone who lives in the house and discuss the new puppy, the rules of the house, and the new routine. Will

some rooms be off limits to the puppy? What sort of sleeping accommo-
dations will the puppy have? Will the puppy be allowed on the furniture? Who will feed the puppy? Will you be crate-training the puppy?
How will you introduce him to the other pets? How will you approach
housetraining? Where and how will the puppy be confined when no
one is home? And don't forget to discuss puppy-proofing: you'll need to
try to block off electrical cords, store ground-level books on a higher
shelf of the bookshelf, and move the valuable antique coffee table into
the guest room for a while. You've got your work cut out for you.

It helps to write everything down. We all forget, and we can all use
encouraging reminders to be consistent and fair. If you write the game
plan down and everybody goes through the rules and guidelines and
understands them from the outset, you'll give yourself a better chance of
being a better, more consistent companion and caretaker to your puppy.
You'll also give your puppy more of a chance of meeting your expectations. A long and successful relationship should be your reward.

As the puppy gets older and blossoms into a well-trained, well-
mannered dog, you might be able to change the rules and the routine
some. When Freeway and Leilani were young, the kitchen was off limits, but as they matured, I lightened up on that rule. As dogs mature, the
rhythms of the household will change. Over time you will get to know
each other, learn to anticipate your dog's actions, and you'll both learn to
trust and understand each other. But in the beginning, it is essential to
put a system in place. With that system you can gently teach the dog
what is expected of him.

If you have kids in the house, you'll have to spend some time training them, too. It takes a lot of patience, but you can train a dog to take a
treat out of your hand very gently. Similarly, you can teach a child to
treat a dog gently. Kids have to learn respect for dogs. They can share a
special bond with the dog, but they have to be supervised. There has to
be mutual respect. A lot of people don't know how to approach dogs,
and their kids need to learn, too. The dog can't be the kids' in-home
punching bag or toy. Too many kids think that dogs are stuffed teddy
bears put on the earth just so we can hug and squeeze them. Kids need
to learn how to introduce themselves to a dog, how to pet a dog, and

how to offer him treats. They need to learn that teasing is unacceptable, and so is screaming and running up to a dog, or pouncing down on a sleeping dog and throwing your arms around his neck. It isn't cute, and it isn't safe. Adults need to look out for the safety of their kids and the safety of their dogs.

When my niece and nephew were small and would visit, they were fascinated by Freeway. That was understandable. But he wasn't always as fascinated by them. They'd spend some time together, with me watching to make sure that neither of them forced themselves on him too much, and then Freeway would disappear. I would find him hiding in the closet in my room, his sanctuary. When the kids asked, "Where's Freeway? We want to play with him," I'd say that he was resting. "Let's give him some space for a while." As a society we feel that dogs should just naturally want to be with kids, but I wasn't going to force Freeway into a situation he wasn't comfortable with. Under no circumstances would I have allowed the kids to go into that closet. Forcing the issue is what gets people, and dogs, into trouble.

When a child is educated about dogs, the bond can be wonderful. Children love taking care of dogs (but remember, it should always be an adult's responsibility). They love to feed them and walk them. They can also be dazzled by training. When I first began experimenting with click-and-treat training with Nipper, I showed a friend's young nephew how to teach Nipper to touch a hockey puck with her nose at the sound of the clicker, then get her to repeat it with a signal, a click, and a treat. They both loved it. The little boy eventually got her to pick up the puck and bring it to him. He was so jazzed that he could teach a dog a trick. Positive experiences like this are what we want kids to carry with them into adulthood, because someday, they are going to be the decision-making pet owners. For the good of dogs, we want them to do it right.

THE PUPPY'S ACCOMMODATIONS

First you plan, then you gather your supplies. That's a logical order. Again, writing things down can help. Take your shopping list to the pet supply store and prepare for the arrival of your new puppy. You'll need toys, grooming supplies, bedding, food, collar and lead, and a crate if you'll be crate-training—and that's just the beginning.

One of your first concerns will be your pet's food. It's best not to make drastic dietary changes during this transition time, so find out what kind of food he has been fed and continue with it for a while. This doesn't mean you have to feed him this food for life. Just take your time introducing the new food. You can really upset a puppy's delicate tummy if you suddenly change his diet, so when it's time to make the transition, gradually switch over to the preferred food by mixing it a little at a time with the old food until all the puppy is getting is the new food. Those first days in a new home can be stressful enough for a puppy. If you add gastrointestinal upset and diarrhea to it, you'll undoubtedly think the puppy is sick, resulting in even more stress and, possibly, unnecessary trips to the veterinarian. So easy on the treats and take your time switching foods.

Consider crate-training your puppy. A lot of people don't like the idea of "putting a dog in a box," and yes, crate-training can be abused, but I think crate-training can be a great thing. Don't use the crate for punishment or just to get the dog out of the way for hours at a time. That is where the crate becomes cruel. Look at the crate as a temporary den, or haven, for your dog. A crate will provide a puppy with a secure and cozy place to sleep, but it will also let him know that someone else in the house is the boss, not him.

Eventually, once your dog matures, you might decide it's okay if he sleeps on your bed—Nipper earned that privilege at about the time of her first birthday. Many trainers disapprove of that idea even though thousands of people do it. (Think about the term *three-dog night,* a night so cold you need three dogs to keep you warm.) But for now, the puppy needs the structure of a more humble sleeping space, either in a crate or an exercise pen—something that will keep the puppy safe and secure at night and during the day when you're not at home to supervise him. A crate gives the puppy his own little corner of the world, where he can sleep and hide and feel safe.

The crate you choose should be large enough for the puppy (or dog) to walk in and turn around in. If yours is a large-breed puppy, you may

It's an exciting day when a puppy comes into its new home, but it can be a sad day for the breeder who has to say good-bye. I got to know each of Leilani's puppies well, and I'd cry when they'd leave to go to their new homes, hoping that I did a good job matching them with their new families.

want to purchase a small, inexpensive crate for the puppy months before purchasing the full-size model, or buy the crate he'll need as an adult now. If you follow the latter plan, you can make the crate cozier inside for your puppy by padding it with towels and blankets and toys. You should outfit the crate this way anyway, of course, to make it a comfortable bed that your puppy will view as a sanctuary.

> ### NEW-PUPPY SHOPPING LIST
>
> - Puppy food
>
> - Food and water dishes
>
> - Grooming supplies (brush, comb, nail clippers, puppy shampoo)
>
> - Safe chew toys
>
> - Buckle collar, lead, and identification tag
>
> - Dog crate

As for toys, don't think you have to spend a fortune on them. I do tend to go a little overboard with toys myself, but I have found that the toys my puppies have been most interested in are things you never think about, things just lying around the house: Cardboard boxes are a favorite with my dogs. These keep them busy for a long time, both as chew toys and hiding places, and they're easy to clean up once they've been shredded by sharp puppy teeth.

Sometimes the toys your dog finds lying around the house aren't toys at all, but dogs don't know the difference. So you must keep anything that you don't want to become a puppy toy out of reach. Puppies are not discriminating. It's amazing what they can do to books, for example. And if you give your dogs stuffed toys to chew on, such as a stuffed dog, you give up the right to get mad at them if they wander into your valuable collection of teddy bears. The remedy is quite simple: close the door to the teddy-bear room—always.

Prevent problems *before* they happen, before you end up getting angry. Do everything you can to keep your dogs—and your stuff—out of trouble. Know what your puppy is doing all the time, and as soon as she starts gnawing on something you'd rather she not gnaw on, such as a live electrical cord or the couch, make a quick substitution with something that is acceptable. Make the substitute seem much more interesting and more fun to play with than the original object of her attentions— and while you're at it, get that electrical cord out of her reach. Don't give your dog time to protest or even to think about the switch, and praise her for chewing on the right things.

It's your job to protect your puppy and to keep life interesting. You can do this by offering her a variety of safe toys. You can even rotate the toys so that old favorites become new again when you haul them out of the closet after a few days' hiatus. Different puppies prefer different toys, and those tastes can change from day to day. Some like stuffed fleece toys, some like rawhide bones, some like squeaky toys, and some lose interest as soon as the squeak is out (which can happen quickly if your pup is an enthusiastic chewer). The benefit of toys is that they entertain the puppy, while also satisfying her need to chew and may thus keep her from the serious problem of chewing the wrong stuff.

THE FIRST NIGHT AND BEYOND

It's hard to think of anything much more exciting than bringing a new puppy home. It feels like a cause for celebration. But you have to get down to business right away. Start establishing some structure and routine for the young dog from the very first moment. Later on, when you've gotten to know each other better, then you might be able to take some liberties and alter the routine a little, maybe even have a welcome-puppy party. But in the beginning, the structure and the routine will help her understand her place in her new family and offer her a sense of security that she really needs right now.

Think about how and when you should bring your new pet home. For most people, the beginning of a weekend is ideal. Don't bring her home in the middle of Christmas or a big, noisy block party. Don't be too excited and show her off to friends and family. Wait a few days. Allow her to adjust to her new surroundings and the people and other animals she'll be living with. This is her family now. It's important that everybody get acquainted in the least stressful way possible. Her society debut can wait.

Get into the housetraining routine and start feeding her on a schedule right away. If the puppy wants to play, then play, but keep the games kind of mellow in the beginning. When she wants to take a nap—and puppies do need to nap throughout the day—show her to her sleeping place and allow her some peace and quiet. This will help her understand

Puppies are wonderful, but they do grow into dogs—very quickly. I loved having a pile of Leilani's pups on top of me, but imagine trying to do this with ten full-grown Danes! Enjoy puppyhood while it lasts, but get a dog because you love dogs—full-grown adult dogs—not because you find yourself enchanted by a cute, cuddly puppy.

that there is a schedule in this house that she can depend on. Establishing the routine from the beginning will help you and the puppy settle into a sense of normalcy right away. Soon she'll be telling *you* when it's time to go to bed.

When Nipper joined our family, she was nervous. Here were these huge creatures that she could tell were dogs, but which were different from anything she had ever seen before—Freeway, Ryan, and at the time, Murphy. I didn't worry about Freeway and Ryan. They had lived through countless puppies in our house, always accepting of everyone who came through the door. But I was a little worried about Murphy, who wanted to play but was too big and too rough for Nipper. At that point, all Nipper wanted was to stay in my arms, and that's where I thought she should be, too—without coddling of course.

During those first nights, you may not get much sleep as the puppy struggles through the anxiety of being separated from her family. This is actually one time when seeing the world through your puppy's eyes can cause problems. You can't help but pity the poor thing. She's away from her family and nervous about her new surroundings. It's tempting to baby her, to let her do whatever she wants, to let discipline wait until tomorrow . . . or next week . . . maybe next month. Follow these natural sympathies, and you're in for trouble.

Your heart may be in the right place, but now it's time to resist that babying impulse and get started right away in establishing your relationship and the routine in the puppy's new home. You want to get these messages across to her: "I'm here for you. You're not abandoned. You're not isolated and alone. But I have certain expectations and I'm going to help you learn what those are." If you're clear and consistent about it, even young puppies are capable of understanding this message. They long for that structure. By sending a consistent message, you're building a strong foundation from day one. You can do plenty of cuddling and cooing with your puppy, of course, but you need to get to work right away on housetraining and setting her physical and behavioral boundaries.

Be warned: puppies can be very persistent. Their cries can break your heart—and shatter your eardrums. When your puppy realizes that she can't snuggle under the covers with you that first night at bedtime— and she can't!—she may protest so loud that the neighbors think you're torturing your new pet. But don't give in. You're either training *her,* or she's training you. Remember that.

Nipper's first night went pretty smoothly. I put her in her little puppy crate with a towel and toys and a hot-water bottle (to mimic mom's warmth; sometimes it helps to use a ticking clock, too, to suggest a heartbeat). Then I set the crate down next to my bed so she could see me—not on the bed, but next to it. Whenever she'd start complaining, I'd stick my finger in her crate for reassurance, and that would quiet her down, but I wouldn't take her out of the crate. She was learning from that first moment that she wasn't being abandoned, but also that tantrums would not get her what she wanted. She eventually learned— and quickly—that if she wanted out of the crate, she should not cry; only when she was quiet would I let her out. The lesson began during that first night, and I firmly believe that this is the reason she'll now settle down so quickly on planes. What you do from the very beginning definitely makes a difference in the long term.

THE HOUSE RULES

If you're going to live peacefully together, in the house or out and about as part of society, you have to set rules and you have to be consistent. You also have to inform visitors how to approach and treat your dogs. The rules must apply to everyone, people and dogs.

Let's say I have a new puppy in the house and the rule, for now, is that the puppy cannot sleep on my bed because we're in training mode. Later, when the dog is older, I might lighten up because we will have reached our stride in bonding and communication, but for now, I expect everyone to honor the house rule. It's too frustrating later on to tighten up the rules on a puppy that has been allowed too much freedom and independence. He just won't understand when you say, "Well, I *used* to allow you on my bed when you were a puppy, but now you're just too big. You're banished to the other room or the backyard." By honoring the rules from the beginning, you prevent the confusion and frustration.

For me, this idea of rules takes on special significance because of my travel schedule. I can't always be home with my dogs so I have to rely on other people to take care of them in my house. I have to make sure that these people are informed about the rules and honor them. I insist on it in the name of consistency.

I also set up situations that give me an opportunity to teach my dogs the house rules. When Ryan and Freeway were young, I would have dinner parties, which were less for me and more for the socialization of my dogs, an opportunity for the boys to see people come into the house and have a meal, while my boys practiced staying in a down-stay during an entire dinner. It was a great way for them to get accustomed to the house rules. Thanks to those dinner parties, I know I can have guests with the dogs right there in the house, in the dining room even, with never a problem. I feel secure, the dogs feel secure, and my guests feel secure. Well, *most* of them do. Now with a house full of young dogs again, well, I guess it's time to start sending out some dinner invitations.

Here are Donna's puppies—a handsome bunch—looking apprehensive on their first visit to the veterinarian's office. I always try to make this the most positive experience I can, which means making sure that they get plenty of cookies from both me and the veterinarian. That way they'll want to go back again, again, and again, even if a shot is involved.

So here are my house rules:

Everyone must get along. This is the fundamental law of the multidog household—probably the most important house rule of all. Everybody has to get along together or changes have to be made. I mean, I will tolerate some uncooperative, unmannerly behavior from temporary canine guests—foster dogs, rescued dogs, or dogs belonging to friends—but *my* dogs have to coexist peacefully.

If your dogs don't get along, it's just exhausting. Jealousies and flare-ups are natural from time to time, but you learn to know the difference between temporary arguments and permanent hatred. When dogs need to be kept permanently apart, there's so much forethought involved: How will you feed them? Who goes where and when do they go out? How do you move the dogs from room to room? You have to be constantly thinking a number of steps ahead before you make a move to make sure the archenemies don't come into contact with each other; otherwise you have a riot on your hands. I've had to do this from time to time, and managing it became instinctive, but try to explain it to someone who's watching your house and your dogs! No one will have the same degree of love, concern, and protective thoughts for your dogs as you do.

I've had dogs that couldn't get along, dogs that wouldn't get along— dogs that could kill each other if I didn't keep them apart. Because of this, I have had to make some regrettable changes along the way: I have had to place dogs with other families when their behavior was too disruptive, as was the case with my Great Dane Murphy. At two and a half, she was causing too much trouble for my two older Danes, Ryan and Freeway, challenging them constantly for the leadership position, which she figured was rightly hers because of her superior strength and stamina. When she wasn't challenging them, she was trying to play with them, and they were too old to be interested.

Finally I made the tough decision that Murphy had to go. When making decisions like this, it's the dogs who have lived with me longer who have to take priority. She was making their lives hell, and the harmony in the household was shot. The story has a happy ending—I wouldn't have it any other way. Murphy went to live with a family that loves her dearly, a family that was better equipped to deal with her youthful energy in such a large package.

Some multidog situations can accommodate dogs who don't get along with each other. I know breeders with large kennels where mutual respect and admiration among the dogs aren't requirements, and it doesn't really matter who gets along, but that's not what I want in my house. We have a more intimate, day-to-day arrangement, and we have all learned to get along. It's what makes us a family.

Consider the consequences of your actions. When you live with a large dog, you can't leave a roast to thaw on the kitchen counter, go run some errands, and expect that it will still be there when you come back. When you live with more than one large dog, well, the teamwork they'll use to get what they want is astounding.

Obviously I'm speaking here from a specific experience. But in my defense, I didn't leave the roast on the countertop. I left it in the sink, where I mistakenly thought they couldn't possibly reach it. But Ryan was apparently on a mission. He found the roast, retrieved it with what must have been some pretty acrobatic contortions, and shared it with Donna and Freeway. Ryan always shared. They devoured the frozen roast together and left only the plastic wrap and the foam base—licked perfectly clean, of course.

Bags of potato chips, loaves of bread: I've learned my lessons. Now that I'm living with three smaller dogs and one Great Dane who's not as limber as he used to be, you might think that I don't have to worry any-more. Well, Nipper can almost jump up on the counter. I can see it now: she jumps up, grabs the forbidden fruit, tosses it to Speedo, who tosses it to Mikey, and the rest is history. Fortunately, because of my history with my bigger guys, I'm already in the habit of keeping things off the counter. I just have to learn that I can't relax that policy now. Anyone who is here taking care of the dogs knows that food can't be left on the coun-ters or in the sink. The only places where anything will be safe are in the oven or refrigerator with the doors closed—until the dogs figure out how to open those, which really isn't out of the realm of possibilities.

WRITE IT DOWN

To ensure that everyone obeys the house rules, write them down and post them in a prominent place where everyone can see them and enforce them. No excuses: the house rules apply to everyone.

Manners will be observed. I like my dogs to have manners. When you have as many dogs as I do, it's a necessity. But teaching manners is just as important for people with only one dog. It's annoying to walk into a house and be accosted by dogs who want to bite your ankles or knock you over or won't stop barking. It's nice when dogs greet you with enthusiasm, it's a good feeling to know they're so excited to see you, but when the greeting period is over, the dogs need to listen and behave.

The goal is to make your dogs a pleasure to be around, not a nui-sance. It's the owner's job to teach them how to live up to that. For example, you're just inviting trouble if you feed your pet table scraps from the table. If somebody complains about your dog begging at the table, then it's a behavior that you taught. The same goes for a dog's jumping up on you. This may be cute when the dog is a puppy and only comes up to your knee, but to have a dog the size of Freeway jump up on you . . . well, he could knock you through a sliding glass door. That's not so cute.

You have to teach the puppy early on what is acceptable and what isn't, and make sure everyone in the house knows it, too. House rules are for everyone, and everyone will benefit. Well-mannered dogs and the people who made them that way can be a joy to be around. They're also good PR for all dogs. Dogs who behave help to make dogs in general welcome additions in public places, and they increase society's respect for canines. I'm all for that.

House rules will be enforced both at home and on the road. Wherever we are, whether at home or in a hotel room in New York City, house rules apply. This is true even if I have to inform other people about the rules, too. Once when I was in a critical training stage with Nipper, I took her with me for a television appearance. I left her in her travel crate backstage, and when I came back, one of the crew members had taken her out of the crate and was cuddling her.

"She was whimpering," the woman told me. "I couldn't just leave her there like that crying. I felt too sorry for her." I know this woman's intentions were good, but I tried to tell her nicely that the message that gives the dog is that all she has to do is cry and make noise, and she'll get taken out. That's not the message I want my dogs getting, and I don't want them getting mixed messages either. The house rules extend beyond the house, and I do my best to let everyone know just what those rules are.

I've had to do this when I visit some breeder friends of mine in Northern California, too. They don't have a problem with feeding their dogs table scraps—and doing it right from the table. It's a rule of their house that dogs can and will be fed from the table. But it's not good manners, and it's not good for a dog's health. I have to remind my friends when I'm at their place that their house rule does not apply to my dogs.

They honor my rule, and I appreciate it. My dogs don't appreciate it, of course, but that's to be expected.

For me, the proof that I'm doing the right thing is the freedom my dogs enjoy, whether we're at home or on the road. They don't have to be put away in a crate when guests come to dinner, and when we're sharing the close quarters of a hotel room, it's peaceful and cozy, even when I order room service. Nipper can sit with me on the bed while I eat a hamburger and watch TV. She'll just lie down right beside me and leave the food alone. That's amazing, really. But it only comes from consistent observance and enforcement of the house rules.

SEVEN

HOUSETRAINING MADE EASY

I don't understand why people have so much trouble housetraining their dogs. Housetraining is easy if you think like a dog and you're patient and consistent.

Mention housetraining and you hear groans and moans. Go to an animal shelter and see yet another dog dropped off because his owners just couldn't get him to understand that the living room carpet is not his bathroom. See all the dogs permanently sentenced to life in the backyard or chained to a tree. All because of an owner who could not hold up his end of the dog/owner contract.

A FRUSTRATING PROSPECT

When owners have housetraining problems with a dog, it is almost always because the owners aren't communicating clearly enough with the dog. Or perhaps they are doing only half of what is required to get a dog trained. Sometimes it's actually a miracle that certain dogs are ever able to be housetrained at all, considering the fuzzy signals people give their pets to housetrain them. A puddle in the corner of the living room is usually the sign of a dog who doesn't have the first clue about what is expected of her. It's not a malicious act. She just doesn't understand—if she did, she would at least leave the puddle by the door. Finally, dogs like this give up, and out of desperation, some figure out how to housetrain themselves. But it shouldn't be that way.

When we have an "accident" in our house, I take responsibility. Usually the dog is making an attempt to please me, to do what she thinks

I want her to do. This is the case when I find a puddle by the door. Now, how can I possibly get mad at her? She was obviously trying. She was moving in the right direction, but I wasn't there to help her succeed. I wasn't paying attention. This is a signal to me that I am lacking in my consistent handling of the situation and I need to reevaluate the routine we have set up for housetraining. I'm glad to say that in my house, accidents are rare, but sadly, it's a pretty common situation in far too many dog-owning households because the owners just haven't been consistent in housetraining their dogs. The good news is that there is a remedy. It's never too late to get a dog housetrained.

A lot of owners complain about the challenge of housetraining, even though they haven't really done much of anything toward getting their dogs trained. For some reason, they think housetraining happens naturally. They figure that sooner or later dogs just read our minds and realize what we expect from them. They think that just sending a dog outside by himself is all they have to do. They open the door, the dog goes out and chases some birds, comes back in, and his owners assume he did his business. He didn't do his business, of course—he chased birds. Later, when the urge strikes him, he'll use the dining room floor for a bathroom, and his owners will be furious.

Dogs aren't cats, who naturally know how to use the litter box, no explanations necessary. For dogs, explanations *are* necessary. Like it or not, you're the one who has to do the explaining, and it can be time-consuming.

Housetraining is something you commit to when you bring a puppy—or an older dog in need of a refresher course—into your household. It's not fair to ignore this responsibility, because you'll just end up being angry and frustrated with your pet. See the situation from your puppy's perspective, figure out just what your pet needs to know to carry out your wishes, and figure out how you need to communicate this through words and actions. You'll find it can be a rewarding experience to achieve this together. This may be the first victory like this that you share, and it can launch a beautiful partnership.

Housetraining requires time, energy, consistency, and observation. It also won't happen overnight, even if you are doing everything right.

Some breeds are notoriously more difficult to housetrain, and so are some older dogs, usually because of the harsh "training" methods used on them before they landed in your more compassionate, more capable hands. However you slice it, though, you can't really expect perfection until the dog reaches eight, ten, even twelve months of age. At that point, assuming you've done everything well, full understanding clicks in, along with the dog's ability to consciously control his bodily functions.

I had a little bit of trouble housetraining my Border Terrier, Mikey, when he first came into the house because of his insecurity marking, which is entirely different from eliminating because a dog hasn't been housetrained. This didn't worry me because I knew why Mikey was marking: he felt vulnerable in this house of big dogs, and he was trying to say, "Hey, there are all these other dogs here, but this is my house, too." It didn't last long, but it might have become permanent if I had yelled at him or punished him. Interpreting my punishment as a negative reaction to the act of eliminating, he would have become afraid to "go" in front of me and would instead have learned to hide his little presents around the house. Rather than punishing him, I worked with him in other areas to beef up his sense of security and safety. As soon as he felt more secure, which comes from consistent handling, a predictable routine, and work in obedience training, he didn't feel the need to mark anymore.

Submissive urination is also different from imperfect housetraining. A lot is going on with a puppy. If she's in a new environment, and she's feeling intimidated, submissive urination often results. If your puppy starts doing this—squatting and peeing to show her submissiveness— you mustn't punish her. You mustn't yell at her or behave aggressively in any way—anger will only upset her even more, make it worse, and cement the habit, maybe even permanently.

A better remedy is to ignore the dog and walk away. If you're petting her when she begins to urinate submissively, immediately stop petting her. Then, when she stops urinating, start petting her again. It works, but it takes time and—yes, that word again—consistency, but it worked with a dog I bred named Sebastian. He ranked tenth in the dominance hierarchy of his litter of 10, so his insecurity was understandable.

As soon as Leilani's pups started eating solid food, I established a routine for them. Chow time was a communal affair, when they dined out of a long trough on moistened, mushy puppy kibble. After dinner we'd go outside for a romp, which helped to introduce them to the housetraining routine (and made cleaning up after ten puppies a little easier for me).

But his owners worked with him with the "ignore it" method, and he snapped out of it. He got the picture that, in their eyes, he was not number ten but number one. They were patient. If you deal with the habit gently and resist the temptation to punish, you will allow the dog to grow out of it.

"RUB HIS NOSE IN IT" AND OTHER HORROR STORIES

Housetraining is probably the number one area of dog care where owners regularly vent their frustrations and anger—and totally confuse their dogs. Don't rub the dog's nose in it. Don't punish the dog hours after he has soiled the carpet when you were late coming home and he had no way to go outside. Don't think that the dog soiled the rug just to make you mad. I have to confess that at times I've had those feelings, too, irritated by repeated accidents from a dog that I could have sworn was perfectly housetrained. It's a common mistake to take the dog's accident as a personal affront. We all project our weaknesses onto our dogs, but dogs really aren't as devious as we are.

You can do so much damage to a dog by believing ridiculous ideas and subjecting your pet to them. And that damage can take months to correct. Just the thought of subjecting a really sensitive dog such as a Great Dane to the "rub the nose in it" method . . . horrible! What do proponents of such ideas think this teaches dogs? That people are barbaric idiots, that's what it teaches them. The dog ends up in utter confusion, wondering just why this person he trusted is doing this to him. And how could he ever trust his owner again? How could he ever feel the same respect for this person?

The attraction of quick schemes comes from our fundamental impatience. We want our pets to be housetrained and housetrained *now,* the great American quick fix. Here's the real fix and it ain't quick: If you want to housetrain a dog and reach that level of perfection, you have to pay attention. You have to watch him—all the time—for signs that he's about to go. When you get him outside, you have to be there to watch him as he eliminates, then praise him when he does. Praise him lavishly.

Living with dogs is very glamorous—not! Bathroom clean-up duty is just another issue to consider when you choose to live with dogs, and one that you can't ignore, even though a lot of people try. Dog ownership is not always pretty, and it's not fair to be the one bad apple who neglects to clean up after his or her pet in a community of responsible owners.

Celebrate his doing it in the right place at the right time. And don't yell when he slips up.

Another wives' tale that might be linked to housetraining is the idea that crate-training is cruel. Although some people overuse the crate, it can be a wonderful housetraining tool when we use it correctly. After you take the dog out of the crate to go to the bathroom, praise him for doing his business, then let him live like a normal dog with you. Don't immediately put him back in the crate. Use the crate as a tool, not as a device that replaces your responsibilities as an owner. Make the crate a pleasant place where he can go to feel secure.

The crate can be a valuable tool if you're housetraining an older dog, too. Maybe a previous method didn't work with the dog, or maybe you've taken in a dog who has never even been introduced to house-training. The crate can be sort of a novelty that tells the dog, "We're going to try something different now." You change your whole method, and the crate plays an important role in that. Remember that before you do anything, you have to help the dog or puppy get acquainted with the crate by making it comfortable and cozy and rewarding your pet for spending time inside it. She has to see it as a positive thing. Remember, it's not solitary confinement.

EFFECTIVE ACCIDENT CLEANUP

No matter how diligent you are, you need to accept that when you're housetraining a puppy, some accidents will happen. Clean these up with enzyme products that help remove the scent and prevent the puppy from returning to the spot again later.

ELIMINATING ON COMMAND

You can teach a dog to eliminate on command. This can be a foreign concept to people, unless they've had a trainer who's introduced them to it. It's not something that's widely known or widely discussed. I picked it up on the show circuit. If you're showing a dog, it's nice to be able to take him out to the grass before you are called into the ring and ask the dog to empty his bladder and bowels with a simple command. Then you can be more confident knowing that he has done his business before you go into the show ring, and there won't be any surprises while the judge is evaluating just how spectacular your dog is. A surprise like that can really put a damper on the overall image you're trying to present.

What's also nice is that this is one of the easiest commands you can teach a dog. It's a command for a natural function, so all you have to do is wait for the dog to perform that natural function, give the command when he does, then praise him for doing what came naturally. What could be easier? It sure comes in handy when you're traveling, too. You can jump out of the car at a gas station or rest stop, give the command, the dog does his business, then you're back in the car and on the road again.

Necessity is what inspired me to teach my Great Dane Donna to go on command. We just figured it out naturally together. Donna hated cold weather, so she wasn't too excited when we visited the Pacific Northwest once when it was snowing. I would take her outside and she would just stand in one place and shiver. I decided to use this opportunity to teach her a new command, and she seemed grateful for it. When I would give the "Go potty!" command, she knew what she needed to do to get out of the situation. It gave her some guidance. It took her mind off her misery of being out in the cold, which sort of just paralyzed her both physically and emotionally. She knew if she obeyed the command, she could get back inside as a reward. The command got her attention. She learned quickly what I wanted from her, and just how beneficial it could be to her.

THE FRANCES LOUGANIS HOW-TO OF HOUSETRAINING

Housetraining comes naturally to me because I had such an excellent mentor: my mom. When I was growing up, she was wonderful at housetraining our dogs. As soon as the dog woke up in the morning or from a nap, she took him outside where he was supposed to go. As soon as the dog finished eating, out they went. She'd stay out there with the dog, making sure he did his business. Then she'd praise him when he did. She knew what she was doing, and she made the necessary effort to do it right. There was never any fuss, never any frustration, and hardly ever any accidents.

I was very young when I witnessed my mom in action at this, but by watching her I learned firsthand about the consistency that housetraining—and any kind of training—requires. Obviously it left a long-lasting impression on me. I've carried on the same tradition with my dogs, and I guess that's why I can't understand why housetraining is such a problem for people. But so many people go only halfway with what they need to do.

People want an easy recipe for housetraining, and really the recipe *is* simple: The puppy is taking a nap in the crate or similar confined area such as an exercise pen in the kitchen. She wakes up, you take her out of the crate, carry her outside, put her down, and she does her business. Then you reward her with a rousing game of chase or fetch. The thing is: *you have to follow this routine after each and every nap, each and every meal, as soon as she wakes up in the morning and before she goes to bed at night.* It's consistency that turns this simple recipe into the perfect soufflé.

If it's a puppy you're training, she'll be sleeping a lot, so it's not like you have to hover over her all the time. You have to be sensitive to the rhythms of her day and the restrictions of her tiny bladder. She can't

My mom, Frances, sitting with her little namesake from Leilani's litter of ten. Mom was always a natural at housetraining dogs and she taught me well. Like a drill sergeant, she knew you have to keep puppies on a schedule: eat, go out, wait, praise, play, go out, wait, praise, nap time, go out, wait, praise. It's a recipe that works.

physically hold it in while you're at work all day. When she is awake, you should be watching her closely for the telltale signs of sniffing and circling. The same is true of an older dog that you're housetraining. His bladder may be bigger, but you can't allow him free run of rooms where you can't watch him. You have to be able to spot his signals, because he needs the consistency just as much as the young puppy does if the housetraining is going to be successful.

Be sensitive to the underdeveloped puppy brain, too. It's easy for a puppy to get distracted. He may understand what you're asking him to do when you set him down in the corner of the yard that you have decided will be his bathroom, but there may just be too many fun sights, sounds, and smells more interesting than squatting and eliminating in a particular place. Here, too, the command can come in handy. That simple word—*potty* or whatever you decide to use—can grab his attention, help him focus, and remind him why you're there. There will be plenty of time afterward to play.

The major rule of thumb in housetraining is *no punishment.* Whether you're training a puppy or an older dog, this is a time for *positive reinforcement only.* If you are going to correct the dog—and correction is sometimes appropriate—it can only be when you catch him in the act. I can't even count the number of people who have said, "My dog had an accident while I was at work and, boy, was he ashamed," when his owner got home two, three, four hours later. Dogs don't remember what they did. They react to the owner's obviously negative body language and tone of voice. Explain this to the owner, though, and you'll be talking to a brick wall. "My dog *knew* what he did and he felt guilty." Tells you more about the owner than the dog, doesn't it?

If you can't catch the dog in the act, don't even bother saying anything. When you *do* catch him in the act, use positive correction, which is different from punishment. Catch him in the act and startle—don't terrify—him, by loudly calling out anything but his name. Shocked, he will usually stop the flow. This will give you the opportunity to whisk him outdoors to finish up in a more acceptable spot. You haven't punished the dog, but you have gotten his attention and taught him, in a positive and immediate way, what you want him to do—and what you don't want him to do. Sure you'd rather not have to do this. You'd rather he not start going on the floor in the first place. But when he does and you're there to see it, you have a golden opportunity for effective teaching.

A MESSY GAME

When your dog does mess in the house, and he will, remove him from the scene of the crime before you clean up the mess. Otherwise, he may get the idea that he has invented a great new game for you.

This type of correction and teaching was really tough with my deaf Dane, Ryan, though. When he was a young puppy, I couldn't yell to him or make some other loud noise to get his attention when I'd catch him in the act the way you can and should do with a hearing dog. With Ryan, I'd have to grab him to get his attention, so I had to be quick on my feet to get across the room in time to catch him in midflow. It was worth the effort. He learned quickly, and he knew it wasn't punishment. I wasn't shaking him or anything like that. I was just getting his attention abruptly and dramatically with my touch. Then I'd pick him up and put him outside to finish up, where I'd praise him lavishly. Dogs learn quickly if you give them a chance. You just have to be clear in what you're trying to teach them.

Nipper was a quick learner, too, but she got the lesson a little confused. Whenever she had to go "potty" (our command) or gave me the signal that she was about to go, I would pick her up, take her outside, put her down in the appropriate spot, and she would go. Then I'd give her a treat, a reward and praise. But somehow she wasn't associating the elimination act with her being moved suddenly outside or with the feel of the grass between her toes. She was associating the routine with my putting her down. So even when we were in the house, if I picked her up and then put her down on the floor somewhere, she'd "go potty"—even if it was on the carpet! Wherever I put her down, she assumed that that's what she was supposed to do, and that's where she was supposed to do it.

I put myself in Nipper's position, and I could just hear her reasoning: "Well, every time he puts me down, I get praised for going potty, so I'll go potty." In her mind, she was doing what I was asking her to do. She

Before we are called into the show ring to strut our stuff, I take Donna for a walk to encourage her to do her business. This is just one situation where teaching a dog to "potty" on command comes in handy.

could hardly be blamed for that. I couldn't punish her for doing what she thought was the right thing. I had to change my method.

The change was subtle. I would carry her to the doorway and put her down right next to it. Then, before she had time to do her business, I would enthusiastically call her to me and run to "the spot." The lightbulb flashed in her little head right away. Just this small change showed her that what mattered was her being outside, not just being put down. Soon we got to the point where I could just open the door of the crate and she'd run outside. What was critical was the routine and my involvement.

Nipper wanted to figure out what I was asking her to do. All dogs do. But to help them in that, you have to be part of the process—*every step of the way.* You have to watch the dog and interact with her. You have to put yourself in her thought process. And you have to be patient. You have to hang out there with her for a while and give her a chance. If you really want to be foolproof, you have to watch and see her go. That way you can praise her, and that way you know firsthand that she's understanding and making progress.

One friend of mine would take his puppy out and immediately bring him back in the house as soon as the pup eliminated. Once inside, the puppy would eliminate again, completely frustrating his owner. Obviously once was not enough for this particular puppy, so his owner had to learn to be more patient. You can't assume just because a dog, especially a puppy, eliminates once that his tank is empty. It's the rare dog that is finished in a single squat or lift of the leg. My friend had to learn what *was* enough, what was normal, for his puppy and keep him outside until he was finished. Once he figured this out, the problem was solved.

As your puppy gets older, he won't have to eliminate as often during the day, but don't expect 100 percent reliability until sometime around your puppy's first birthday. In the meantime, you have to stick with the training regimen, morning, noon, and night. You have to stick to the schedule, feeding the puppy at the same times every day and taking him outside regularly. And stick to the routine: "Okay, puppy, you've eaten. Let's go outside." "You just woke up from a nap. Let's go outside." You have to praise, praise, praise. And you can thank my mom for her secret recipe.

EIGHT

EARLY EDUCATION

Sometimes I can't believe how many hours I spend training dogs: hours in class, hours at home. Spending long hours training is nothing new for me. It's something that has always been a part of my life. Now I'm even more comfortable because those training hours are spent for and with my dogs. I love it, and the dogs love it. It keeps our relationship fresh, it builds canine confidence, and it helps my dogs become the best citizens they can be.

Training is an ongoing thing, like conditioning for athletic activity. We all get rusty and out of shape if we don't keep up with our training in any kind of endeavor, whether it's diving, skiing, or mountain biking. The same is true for dogs. Once I was joking around with a friend about the differences between having dogs and having kids. I said, "Well, at least you don't have to send a dog to college." My friend said, "Yeah, even if you do send the dog to an obedience class, it's only a one-shot deal."

I disagreed emphatically.

My friend's comment mirrors the mistaken belief of a lot of people. Training is for a lifetime. It begins during the earliest stages of puppyhood, and there's no "one-shot deal" for the well-adjusted, well-trained dog.

A NATURAL APPROACH

I wasn't always so enthusiastic about dog training, but that was because of the attitudes behind the training I was doing. My own journey into formal training began when Freeway was a puppy. Figuring I was doing the responsible thing, we attended classes that employed the old jerk-the-chain, demand-100-percent-compliance method. The point was to get through it and become top dog over your dog. It was a chore and certainly wasn't fun or rewarding for either of us. It was also rigid, ineffective, and frustrating. Training doesn't have to be that way.

I started looking around at other trainers and saw that some out there were really joyful in what they were doing, and I saw that their dogs shared that. I started researching the behavior of wild dogs and reading books by behaviorists and trainers such as Ian Dunbar and Karen Pryor. I learned that dogs don't have to be forced into obeying our wishes; they *want* to work with us. They want to please us, they want to communicate with us, they want to be our partners. The key to achieving that isn't force and dominance, but positive reinforcement.

In positive reinforcement, which some people now call affection training, you give the dog positive associations with what you are teaching him to do. It emphasizes rewards not punishments, and it can work miracles. It can make for an incredible bonding experience based on mutual respect and trust. Positive training gives you the opportunity to get to know your own dog in a different way—as an equal. It was a revelation for me, and it helped me work toward the type of relationship I was looking for with my dog.

This is not to say that I agreed to share the leadership position in my household with my dog. If you don't let your dog know that you are the boss, or alpha, dog in the house, you can get yourself into big trouble. But even when you're asserting your leadership over your dog, you should be positive about it. Some theorists say that you need to barge on in and "show that dog who's boss" at the first suggestion of disobedience from the dog: wrestle him to the ground, flip him on his back, and bite his neck.

I prefer something a little less severe. You can assert your dominance in a gentle, subtle way that won't result in your having to make a trip to the emergency room. I make it a game. (You have to with dogs the size of Great Danes.) I would get on the floor with my Danes, hug them, and when they relaxed, lie on top of them and roll them over on their backs. Then it would be praise time. "Good girl!" "Good boy!" Noogies on the belly. (We all have our special ways of showing affection, don't we?) I would do this when they were puppies and when they had grown into one-hundred-plus-pound adults. While they enjoyed the activity, it would gently reinforce their understanding of our family's pack order. Then a Jack Russell Terrier joined the household—a tireless, dominant-minded Jack Russell at that. (There is no other kind.) With her, my subtle tactics didn't work. There I was having this struggle for dominance with a tiny puppy that I could've squashed like a bug or drop-kicked across the room. And I was at a complete loss.

When I'd try to get Nipper on her back, she'd try to bite me with those needle-sharp teeth of hers and do everything in her power to escape. I couldn't lie on top of her. She weighed what . . . seven pounds? She wouldn't stay still long enough for me to praise her. Then I got an idea from a program I watched about training dogs to do tricks. The narrator pointed out that when you teach a dog to roll over, you give him a treat reward and you're actually rewarding him for being submissive. So I tried it with Nipper. It worked. As soon as she got accustomed to being in a more submissive position, she realized we weren't going to squash her like a bug, and she calmed down a bit. Training and learning tricks became more interesting to her than fighting for the position of top dog. The treat was the charm, a very positive charm.

Now, I don't believe that *all* training can be positive or even that you can do treat training 100 percent of the time. At times you definitely have to give some negative feedback. A dog will always test you, push you, try to manipulate you. But correction should be reserved only for situations that legitimately call for it. For some dogs, a yank on the choke chain or even a raised voice can be devastating. For others it's only a slight annoyance. My Dane Ryan was one of the best puppy trainers I've ever known. Sometimes giving a throaty growl was all he needed to do to tell the puppy to back off. Ryan never let a puppy get away with anything. It was all in his regal alpha-dog attitude. I learned a lot from him.

Evaluate your puppy and the situation and react appropriately. Remember that puppies need consistency, but they also need some special handling. They are delightful little bundles of energy and life, and it's not your job in training to break that puppy spirit. It's your job to tap into that spirit and channel it in positive directions, to teach the puppy

Ryan always loved puppies, and he was one of the finest puppy trainers I've ever known. I paid close attention to how he handled the pups who would bask at the feet of the master, and I learned how I could use his techniques to enhance my own effectiveness as a trainer.

how to be a dog. This helps to build a lifetime foundation of trust that will enhance your training and your relationship.

LONG-TERM TRAINING

Dogs are beautiful creatures, but a dog's training and behavior are much more important than its external appearance. You have to care about a dog's heart and soul. You have to look at every dog as a work of art that will never be completed. You stay with the dog and work with her. Then, one day, you look at this animal that you live with and train with and realize that you've helped to influence what she has become. You've helped mold her behavior. You've helped her work toward her potential.

Obedience training plays a key role in this, and I believe that it's a must for every dog. It builds confidence in a dog and builds the bond between the dog and his owner. It also provides dogs of all ages with exercise, which can be really valuable for young dogs and older dogs who might not be physically able to participate in more traditional forms of exercise. Training helps dogs get along in the world, to tolerate and enjoy a variety of people and other dogs, and to be better citizens. It makes a dog more adaptable to change and more welcome out in public.

FUN AND AFFECTIONATE TRAINING

Affection training is the new catchphrase that everyone uses but few understand, let alone practice. Be leery of a trainer who refuses to use treats as rewards or who emphasizes force and dominance over positive reinforcement. Success takes time. If you're not having fun working toward that goal, then find another instructor.

Ongoing training is good for the owner, too. It helps you deal with problems that can come up when you live with dogs. It also helps you keep your expectations realistic. If you haven't trained a dog in a while, it's important to give yourself a refresher from time to time, too. Things are always changing in the training world. Sometimes it's nice to get out and see what's new. It can be inspiring and helpful. It can also lead you to new adventures. Build your confidence together through obedience training, and you might get interested in taking some new classes for such activities as agility, conformation show handling, flyball, even search-and-rescue. And of course there's always David Letterman's Stupid Pet Tricks.

Obedience classes aren't expensive and they're readily available in most areas. It's hard for a lot of people to make progress through do-it-yourself training. You have to practice at home, of course—otherwise there's no point in attending an obedience class—but it's great to have a good trainer who can help you figure out what you need to be doing at home. It's not unusual for me to be attending two different obedience classes a week, working on different things with different dogs. The trainer can also be your cheerleader, encouraging you to be patient when you're working on specific problems—just as my trainer did when I was having trouble convincing Nipper during our first few weeks together that I was top dog. I don't think I could have worked through it alone.

The class environment can be fun, too. You can set up situations for practice in a supportive environment that you might not be able to arrange at home, and you can meet other people who share your passion for dogs. To really make it work, though, you can't be afraid to be emotional and animated and dramatic. In training class, some people are afraid of how they're going to look, in lavishing their dogs with praise and jumping up and down and squealing in high-pitched voices to get their dogs' attention. Dogs pick up on our emotions, tones, and behavior, not the specific words of our spoken language. In the training process, you're going to look foolish sometimes when you're trying to get your messages across to your pet.

I especially love the first day of class. The guys are trying to be cool, while the women are more openly affectionate and animated and accessible to their pets. But once the guys realize that everyone in the class looks like a fool, everyone relaxes a little—even the dogs. All in all, the experience should be fun for both you and your dog. If it isn't, find another class.

PUPPY PRESCHOOL AND BEYOND

It used to be that dogs didn't start their formal obedience training until they were about six months old or so, which is a waste of opportunity. Puppies start learning from their mothers almost as soon as they are whelped. We can help continue this training when they leave mom and come live with us. Many owners don't realize that they need to start training young puppies right away, even when they come into their new homes at eight or so weeks of age. You have to handle them, set boundaries for them, put them on their backs—all so they will get comfortable and learn to trust you. That's the first step.

The second step, ideally, is a puppy preschool, or kindergarten, class. These classes help introduce puppies to the basic obedience commands and to the idea that they need to get along with other puppies and people. Because puppies have such short attention spans, these classes focus on positive methods of training that seem more like games and play than training. The emphasis is on giving the puppies positive experiences so they will approach later training with a positive attitude, too. If you're too hard on them, they're going to start to fear you, and you lose the trust that is so difficult to rebuild once it's destroyed.

Treat rewards are usually at the center of puppy preschool training and so is a focus on a puppy's natural behaviors. You learn a lot about how mom dogs train their puppies and how you can do that, too. You learn such tricks as moving a treat up above their nose to get them to sit and moving it down to get them to lie down. And it really works. The puppies also meet, play, and wrestle with other puppies, and it becomes a positive experience for the dogs and for the owners, too. In fact, my own puppy preschool class with Nipper helped save our relationship.

When Nipper was between nine and twelve weeks old, I was start-ing to feel that maybe a terrier was too much for me, after all. I just couldn't figure out how to get through to her, how to harness all that terrier energy of hers, and I was thinking that maybe I should take her back to her breeder.

One day in class, it was the same old thing. The play session, which was supposed to help the puppies expend their energy so they could concentrate on the class, had just ended. As usual, there was no way of getting Nipper's attention back. She was gone, out of control—the way toddlers get sometimes. I was at my wit's end, never having dealt with anything like this before. Then it hit me: she needed a time-out.

Without a word, I picked up my wild little toddler, sat down quietly, away from the group, and placed her on my lap. She threw a tantrum, a genuine, full-blown tantrum. She squirmed into every imaginable posi-tion, snarling, trying to bite me, totally out of control. I stayed cool, but beneath my cool exterior all I could think was, "What have I gotten myself into?"

Then I reached down and placed my hands firmly on her tiny shoul-ders so that she couldn't jump off my lap. She wiggled around, of course, and tried to gnaw on me, but I stayed still and quiet and calm and contin-ued to hold her firmly. Finally she figured out that I meant business. I wouldn't be letting go, no matter how hard she tried to escape. Realizing the futility of her struggle, she surrendered and started to settle down.

Group training sessions offer unique opportunities for learning. Here Donna is watching Brutus, who is setting an example of what they are both supposed to be learning. Working together, the dogs learn to ignore distractions—and sometimes the other dog is the distraction. They also learn to connect the commands with their names, so I can have two dogs with me, and one knows she is supposed to do a down-stay while the other remains standing.

Because of my calm demeanor and my firm hold on her shoulders, she understood that I wasn't going anywhere, and neither was she. When she relaxed completely—which by a miracle she actually did—I loosened my hold on her shoulders and she curled up in my lap and closed her eyes! That was our turning point.

We have made nothing but progress ever since. I had figured out how to reach her, and from then on, the time-out was my salvation. I stayed persistent. Whenever she would get all wound up, all I had to do was put her in my lap and place two fingers gently on her shoulders and maybe tap my fingers once or twice—that's all. She'd circle and plop down. It took lots of time and aggravation to get to that point, but we figured it out together.

Puppy preschool can also obviously be a dramatic training experi-

At a photo shoot where I was demonstrating training methods for the organization Last Chance for Animals, Murphy appreciates the play session we share in the midst of our more serious work. There's nothing more boring than a repetitive training session—for both the dog and the trainer. Keep it fun and varied, and you keep it interesting.

ence for the owner, as well. For some, it's the first formal training experi-ence they've ever had. They get to see in this setting how much fun training can and should be, not the strict, rigid, boring thing that so many people think obedience training is. It's a great introduction, and I am always hoping that it will inspire the puppy owners in the class to keep on with their training—maybe even go into other things, such as agility, field trials, or search-and-rescue.

Being enrolled in a puppy preschool class gives you the opportunity to confer with an expert, as well as other owners, on problems you might be having at home, such as housetraining—things they're probably not going to be discussing in a more formal training class for older pup-pies and dogs. You also learn which behaviors are acceptable and which aren't: mouthing versus biting, for instance.

Puppies are oral creatures, some much more than others. Part of the way my deaf Great Dane, Ryan, would communicate with me was by grabbing my arm in his mouth. This was his way of both getting my attention and showing me affection. He never bit down hard, just used his jaws like a hand. Nipper, too, learned to do this (probably from Ryan), and for me, it's okay if my dogs mouth me. For some people, it isn't acceptable. You can and should work on this early in puppyhood, either teaching the puppy not to mouth or showing him how to do it acceptably, and figure out the parameters together.

The dog's entire family needs to be involved in his training. Everyone who lives with the dog has to learn the right commands and commit to the consistency that the puppy requires. You have to work as a synchronized team. Write everything down if you have to. Get it documented. Make lists and charts, hand them out to family members and tape them to the front door or the refrigerator or the household bulletin board. Anything to prevent confusion in the dog. The more you all work together, the better prepared you'll be to face whatever lies ahead, such as canine adolescence, a show or agility career, or even a move to another home or an unexpectedly lengthy kennel stay. Obedience training is one of the most valuable gifts you can give your dog.

EVALUATING TRAINING METHODS AND TRAINERS

Believe it or not, there are still trainers out there who recommend that you smash a dog's head against the wall to deal with aggression problems or punch a dog in the face if he growls at you at dinnertime. You won't find these methods in books, but their practitioners are alive and well, and in my opinion, trainers like this should be punched in the face themselves. Dog owners have to choose what is acceptable and what isn't and steer clear of recommendations that they beat a dog into submission with a rubber hose (as was once recommended to me). It's horrifying to think that some dog owners out there know so little, they assume that whatever an expert says must be okay. But lots of good trainers are out there, too, and the more you know, the more likely you'll be able to find them.

As my dogs have taught me, every dog is unique. They all have their own personalities, their own idiosyncrasies. You have to take this into consideration when you're training a dog. What works for one dog won't necessarily work for another. You also need to know enough to recognize when a trainer's methods are inhumane and potentially damaging to a dog. You have to do your homework.

What you'll learn while you're doing that homework is that trainers and behaviorists can differ significantly. A behaviorist can usually teach obedience, but a trainer may not be able to deal with behavior problems. If you're dealing with a severe problem, you really need to make sure you're working with a qualified behaviorist.

Beware, too, of people who claim to do "affection training," which has become kind of a trendy catchphrase. Observe the training session before you sign up, because a lot of people say they're doing affection training no matter what kind of training they do. Dog training is evolv-

A dog is never too young, or too old, to learn her manners. Here Nipper works on her stand-stay, all the while licking her chops in anticipation of the treat that awaits her for a job well done. Trained on a grooming table this way, Nipper's elevated position helps keep her attention on me and brings her closer to my level. When you're towering over a small dog, she has to stretch her head way back at an uncomfortable angle to see you, and she may not be able to concentrate as well on what you're trying to teach her.

ing. Most enlightened behavior experts today encourage positive reinforcement as the core of an effective training program. Positive reinforcement takes longer, but requires the dog's active learning rather than manipulating preprogrammed responses through force.

When you're observing and evaluating training classes, pay attention to the techniques and even to the equipment being used. Pronged pinch collars, for example, have become popular these days, probably because people see them as an easy road to quick training; those prongs at the throat can be pretty convincing. The pinch collar, if used by someone who knows what he or she is doing, can actually be more humane than the chain choke collar because at least it can't strangle the dog, but both collars can be abused. Pinch and choke collars should also be used, if they're used, only on physically mature dogs. They can damage the muscles and tissues of a young dog, so I'd be wary of a trainer who recommends them for puppies.

TRAINING COLLARS

Chain choke collars and pronged pinch collars are *training* collars that should be used only for training sessions and walks, never as a dog's everyday collar. They are designed for quick engagement in conjunction with a given command, not for a constant pull on the lead that keeps them tight around the dog's neck. They should be used only as attention-getters, not as instruments of punishment.

I'm skeptical about the idea of protection training for companion dogs. I did some with my first Great Dane, Maile, but I'd never do it again. Most dogs are instinctively protective and will come to their owners' defense if the need ever arises. But with all the bad press that comes from canine aggression, it's not wise to encourage a dog to bite, especially when we're trying to teach puppies to control that impulse.

There are excellent trainers out there for protection and *Schutzhund*, but handling dogs trained for these aggression-oriented vocations is beyond most pet owners' talent, knowledge, and ability. This is a potentially dangerous area, so it's important to know where you stand on it before you choose a trainer. Why get involved in something that really is not what attracted you to dog ownership in the first place and that could lead to trouble sometime down the road?

It's beneficial when you're looking for a trainer to use your powers of observation—and then to rely on your common sense. You can find trainers teaching their classes privately or through city programs, in obedience-training-club activities, and in the obedience-competition ring at dog shows. When you're able to watch several together, you'll see the dogs who perform like robots, and you'll also see the dogs who are really special, the dogs who sparkle. They're excited about what they're doing and have really wonderful attitudes. Whoever is training those dogs is the kind of person I want to work with.

It's always a good sign when a trainer or behaviorist admits that he or she is still learning. Even if we spend our lives trying, we can never know everything. I feel most confident with someone who admits that he or she is still on the same journey. This is also probably the person who will be more likely to give the dogs the respect they deserve, who'll be willing to admit that not every dog is cut out by the same cookie cutter. Major differences exist among breeds and between individual dogs. All are not created equal, or at least not identical.

Not every dog learns in the same way. Sometimes it's a physical thing. A Jack Russell Terrier is as nimble as can be and can do whatever you ask her to do at a very young age, but Great Dane puppies take a while longer. Larger dogs go through a kind of gawky stage, in which they understand what you want but they have to gather themselves up just to get themselves into a sit. We need to get to know the dog to find out what will work with him and what won't—and what he's capable of doing at a certain stage of life.

BREED-SPECIFIC TRAINING

If possible, try finding a trainer who has experience with your dog's specific breed. This may help you get a head start in understanding the temperament of and most effective training methods for your dog.

Consider one exercise that is designed to teach a dog to control his play biting: The dog bites you and you yelp like a dog or say, "Ouch!" If the behavior persists, say in a firm voice, "Enough! I'm not going to play with you anymore." Then you walk out of the room, close the door, and leave him. That's a powerful message for some dogs, but it would never have worked with Nipper. She would just have shrugged and found something else to do, happy making her own new discoveries. That's what led me to her "time-out" exercise, my personal way of dealing with her. It worked for us, but it might not have with another dog. The same applies to disciplinary methods. Some dogs may stop whatever they're doing when you rattle a can filled with pennies, but for other dogs, this may just make the activity more exciting and give them something to bark at.

There is no one ideal training method. I spend a great deal of my life studying, researching, and practicing various training techniques and ideas. My philosophy is embodied in my dogs. A unique combination of techniques and theories have molded each of them into who they are. I collect the best of what I find from the best trainers and behaviorists in the field, the common thread being anything rooted in empathy for the dog, trust, respect, and positive reinforcement. Otherwise, it will be ineffective, and it won't address the dog's individuality.

Along the way, I've made some mistakes, but I've tried to learn from them. Freeway hated the old jerk-the-chain method, and finally we just stopped. If I had known more about treat training and more positive methods when Freeway was young and impressionable, he would have been a lot more responsive. But we got through that negative stage. Now he wears a flat collar, and if I ask him to do something, he usually does it. He does it willingly because he's my partner. He knows I'm not going to force him, and he obeys because he wants to.

As for Nipper, she's a tougher spirit. She has a harder head. Creative as she is, she loves the goofy little tricks that we work on with click-and-treat training, but I have known other dogs that would rather eat the clicker than obey its every command. Sometimes you have to try a variety of methods before you get it right. Dogs get bored easily. You need to keep training interesting, to teach them new games as well as obedience commands. If they're really intelligent dogs, they'll figure it out, and then they'll start in on training you.

Nipper is one of the challenging ones. She manipulates, she's fascinated by everything, and she really keeps me on my toes. I have to work to stay one step ahead of her. When you work with dogs, you have to be able to switch gears if necessary to prevent boredom and to make progress. You have to be willing to try something new. Each dog is an individual.

The well-trained dog is made, not born, the product of hours and hours and months and months of training—training that begins during the puppy's first weeks of life. It doesn't happen overnight—no matter how much we wish it would—and it will continue on for the life of your dog.

NINE

PUPPY HEALTH AND WELL-BEING

Living as I do with HIV, health is a pretty important subject for me. I believe that my dogs are reflections of my own attitudes toward maintaining my health. I work out every day, and I want my dogs to get some type of exercise every day, too. I try to eat right, and proper nutrition for my dogs is a vital concern for me, too. I have to stay attuned to my health and wellness every day, and I do the same for my dogs.

When I was growing up, a dog who lived to age ten was considered old. But today, more and more dogs are living happily and healthfully well into their teens, partly because of all the amazing strides veterinary medicine has made in recent decades, and partly because of all the intensive research that has gone into uncovering the secrets of proper canine nutrition and formulating foods that embody those discoveries.

We're lucky to have this knowledge, these services, and these products at our fingertips nowadays. But how we manage our dogs and their health is crucial. Basically, what is good for the puppy is usually good for the owner—and vice versa. Preventive medicine, optimum nutrition, and regular exercise are all important factors in what makes a healthy puppy and a healthy dog. That's why I begin paying attention to all of these issues just as soon as a new puppy joins my canine family.

HEALTHY FROM THE START

We all want our puppies to be healthy from the start, but be warned: when you're establishing a healthy foundation for your puppy, you have to realize that preventive health care is not cheap. People sometimes complain that dogs are too expensive to purchase or to adopt. They can't believe the prices charged by breeders, or they rebel when animal shelters and breed rescue groups charge adoption fees. These people rarely understand that's only the beginning. If you can't afford the initial cost of the dog, perhaps you shouldn't get a dog in the first place.

If you're going to invite a dog into your family, it isn't fair to skimp on his care. You have to offer him a high-quality diet (high-quality, name-brand foods, which are what you should feed your pet, will cost more than generic foods); you may have to pay for kenneling or pet-sitting from time to time; you will have to purchase such supplies as toys, grooming products, and bedding; and you will absolutely have to take your dog to the veterinarian for both regular checkups and unexpected sickness or injury.

This is from someone who has probably put several veterinarians' kids through college. I've dealt with everything from minor respiratory infections to heart murmurs to bloat to spinal surgeries that cost many thousands of dollars. I don't hesitate to call the vet when I suspect something might be wrong, and we've actually dealt with some pretty serious conditions through the years. My dogs and I are well-acquainted with our veterinarians—we've worked with both generalists and specialists—and they are well-acquainted with us. That's how it should be, if you ask me.

It's invaluable to find and work with a veterinarian whom you trust and with whom both you and your dog get along. Shop around if you have to. You won't necessarily click with every veterinarian you meet, so since this is a long-term relationship that involves a member of your family, you want to find someone you feel comfortable with. It helps if that person is also comfortable with your dog. That's not necessarily a given.

I have always appreciated a veterinarian who doesn't talk down to me, who doesn't try to hide anything from me. I've always been interested in medicine and biology, and because of my own health, I've worked hard to keep up with advancements and terminology and treatments. When veterinarians talk to me about what's going on with my dogs, I understand what they're talking about. I expect my doctors to give it to me straight, and I expect the same thing from my dogs' veterinarians. I want someone who will answer my questions honestly, and I want all the necessary information so I can make informed decisions. I want to know what's going on.

No veterinarian can do this alone. You have to play an important role in the health and well-being of your dog. You have to be familiar with what is normal and healthy for your dog and what isn't, so that as soon as you notice something that suggests a problem—a lump or bump or change in attitude or appetite—you can get the dog to the veterinarian as soon as possible. The earlier you get treatment for such things as tumors, parasites, and canine bloat, the better chance the dog will have of coming through it okay. Early detection can determine whether a dog survives a serious condition.

This means getting to know your dog, developing a baseline for your dog's health that you can use as a gauge from then on. It's important for the overall health and longevity of the dog. So take advantage of the puppy years for this. This is the ideal time to get to know your puppy, nose to tail. Your familiarity with your pet's health baseline will play an important role in the health care he receives throughout his life.

Get to know what your puppy's eyes should look like as far as color and clarity, get to know the texture and markings and geography of his skin, the texture and uniformity of his coat, what his ears smell like, and yes, even the consistency of his bowel movements. Pay attention to his eating and bathroom habits, his attitude during different times of the day, his sleeping patterns, his play habits, and his likes and dislikes. Changes in any of these, even subtle changes, could be valuable signs if your dog becomes sick. It's your job as a responsible dog owner to pay attention. Your veterinarian will be an important person in your pet's life, but you're the one who lives with him and is in the best position to notice the little things that will call for the veterinarian's attention.

With the exception of those unfortunate puppies who contract parvovirus or develop hip dysplasia or juvenile cataracts during their first year of life, puppyhood should be a healthy time. Veterinary visits are for the most part preventive, for vaccinations, perhaps parasite control, maybe a quick trip when you suspect the puppy has swallowed your mom's diamond ring. This is also the ideal time for spaying and neutering—for the female, preferably before her first heat cycle at about six months of age. Spay and neuter within the first year and you reduce your pet's risk of developing various cancers—mammary and testicular cancer, to name two—and life-threatening infections later in life. While it's not fun to think of your puppy "going under the knife," puppies are phenomenally quick healers, and the long-term health benefits of these common procedures far outweigh a puppy's temporary discomfort—and an owner's temporary fears.

PUPPY VACCINATIONS

If you're lucky, the only major medical issue you'll deal with when your dog is a puppy is vaccination, the cornerstone of a dog's preventive medical program. Some people out there don't vaccinate their dogs. They believe they can protect their pets holistically. I don't know about that. I do know that living with HIV as I do, my comfort level requires protecting my dogs with vaccines.

However, I absolutely believe in alternative therapies, such as acupuncture and herbal remedies. One of my favorite veterinarians practices a combination of Eastern and Western medicine. That's how I think alternatives should be used—in addition to more traditional therapies, not instead of them. I vaccinate my dogs for their benefit and for the benefit of other dogs, as well. I would hate to think that one of my dogs, unprotected by a vaccine, was responsible for spreading something devastating such as parvovirus or distemper to other dogs in the community. Vaccines are not guarantees of protection, of course, and some dogs have contracted parvovirus even though they have been vaccinated. But if all dogs were vaccinated, all dogs would be safer. I want to make sure that my dogs contribute to that chain.

A puppy's actual immunity status can be a little iffy during her first months of life. It can take a while for mom's maternal antibodies to leave the puppy's system and allow the vaccine antibodies to take over. That's why a series of vaccines is necessary. Vaccinate before you begin attending a training class (a good trainer will require proof); vaccinate before kenneling; vaccinate before traveling (pockets of disease might exist wherever you're going); and vaccinate before you take your puppy out

Part of the preparation that makes life easier for an adult dog is ensuring that a puppy's early experiences, such as visits to the veterinary hospital, are as positive as possible. I also introduce my puppies to a variety of surfaces—grass, sand, concrete, carpet, and the cold slippery metal of the veterinarian's examination table—to help them gain confidence in and comfort with the world around them.

to any large public event, such as a dog show, a weekend festival, or even a local park or beach. Prevent your puppy from investigating the feces of other dogs, too, because these can be prime carriers of disease.

Vaccine protection begins with a series of four vaccines administered to a puppy about three weeks apart, beginning at about six weeks of age. After that the dog should receive a booster every year for the rest of his life. The standard "puppy shot" is usually a single vaccine that includes distemper, parvovirus, coronavirus, infectious canine hepatitis, leptospirosis, and parainfluenza. The puppy can't be vaccinated against rabies until he reaches four months of age. Depending on the vaccine, the rabies vaccine is then followed by boosters either every year or every three years.

In most areas, vaccinating for rabies is the law—and a requirement for license registration. This is where you see canine disease as a public health issue for both dogs and for people. We don't want dogs to contract a horrible disease such as rabies, which is 100 percent fatal, and we certainly don't want a person to have to go through the trauma of being bitten by a dog with an unknown vaccination status. When a vaccinated dog bites someone, it usually has to be quarantined to make sure that it exhibits no signs of rabies. But if the dog is not vaccinated or his vaccination status is questionable, the dog has to be destroyed so he can be tested for the disease. Any way you look at it, rabies, or any other canine disease, is not pretty. In my mind, the simple way to avoid dealing with it is to make use of medical technology and vaccinate.

VACCINATING FOR PEACE OF MIND

If you're adopting an older dog with an unknown background, it's wise to have him vaccinated as soon as you bring him home. If you're adopting him from an established breed rescue organization or a reputable animal shelter, then you can probably rely on the claim (and written proof) that he has been vaccinated. But if there's any question, play it safe and have the dog vaccinated. It won't hurt him, and it will give you peace of mind.

While those vaccines are mobilizing your pet's immunity, *you* have to be the guardian of your puppy's health. When I was breeding, whenever somebody would come in to see the puppies, I would spray bleach on their shoes or have them remove their shoes when they arrived at the house and leave them outside. (Some breeders won't even let people walk up the driveway until they've had the bleach treatment.) Then I'd have them wash up with antibacterial soap before they could see the puppies. You do everything you can to protect puppies, whether they are puppies that you have bred or puppies you have just purchased or adopted as companions. Some things are just common sense. You don't, for example, take a puppy to a park, the beach, or any other public place like that before he's been vaccinated. That's reckless behavior.

ESTABLISHING HEALTHY EATING HABITS

Many of the advancements in canine health and the increased longevity of dogs may be linked directly to improvements in canine nutrition. Feeding a puppy and feeding her right is just about the easiest thing you can do. But that ease comes from starting out with healthy, commonsense nutritional habits from the very beginning. It's when you stray from what responsible dog owners and canine nutrition experts define as best that you get in trouble. That's how dogs end up obese, finicky, and all-around unhealthy.

I feed my dogs and my puppies twice a day, morning and evening (young puppies may require three meals a day), a combination of kibble and canned food, but kibble alone is fine, too, and it's good for the teeth. The daily ration divided into two or three meals a day helps prevent canine bloat (one of my greatest fears), and it helps prevent hunger pangs in the dogs. I never feed my dogs junk food, never feed them table scraps, and I never feed them generic foods. I follow these rules from the moment a puppy comes to live with me.

All my puppies ever know is a diet of high-quality, complete, and balanced dog food—with a few healthy dog treats thrown in now and then. I try to shield my dogs from finding out about anything else. A dog who has never sampled pizza or Chinese food off his owner's plate has no reason to beg for it and refuse to eat his own food as a way to coerce you into sharing yours. I also take it easy with the treats. Treats can be great for training, but I try to reserve them solely for that. Obesity comes from too many treats—especially when those treats are table scraps. Don't fall into the treat trap.

We tend to want to imagine that what is good for us is good for our dogs, but this can be dangerous when you apply it to our compulsion for variety in our diets. Contrary to what we might imagine when comparing ourselves to them, dogs don't need variety. Any change in diet can lead to severe digestive upset. Constant change can turn your pet into a finicky dog. When you live in a house with four dogs, you just don't have time for that. The same holds true for the one-dog household. It's not good for a dog's health and it's not good for an owner's sanity.

People naturally think, "Well, I wouldn't want to be fed the same food every day. I'm sure my dog doesn't either." It's not the same. Go ahead and empathize with your puppy, but be careful not to carry it to the extreme. Remember that even though you and your puppy can thrive on some of the same nutritional inputs, you are not a dog. So choose a good, high-quality food that your puppy likes (some dogs do better with some foods than others), one that is complete and balanced and has been tested according to feeding trials established by the Association of American Feed Control Officials—and stick with that. Then don't switch around. There's no need to.

Instead, concentrate on how you're feeding your puppy and what sort of nutritional foundation you are setting for her future. Puppies have small tummies and speedy metabolisms, so divide their rations into several daily feedings and make sure they always have access to fresh, clean water. Remember that water, too, is a critical component in the healthy canine diet. You might also want to think about elevating the food dish if your dog is a large-breed dog (or a floppy-eared dog such as a Basset Hound, whose ears may fall into the food dish at mealtimes). With large-breed dogs, the belief is that an elevated bowl will provide a smoother track to the stomach, which could help prevent bloat and gastrointestinal problems.

You should also pay attention to the research that has gone into advancements in canine nutrition—much of it from the pet food manufacturers. Canine nutrition and the formulation of balanced dog food has become a bona fide science. If you go with a high-quality product, you probably won't need to supplement with vitamins or other nutrients. The quality foods are usually "complete and balanced." If you're interested in supplementing, maybe because your dog is involved in some special type of activity such as sled dog racing or has a health condition that might be related to a nutritional deficiency, work with your veterinarian and do your own investigating, too. More of a nutrient doesn't necessarily mean better, so don't supplement because of rumor or hearsay. You can do terrible things to your dog that way and throw her whole diet, and thus her system, out of balance.

Be especially careful with supplementing where puppies are concerned. An unbalanced diet can do great damage to all those developing tissues. A better idea is to feed one of the puppy foods that has been especially designed for growing dogs. Formulated to provide balance as well as energy to growing pups, these are far superior to the practice of just loading the puppy up on vitamin and mineral supplements—safer, too, and less costly. Leave the nutritional research to the experts and take advantage of what they discover.

Some people sustain their dogs on home-cooked foods that include all the necessary nutrients. I actually tried that myself for a while, of course using professional recipes to make sure I was including everything my dogs needed. I enjoy cooking and I have big commercial pots and bowls and equipment, so that wasn't a problem. A batch would last for three

I prefer natural ears on Great Danes (and I'm not alone; ear cropping is actually illegal in some countries), but if you want to compete seriously in the American show ring with certain breeds—Danes and Dobermans, to name two—you pretty much have to crop their ears. If you do decide to crop, work with a veterinarian who is an expert at it and who can help you understand the aftercare required to make the procedure a success.

I am a proponent of combining both Eastern and Western medicine for dogs. This includes exploring alternative, natural remedies for certain health problems, but also taking advantage of medical technology and ensuring that all my dogs have been vaccinated—a practice I pursued most recently for bright-eyed Mikey here.
(Photo copyright © Pompano Bill)

days. Every third day I was cooking and I would store it in the refrigerator. But I couldn't ask somebody else to feed my dogs that way if I had to be out of town. So with my travel schedule, I had to stop. I would probably have gotten tired of it anyway, but while I did it, I enjoyed it, confident that I was personally supplying my dogs with a balanced diet.

TREATS AND CALORIES

Remember that treats are food and food means calories. By reducing your pet's daily ration to compensate for the calories he gets from his daily treats, you can help prevent treat-related obesity.

Your puppy, and later your dog, will do fine on a high-quality commercial product. Just make sure you establish how you will be feeding early on—and most important, take it easy with the treats and don't overfeed. While your dog is a puppy, commit to establishing healthy eating habits that will last a lifetime.

A PUPPY'S EXERCISE PROGRAM

Puppies are bundles of energy, so of course they need exercise, right? Puppies may seem to be full-grown physically, but internally, a lot of important developments are still taking place. Their muscles, joints, and bones are still growing and strengthening. Strain them with inappropriate exercise, and you could do permanent damage. Stick to an age-appropriate exercise regimen, and be patient. Eventually your dog will be up to speed.

Remember, too, that even a puppy who seems full grown doesn't have the necessary stamina yet to do such things as jog or run beside you while you speed along on in-line skates. It's easy to get lulled into thinking that our dogs can do anything. Many can, but with limitations. Walks and hikes are excellent activities for a puppy—but only in moderation. The walks should be short and the hikes not too taxing. This was another lesson I learned the hard way—this time with my Great Dane Brutus.

I took Brutus on a hike one day when he was a puppy, a large puppy. I soon realized, because he told me, by panting and slowing down, that it was too warm and we had gone too far. Practically in midstride he decided enough was enough. He stopped suddenly and just plopped down on the ground, panting and breathing heavily. He wasn't willing or able to go on.

Fortunately, a friend had come along on the hike, too, so one of us stayed with Brutus while the other went and got a car. But I still wonder, what if I had been alone? I would have been stranded with a one-hundred-pound puppy, who for all I knew was suffering from heatstroke. I couldn't carry him home, but I wouldn't have been able to leave him there either. I sure learned a lesson that day: don't be fooled by a puppy's apparent physical maturity. He is still a puppy, inside and out. He may be a big strapping guy who seems filled with endless, boundless energy, but don't be deceived. He could be bouncing off the walls—or along the trail—one minute and plopped down sleeping the next. Be ready. Don't overtax him, and don't wander too far away from home.

The first two years or so of your puppy's life is no time to be running marathons together. Even running a mile may be too much. This is the time to be working on your partnership, the foundation that more rigorous physical activity will someday be built on. Game playing (hide-and-seek, fetch) and obedience training, along with moderate walks and hikes, will probably offer your puppy all the exercise he needs during this stage of life. This will help condition him physically, expend that puppy energy of his, and also gently stimulate his developing tissues rather than damage them.

Allow the puppy to go at his own pace. If you're at the park, let him run around, but when he gets tired, respect his fatigue and go home for a nap. When you're playing games or teaching him a new trick, don't force him to continue if he grows tired or bored. Before you run a mile, you walk it, right? It's the same with dogs: they need gradual conditioning plus attention to physical capabilities at a given time and stage of life.

Bringing a new puppy into your life can improve your own health—if you let it. As I think I have made abundantly clear by now, just throwing a dog out into the backyard to "exercise himself" doesn't cut it any more than it would for you. You need to be an active participant. Condition gradually with your pup, exercise intelligently together, and you'll feel better and healthier yourself. Sometimes just knowing that you have to get your dog exercised every day can be a great inspiration to keep you attentive to your own daily exercise needs.

PART THREE

THE PRIME
OF OUR LIVES

TEN

A WHOLE NEW WORLD

Congratulations. You've made it through puppyhood. It's been a challenge, and sometimes it's been a pain. You feel that you yourself have been through a strict training regimen making sure you set a good example for your pup, through difficult-to-maintain consistency and increasingly devoted commitment. Now here you are with a dog that's somewhere around two or three years old, and you realize that something has changed. You've reached a new stage. Welcome to the middle years: the prime of your dog's life, and a golden time in your own life, one that you will remember as some of the best years you've ever spent.

Your dog is now physically able to do just about everything and anything you ever dreamed he'd be able to do (with the right conditioning, of course). Your dog is also emotionally and intellectually able to understand what you expect of him (with the right training and communication, of course). Your daily routine is in place and second nature to everyone, you've learned to read each other, and there is no question that the dog is a member of the family who knows his place and yours. It really is a whole new world, and you're going to have great fun together.

BEYOND PUPPYHOOD

If puppyhood was a time for training and routine, now is the time to reap the benefits of your investment. You've respected your dog's need for some time to grow up both physically and mentally. Your dog has worked hard, with your guidance, and he has developed the confidence he needs for this new stage of his life and your relationship. He now

Showing should be fun, and to make it fun you have to maintain your sense of humor. Trev'r knew that secret when we were showing. He was always smiling and he always approached the ring with mischief in his eyes. If given his choice, though, he preferred to be out herding the Danes.

enters his prime, a young adult dog with a mellower nature, a seasoned personality, and superior physical structure and stamina. Of course, if you haven't worked on it, he might be entering his prime as a monster. But that, as we have seen, doesn't have to happen.

Things really calm down when the dog reaches about age two. At age two they get it; by age three, it's consistent. Assuming you've been consistent with the routine, the rules are now set and your dog is really adhering to them. He may still try to challenge you sometimes, maybe by pretending he doesn't hear a command or has forgotten how to obey it, but if you've done your work, his resistance will be short-lived. He's just trying to keep you on your toes, and you should keep him on his by continuing with the obedience training, whether you take a class (which you should periodically) or just reinforce your bond in your day-to-day activities around the house. Whatever you do, make sure it's something you can both enjoy.

With your dog in his prime, you can truly become inseparable. You can finally take him jogging with you or have him run alongside you while you ride a bike or skate. Now is the time to get seriously into agility or sledding or herding or any of those great things that the well-trained, properly conditioned dog can participate in. You need to stay on guard, though, and keep thinking about your dog's well-being. Think ahead, stay alert, and take care of your dog. This means even paying attention to the weather to make sure you won't be overheating your dog while you're out playing on a hot afternoon. It also means paying attention to what's going on with your dog and with the other people and dogs around you.

I'm pretty good at looking ahead and maintaining control when I'm out with my dogs. I consider myself their bodyguard. Sometimes something sneaks up on me, something comes around the corner that I don't anticipate—such as an unruly, out-of-control dog or a pack of wild toddlers. When that happens, and it depends on which dog I have with me at the time, I'll either give the unruly dog or the kids a wide berth, or else I stop and use the situation as a training opportunity for my dog.

If I'm out with, say, Nipper, and a wild, ill-mannered dog approaches, I'll stop and work with Nipper on the sit, down, stay. I'll start giving her commands as a way both to train and distract her, while I allow the distracting dog or person to pass without incident, without her or the other dog getting upset. Even if Nipper does get excited, I reward her for glancing at me even for a second. This teaches her that she doesn't have to react to every little thing in her environment, that sometimes it's okay to ignore other animals and people. That's a tough one for a terrier. At the same time I stay alert and ready to pick Nipper up and get her out of the situation if the other dog starts to lunge or act aggressively. (If necessary, I even cover her eyes to prevent her from giving her signature "death stare" that she uses so effectively to provoke other dogs.) I do the same with my bigger dogs. I won't hesitate to lift my 130-pound Freeway into the air if I have to—and I have had to. It's amazing what a rush of adrenaline will allow you to do when your dogs are in danger.

NEW FREEDOM FOR THE WELL-TRAINED DOG

From the dog's point of view, this time of life can be paradise. She's happy that she gets to do all these fun new things, and even better is that she gets to do them all with you. That's the dog's greatest reward. You should be honored.

Take a look at this new world through the dog's eyes. She finally really understands what you're asking of her and that you understand what she's trying to tell you. You can see the pride on the dog's face during those wonderful moments of communion. Now is when the partnership really blossoms and, with the right input, becomes what we always dream the dog/owner relationship can and should be: your dog becomes a full-fledged family member, and she knows it.

I love traveling to France and seeing the way dogs are treated there, especially in Paris, the ultimate dog-as-family-member utopia. Dogs are everywhere you go in Paris—in restaurants, shops, cafés, everywhere—and there's no hype about it, no novelty. Dogs even have their own kind of Parisian attitude there. They'll be sitting at a café table and the waiter will bring them a bowl of water, and it's as if that's just the way they're supposed to be treated. Parisian dogs just assume they belong there—and everyone else assumes it, too.

In France, dogs truly are members of the family, and they earn that status with their behavior. French dogs are incredibly well behaved, probably because they're socialized to be part of everything from the time they're puppies. They're with their owners and other people all the time, which is all it takes. That kind of bond and that kind of public acceptance don't happen without a lot of effort. The dog has to learn, which takes time.

Almost any dog, properly prepared through training and socialization to reach that level, can become an integral part of your life—even when that dog weighs 130 pounds. From the time Freeway came to live with me, we spent so much time together training and working. We were always together. I had a Jeep at the time, and I'd leave the back open when I was home. Whenever I was leaving, he would just run out and jump into the back of the Jeep. He knew I wouldn't be leaving without him. Usually he was already in the Jeep. It was his safe place, his favorite place, his private little den. I had no problem allowing him to be there. It was a unique part of our relationship, one that we had worked out together.

WORK AND PLAY

The prime of your dog's life is also the time when you can begin to use the obedience training you've worked so hard on as a valuable tool. With obedience training comes more freedom and variety for the dog— and more fun for both of you.

In my house, I'm always trying to be creative and build on the foundation of our training to figure out new, exciting things that my dogs and I can do together. Hiking is a good example. If you like hiking with your dog, and you've mastered the basic commands and the training techniques that help dogs learn effectively, you can carry this a step further by teaching the dog to wear a backpack designed specifically for dogs. It doesn't matter whether your dog is large or small. You can't spring this on him all of a sudden, though. You have to do it gradually. I start by putting the backpack on the dog and walking around the driveway. Once he's used to it, after a day or two of practice, then we try walking up the street, and then a little farther up the street. Eventually, when the dog realizes that he doesn't have to try to rip the backpack off his back or chew on it, we start going on real hikes.

Freeway, Ryan, and Leilani used to love when I put their backpacks on and took them hiking up in the hills near my house. It was probably around eight miles or so along the trails, and we'd pick up glass bottles and aluminum cans along the way, put them in the backpacks, and then take them to the recycling center. I would always use that money to buy new dog toys. I believed that they knew they were doing a little job— cleaning up the environment—and they were getting rewarded for it. They were doing their civic duty, and we had fun.

TRAINING STEP-BY-STEP

When teaching your dog something new, such as hiking with a backpack on, getting in and out of the swimming pool, or carrying in groceries, introduce each step gradually and positively. First introduce the equipment (for example, the backpack), then the use of the equipment (the dog adjusts to the feel of the backpack), then the activity itself (hiking with the backpack). The key to success is your patience—and some well-timed treats.

Dogs love being part of projects. They love feeling that they're in the middle of something important—and they love being in the middle of it with you. It's the family thing, the pack thing. Don't waste the opportunity to satisfy that longing of theirs. The dog's prime is the perfect time of a dog's life to get her involved with the family this way. And that's only the beginning.

When they hit their prime, dogs who have successfully been trained for serious vocations finally enter their professions. Everything up until then, the preparation, has been a dress rehearsal. Guide dogs and assistance/service dogs graduate from school and take their place beside their permanent partners; herding dogs are expected to know their way around a herd of sheep; therapy dogs earn their official titles as ambassadors to hospitals and nursing homes; and police dogs start patrolling the streets. Your dog can—and should—have a job, too. He's your companion, but go ahead and put him to work.

Just because a dog is a dog doesn't mean he should be restricted from joining his family in just about everything that goes on in the household. The canine mind catches on quickly, and dogs love new activities. Most dogs are happiest being right in the thick of things, and unlike humans, there are few household activities that they consider boring. You have some groceries to bring in? Train your dog to help. You have a bookshelf to build? Teach your dog the difference between a screwdriver and a hammer and enlist him as your assistant who on command brings you any tool you ask for. Dogs can learn to carry the garbage out, get the newspaper, pull the kids' sled up a snowy hill, retrieve the golf

Someday Bouvier Speedo may make her debut in the conformation show ring, but we're taking it slow. We're enjoying more natural dog pursuits for the time being, like playing in the park. She is enjoying the other dogs and blossoming into quite a clown, exhibiting endearing qualities that make her a delightful pet, and perhaps a better, more well-adjusted show dog someday.

balls you chipped at the park or the tennis balls you shot out of the court, bring you the remote after a tough day, even carry the laundry to the washing machine.

Never underestimate your dog's abilities. While he won't be doing the laundry unassisted—and forget about the ironing—if he's like most dogs, he'll be thrilled, honored, and ecstatic that you are asking for his help. You could probably do the work in less time without his assistance, but what fun would that be? Working with a dog this way can give you a new perspective on things. When you see how joyful your dog is about helping you with chores you consider mundane, they may stop being mundane. You may start to appreciate what you have, and even your household responsibilities, a little more. All this because a dog let you know that your life is wonderful, and he's happy, and grateful, to be sharing it with you.

TO BREED—OR NOT TO BREED

The prime of a dog's life is also the time that you might consider breeding your dog. I've learned some hard lessons as a breeder, but I've also had some incredible experiences. I'm not breeding right now, because for me, it was all so personal and such an emotional experience. I'm still haunted by the hard lessons, and still gratified by those incredible experiences.

When I bred my first litter, Leilani's litter, I took time off from the usual demands of my life so that I could devote myself completely to it. Basically it was like taking a sabbatical from work to take care of my dog and her puppies. Looking back now, I know that that is the only way that anyone should ever do this. Most people who breed their dogs don't, and I've been guilty of that, too. But I learned my lesson, and the experience I had with Leilani continues to be my inspiration. I think back so fondly of that first litter. I was really proud of how it all worked out. Friends were amazed that I had so much knowledge, but I did my homework. I studied and read and asked lots and lots of questions of veterinarians and other breeders, making sure that I would be really prepared for this giant undertaking.

How could anyone possibly approach this halfway? For one thing, the life of Leilani, a dog I loved very much, was in my hands, and so much can go wrong during whelping. I owed it to her to learn all I could and to be prepared for the best as well as for the worst. Considering how wonderful she was to me and to her puppies throughout the whole thing, I believe she understood that and appreciated it. Once Leilani's puppies arrived, I was fascinated by these little creatures that came into the world deaf and blind and totally dependent on Mom. At the same time they had incredible survival instincts to find the food and the warmth they needed.

If you are going to breed a dog, you have to honor the amazing nature of what you're doing. You must become an expert on the breed. You must determine whether your dog is more than just a nice dog who should be bred. Is she a good enough example of her breed in conformation and temperament? Has she received the highest marks in the various

Border Terrier Mikey—the marshmallow—marches to his own drummer, and I respect him for that. He may not be the most outgoing critter, but he has found his niche in the household and he is learning what is expected of him. He has become a unique companion amid a herd of more flamboyant pups.

genetic tests and evaluations of traits that affect the quality of a litter and an entire breed? The same applies to the stud dog. If not, what exactly is your reason for breeding her? Look around and think about what's happening within your household at the time. How will these things affect your dog's ability to be a good mom?

You can't expect Mom to be relaxed and calm while you're remodeling the house or dealing with your own young children. In an environment like that, the mom may become dangerously stressed and ignore her responsibilities. You certainly won't be able to offer the puppies the early care and handling they need to make them well-adjusted, even-tempered adult dogs. That happened with a dog I co-owned. She had five puppies, and only one survived. I was not thrilled about breeding her in the first place, and I should never have agreed to it. It was a nightmare. In the end, when I was feeling angry and sad, I had to realize that even though someone else was caring for the mom and the puppies, *I* was the one who had to take responsibility for the situation.

THE VETERINARIAN'S ROLE

If you decide to breed your bitch, involve your veterinarian immediately in your dog's prenatal care, and discuss delivery in depth. Veterinarians have varying opinions on how intimately involved the owner should be when the puppies begin to arrive. Grill the doctor on the signs of distress you should look for, so you'll know when your dog requires veterinary intervention. For the safety of the expectant mother, write down the warning signs and the delivery details, step-by-step, post them prominently, and keep the veterinarian's number by the phone.

People need to take the responsibility seriously. They need to take on that responsibility themselves. When you decide to breed your bitch responsibly (that's standard dog talk, you know), you agree to become midwife, nanny, and coparent. That's a big job that takes a lot of time. I wasn't able to do that with my Dane Donna's litter because I was traveling at the time, and the experience became another one of those hard lessons. I had to be away during the first few weeks after her puppies were whelped, and I had to rely on other people to do what I should have been doing: socializing the puppies, handling them, and playing with them regularly. I learned the hard way that you can't rely on someone else to do this, unless that someone else is your spouse, partner, or someone else who feels the same way about the dog and her puppies that you do. Donna's puppies missed out on all the early handling that I knew from my first litter was so critical. I let Donna down.

It disturbs me so much when I hear people say that they are breeding their dogs "for fun and profit." "I love my dog's temperament and I just want to reproduce it." That's not a good enough reason to breed. It's also not good enough to think that you might as well breed your dog because all your friends would just love to have one of the puppies. Just wait: as soon as the puppies are on the ground, those friends disappear.

It's also a mistake when people decide to breed their dog so their kids can experience "the miracle of life." Too many of those kids end up learning a sad lesson about pet overpopulation when the family can't place the puppies. Too often they end up going to the shelter or being driven away by less-than-perfect owners. Sometimes the whelping goes badly, and the kids' beloved pet could die.

Breeding right is time-consuming, messy, stressful, and costly. It can be long, grueling, even bloody, and all the necessary genetic tests, as well as the prenatal and postnatal veterinary exams, don't come cheap. By the time the puppies are whelped, you're already in debt, even if you've pre-sold all the puppies. Breeding is not a money maker, and it's not something for the squeamish.

I may decide to breed dogs again. Depending on my Bouvier Speedo's future in the show ring, motherhood may be in her future. Plenty of puppies are out there, and some really great breeders are breeding them. Some breeding programs are run by people who have com-

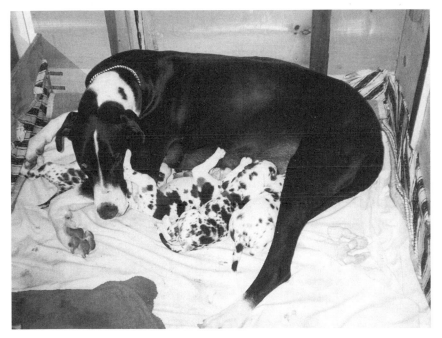

Leilani was a natural at motherhood. I helped by providing her with a versatile and spacious whelping box. Constructed of removable wooden slats, the sides could be raised higher as the puppies grew. The whelping box—located in the small room off my bedroom also known as "the nursery"—offered the new mom a sense of security, and it could accommodate the changing needs of a growing family.

pletely dedicated their lives to their particular breeds. It's a passion, not a whim or a big money-making project. They're like artists who love what they do and can't imagine doing anything else. That's the only kind of person who should be breeding.

But for me, the real issue is the fate of the puppies. I've done everything I can to ensure that my puppies ended up in good, permanent homes. Breeding means that you bring these amazing little puppies into the world, you nurture them, you love them, you play mom to them, and then you send them off to live with strangers. Despite all the promises, despite all the contracts, you never really know what will happen. And in a part of your heart, you never stop thinking about them.

I've gone the contract route and I do the periodic follow-ups. I love hearing about my kids, what they're doing, what problems and even what illnesses they've had, their personality traits, and especially their funny habits. A lot of people who have bought puppies from me are really good about sending me pictures and updating me on what the dogs are doing. But even with all my efforts, some have still fallen through the cracks, such as one poor baby who came to my attention during the writing of this book.

One day I found that one of Donna's kids had shown up in an animal shelter—apparently his owners had ignored the return-to-breeder clause in my sales contract. I sprang the dog from the shelter and brought him to my home. He was underweight, he was infested with all kinds of internal parasites, he had kennel cough that was pushing pneumonia, his ears were infected, he was dog aggressive, and he still hadn't been neutered, which really made me angry. Obviously, he was in distress. I'll never know what had brought him to that stage or what kind of suffering he had endured. I was furious at the people who had adopted him, who couldn't now be found.

We went through weeks and weeks of antibiotics. I took care of him, tried to put some weight on him, did everything I could to get him healthy. Finally, when he seemed to have made it over the hump, when it seemed as if we really were moving in the right direction, I took him in to have him neutered. The next morning, he seemed a little dazed. Something wasn't quite right. He ended up bloating that day, and he didn't make it.

How sad it was. I still have trouble thinking about what it all meant. I'm grateful that he came back to me in the end, but I'm sad to think of the life he had probably led up until then. I tried so hard to nurse him back to health, to renew his faith in how things can be for a dog, and I'm glad that I was at least able to make his last weeks comfortable. But even though I tried, I wasn't able to make sure he lived the life that every dog is entitled to. I just couldn't guarantee that for him. In the end, I couldn't help him, even though I always work so hard to make sure my puppies land in good, permanent homes. Even if just one falls through the cracks, it's hard for me.

So most dogs just shouldn't be bred. Only the finest examples should be, and those are not all that common. Beyond that, breeding can put a definite damper on the prime of a dog's life. Whelping can be stressful and even life-threatening to the bitch, especially if her owners aren't properly prepared or educated, or don't think there's any need to call the veterinarian for help when the dog is in labor and has been straining unproductively for four hours. For most dogs, the prime of life and the dog population at large are best served by two simple procedures: spaying and neutering. There are more important things than pedigrees and puppy profits to be thinking about during your canine companion's prime.

ELEVEN

THE HOME ROUTINE

When your dog reaches her prime, your responsibility really begins. You have your work cut out for you, different from the work you did to help mold your puppy into the wonderful dog she's destined to be. Now, as you approach that destiny, you have to keep the momentum going.

You have to keep up with the foundation of consistent handling you built while your dog was a puppy. You have to keep up with the commitment and the attention, the key components in the sound routine you developed for your dog, the routine she has learned to depend on each and every day. Paradoxically, the more you stick to the routine, the more your dog will be able to deal with just about any variation to the routine. Now is no time to start slacking off. You can undermine everything you've built with inattention.

CONTINUED TRAINING AND SOCIALIZATION

Learning and education remain at the heart of your relationship with a dog who is in his middle years, his prime. At this point you'll hear people saying that they've completed their dogs' training. But training is ongoing. The old expression about not being able to teach an old dog new tricks seriously underestimates the pleasure a dog takes in learning. You'll need to keep working together every day to keep that lifelong quest for education fresh. Dogs thrive on the continued stimulus and the challenge. When they have it, they are not only better companions, but they're also much happier.

You have to continue to have high expectations of how she should behave—and give her ample opportunity to meet those expectations by continuing her education. This doesn't necessarily have to take place in a formal class setting, although it's great when you keep reinforcing it with advanced obedience classes or agility classes. This more mature training is most effective if you do this the way you approach puppy training—by treating it like a game: "Find and follow me." "Chase the ball." "Fetch the kids." "Carry in the groceries." The dog will get bored if all you do is just repeat obedience drills over and over again, day after day.

When you're creative and keep it a game, it's fun for everyone and you build your dog's confidence. I just love that moment when a dog "gets it," when she suddenly understands the rules of a new game that you have come up with. You'll probably be amazed, too, by your dog's sense of humor. I have one friend who does a whole little routine with his dog, in which they act out a robbery: the owner pretends to shoot, and the dog drops and rolls. It's hilarious to watch, and it's clear that both my friend and his dog have a blast doing it.

You can do many things like that to keep it fun. Your dog may even start coming up with games of her own—but you'll have to decide, of course, whether her games are acceptable. Fetching the cat may be a creative idea, but it will probably be too disruptive to the harmony in your happy household. In the meantime, while you're having fun, you will be enhancing your relationship with your dog, solidifying your bond, and reinforcing, in a positive way, that you are a team that works together—and that you are the team captain.

One command that I've found handy—and that my dogs and I kind of came up with on our own—is "no dogs." We use this when we're out somewhere and we're passing other dogs that I'd rather not have an encounter with. This command is great for people who like to take their dogs out in public and into new and unusual situations. When a dog is passing by, I tell whomever I have on the leash at the time, "No dogs. No dogs!" Then praise, praise, praise. All my dogs know this means to ignore the other dogs, and in most cases, it works great.

Unfortunately, I taught this command originally with the jerk-the-chain method. I have learned since then that you can also teach it by saying "no dogs" and praising your pet when other dogs approach. Offer your dog treats when he keeps moving in the right direction and pays attention to you rather than the other dogs, and make the whole thing a really positive experience. Other people who see me going through the "no dogs" routine comment on how well-behaved my dogs are. They don't realize that it wasn't always that way, and it never happens overnight.

Once you have that kind of solid foundation, the sky's the limit. Some trainers might not like that I'm saying this, but this may also be the time to start playing around and relaxing the rules a little bit. I don't mean the fundamental rules of the house, such as no table scraps and everyone must get along, because as far as I'm concerned, those rules are set in stone. But if you've built a stable foundation, you might (and I emphasize *might*) be able to start bending the lesser rules, the way great artists or athletes who have mastered the classic techniques in their field then have the freedom to pursue their own way of doing things.

Where the dog sleeps is one area where I see this done most often—and where it is most often done in my house. The party line says that you really shouldn't let a dog sleep on your bed or even in your room at night because that puts your dog on your same level and makes him feel dominant. But if you've done your work and have done the obedience thing—and are still doing the obedience thing—then it might be okay.

Once you've gotten through your dog's adolescence and gotten to know the dog well and you know whether dominance is a problem, you can lighten up on the rule on where the dog sleeps. If it's on your bedroom floor—or even on your bed—and it works for everyone, then so be it. The important thing is that you remain the boss. If you start with that consistent structure, the possibilities are endless.

MIDLIFE BEHAVIOR PROBLEMS

Friends of mine often call me to discuss problems they're having with their dogs. They usually begin by saying, "I'm so frustrated. We've already been through training but now my dog doesn't seem to listen." The dog is usually around two or so. I tell them, "It just hasn't clicked yet. You haven't given him a chance to learn it, to let it sink in." Think of

The middle years, the dog's prime, are a time of great fun and activity, but even the well-conditioned canine athlete, like Freeway here, needs a rest sometimes. When he wasn't taking sanctuary in the closet, Freeway would crash out on his favorite chair (once I felt confident with his training, I bent the rules a bit and allowed him to get on the furniture). He understood that this did not mean that I was relinquishing my alpha position to him.

how long it takes to learn a foreign language. If you're going to be able to retain it, you have to take refresher courses to keep it fresh in your mind.

One friend had a young, overly energetic Labrador Retriever who was constantly getting into all the typical problems: chewing, digging, and barking, but also some large-scale household destruction. My friend was at the end of his rope. I offered the best advice I could give: increase the daily exercise and get the dog into an obedience class. He took my advice, and the change was incredible. The dog gained more confidence, the bond strengthened between him and his owner, they both got more active, and the dog no longer had to deal with all that pent-up energy that comes so naturally to a Lab. He no longer felt the need to take it out on things he'd find around the house. This is the true value of training: it gives the dog a prideful purpose in life, a satisfying way to lead his life, and a structure for his existence. Add that to the love you both share, and what more does anyone need?

> ## RX FOR A SUDDENLY MISBEHAVING DOG
>
> - Visit the veterinarian to rule out any medical conditions that might be the root of the problem.
>
> - Return to obedience class for a refresher course—perhaps several refresher courses.
>
> - Increase the dog's exercise and mental stimulation: longer walks, jogs in the park, visits to friends.
>
> - Get involved in some new activities, such as flyball, hiking, or agility.
>
> - Lavish your pet with even more attention.

It would be unrealistic and naive to claim that even the most care-fully trained dog can't suddenly develop some type of behavior problem. It happens all the time, sometimes as a result of changes in the household or sometimes because the roots of the problem were never dealt with effectively when the dog was a puppy. If a dog suddenly changes behavior, there's always a reason. It's never that he's just trying to annoy you, and it's never too late to work on those problems and get them taken care of. Assuming you haven't allowed the dog to be the boss all this time, this may actually be easier than you think.

Let's be clear: We're not talking about serious problems, such as a dog who suddenly attacks and mauls members of the family. A family with a dog like that needs serious help from a behaviorist, and it's often doubtful that the problem can be repaired. But if the dog starts barking out of separation anxiety because you have a new job, or if the dog becomes destructive following the loss of a longtime companion dog from the household, or if the dog suddenly decides that your furniture is his favorite food—the problems can be remedied.

First, go the veterinarian and make sure a medical problem isn't to blame for the dog's behavior: maybe a painful back problem or even a

Ryan, Leilani, and Freeway participate in a group down-stay lesson. They excelled in these sessions, but sometimes Ryan would get confused because he relied not on the sound of his name, of course, but on visual cues—and sometimes a visual cue was one of the other dogs. All would be in a down-stay. I would call Freeway to me; Leilani would stay where she was because I hadn't called her name, but Ryan would stand up and come to me because he saw Freeway doing it. Dogs, too, are susceptible to peer pressure.

tumor that hasn't been detected. Then evaluate your life and household to see if anything has changed that might be affecting the dog, to see if his family pack has been disrupted. Once you address this, you can deal with the problem with pertinent information and seek the assistance of a qualified expert: a trainer, a behaviorist, or maybe your dog's breeder. Don't waste your time and your veterinarian's by asking him for behavior advice. Unless your vet has specifically studied behavior, it's best to leave the medical care to the veterinarians and the behavior to the trainers and behaviorists.

THE NEW ROUTINE

Whether I'm at home or away, I'm always wondering what my dogs should be doing at that moment. My personal routine is so erratic, it's not always easy to keep a regular routine going in my household, but I still manage to provide my dogs with structure and regularity. I do whatever I have to, because it's what my dogs need. I often rearrange my schedule for them, such as driving an hour each way between a speaking engagement and the dinner afterward to make sure my dogs are fed and settled. I'll feed the kids, put them in the bedroom, turn on the TV, and then I'm off again for the evening. Some people might say I'm going overboard, that I'm compulsive about my dogs, but that's part of the responsibility I have taken on. That's my life and it's who I am. It's what I give them in exchange for everything I get from them.

Of course, at times you can't stick to the routine, no matter how

If you do decide to bend the rules a bit as your dog matures and allow her access to the furniture, make sure your furniture can accommodate her (and that you can tolerate dog hair on the upholstery). My friends who breed Rhodesian Ridgebacks make sure that for movie night, their furniture will accommodate a pack of large Ridgebacks as well as a visiting Great Dane named Murphy.

compulsive you get about it. Moving is obviously one of those times. Dogs are creatures of habit, which is why moving can be so traumatic for them. It was for Freeway, Ryan, and Leilani when we moved from Venice Beach to Malibu. That was when Freeway decided that the closet would be his haven. He knew that, wherever we were, inside that closet he could be safe and out of the way.

Most dogs go through moving at least once in their life, because many people don't stay in one place for long. It can be confusing for a dog who has lived in one home for several years and considers that place a part of his routine. But if you share a strong bond with your dog, you can help him understand that you're there for him, and that as long as you're there, it must be okay. This is another benefit of raising an adapt- able, easygoing dog.

When you move, you need to pay attention to what the dog is going through and to spend time getting the dog acquainted with his new sur- roundings, both indoors and out. I let my dogs explore the entire house early on, including rooms that may be off limits to them eventually. Outside, I make sure they are on lead and under careful supervision. Set the dog completely free to explore his new environment, and you'll end up with a lost dog, or a drowned one. The pool at the Malibu house was new for my dogs, and sure enough, Leilani fell in. Good thing I was keep- ing an eye on her.

Make sure your dog has familiar items close by, too, such as his bed (with its familiar scents and comfort) and his favorite toys. Feed the dog at the same times and in the same place each day, groom him at the same time, and exercise and play at the same times. Be aware that you may need to go back to the housetraining fundamentals for a while, too, until your dog learns where the bathroom is. Keep things as familiar and pre- dictable as possible, and in a few weeks your somewhat confused com- panion will adjust to his new surroundings and the new routine.

You should follow the same rules when you travel with a dog. Do everything you can to make him comfortable in this strange new place, and keep him on a tight lead.

Travel is another unavoidable event that throws the home routine out the window, but it doesn't have to if you plan ahead. Several years ago I took all my Danes—Donna, Brutus, Ryan, Freeway, and Leilani—on a five-week road trip in a motor home through Canada. I was there to show Brutus and Donna. Inside the motor home each dog had his or her own crate, and I designed a ten-by-fifteen-foot exercise run made out of wire exercise pens so they could get out and stretch when we were camped for the night. I even fed them the way I fed them at home (they couldn't all eat together): Donna first; then Ryan, Freeway, and Leilani together outside; and Brutus inside, often with Donna as company.

I'd get them out for exercise as often as I could, usually as a group, and I'd stop at rest stops so they could stretch their legs from time to time. I could never just lock them in their crates and go, as you sometimes see on the show circuit. I knew them well, and I knew that all five of them had different energy levels and priorities. Freeway was mostly interested in just being with me. Ryan wanted to explore. Leilani was an explorer, too, but a little more cautious about it. Donna was the foolhardy one, and Brutus was the follower. He'd just go along for the ride and follow Donna, whatever she was doing. I used this familiarity to work out our routine on the road so my dogs never felt adrift. Even when we were driving all over Canada, they still had a sense of routine and predictability to depend on.

ADDING A NEW DOG OR ANOTHER PET

Another thing that can dramatically and permanently disrupt a dog's routine is the addition of a new pet. For some pets, the addition of a new buddy is cause for celebration (after an adjustment period, of course); for others, it is the unhappy end of an era. Because the dog in midlife is more set in his ways than a puppy, new additions may be more of a challenge for the young adult dog—and even harder for the older dog. Any way you look at it, from any age perspective, this is not something that should be done impulsively or without a lot of forethought. You have to plan it all out ahead of time, just as you did when you brought your first pet into your house. Only this time, you have the perspective of the resident animals to consider.

There is a difference in bringing a new puppy home and a new adult

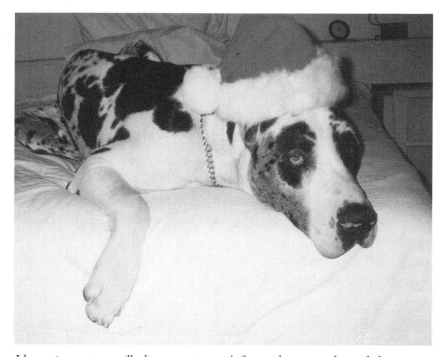

I know it may seem silly, but sometimes it's fun to dress up a dog to help you celebrate the holidays. If your dog will tolerate it, why not? If he will, that's a tribute to your efforts to make him a well-adjusted, adaptable companion. Brutus had apparently shopped 'til he dropped on this particular Christmas shopping excursion, and I, thinking as I always do about training and adjustments, was pleased that his willingness to wear the Santa hat meant that he'd be fine if he ever had to wear a bandage on his head.

dog with a more mysterious past. You can observe certain protocols with the puppy that address his still-developing, puppylike view of the world. But you may want to keep the new adult dog separate from your other pets for a while so you can get acquainted with the dog's personality, fears, and quirks and can observe him for any serious temperament disorders. You may consider this an informal quarantine, too, where you can make sure that the newcomer doesn't have any serious diseases that he could spread to your existing pets if you're not careful.

If you're bringing a new noncanine pet into your house, you have to think of the predator/prey relationship between, say, rabbits and hounds and make sure that all interactions between the dog and the newcomer are strictly supervised. Planning also includes preparing for what you'll do if the new arrangement doesn't work out. I've had that happen, and it was heartbreaking. You must work with all of your pets to establish the fundamental house rule: everyone must get along.

Not every pet owner has the time, energy, or know-how to deal with a multidog or multipet household. The best thing you can do to make it a success is to keep your eye on maintaining the routine, in which there will be comfort and security for everyone—even you. Routine will be your salvation, as will your ability to see the situation through both the nervous newcomer's eyes and the eyes of the existing dog or dogs.

Rely on your instincts. If a newcomer is overzealous with an exist-

If you do your work from the beginning in training and socialization, your dog can enjoy a life of greater freedom. Here Murphy enjoys a sleepover at the Ridgeback house. There's no jealousy, no aggression—pretty amazing when you consider that she is sleeping peacefully within the territory of a fearless breed that was developed to hunt lions.

ing dog or you suspect that jealousy is brewing, keep the dogs separated. If the situation escalates into a fight, you might never get the dogs back together in an unsupervised situation. Do you have room to keep them separated for a while and maybe permanently? Food is territory. Do you understand that you cannot allow your new kitten to wander around the Rottweiler's food dish at dinnertime? Do you have the experience to manage separate mealtimes and separate exercise sessions? Do you have a plan for how you intend to introduce a new pet into a house where a dog already rules the roost? If not, maybe the multipet household isn't the direction you should be going.

It's always come pretty naturally to me—I'm good at the introductions on neutral ground, and at management when problems erupt—but I have had my defeats, too. I've always understood that certain personalities just don't get along together, so they can't be together, but not everyone is willing to acknowledge this. As a dog owner, one of my troubles has been to leave town and have someone else watching the dogs. I'll get back and they'll tell me about a terrible altercation. The caretaker inevitably says, "I didn't think it would be that bad." Well, it can be.

In addition to maintaining the routine when you add a new pet to the household, it also helps to work on training both the newcomer and the veteran. Don't use up all your energy showering the newcomer with attention and neglect your old pal. When I brought Ryan home, he demanded more attention than any other dog I've ever had, because he was deaf. Fortunately, Freeway and Leilani stayed cool about it. I made it a point to remind them through it all how special they were and would always be to me.

A lot of my experience dealing with a multidog household has come from the temporary boarders we've had at the house from time to time. I've had so many different dogs come through that I've been working with or showing or fostering. Sometimes those dogs need extra attention, and sometimes my kids have been jealous. I have to remind them, and myself, that these are just visitors. My permanent guys can usually tell when someone is just passing through, probably because I treat the temporary guests differently and exhibit different body language when I deal with them.

SAFE AND POSITIVE INTRODUCTIONS

When introducing a new dog to the household, be sensitive to both the veteran and the newcomer. Introduce them on neutral ground and bribe them with treats. From then on, make sure that they can both escape from the other in case either one gets aggressive or just starts playing too rough.

As for the newcomer who's here to stay, I try to introduce everybody properly: on neutral ground in a wide, open space with plenty of treats on hand. I work hard during those first few weeks to make sure that everyone is content, getting enough attention, and secure. We stick to the routine and training exercises, and I lavish my attention on my older guys, just as I do on the newcomer. I also make sure that both the veteran and the newcomer can escape the situation if they feel like it. My adult resident dogs always have an escape route and a sanctuary if a newcomer becomes annoying. Don't ever underestimate an existing dog's jealousy or resentment, and never let a puppy harass an older dog.

You can't let a larger, older dog play too roughly with a puppy. The puppy needs an escape hatch, too. When I brought Leilani home, she was small—but not for long. For a while there was a big difference in her size and Freeway's, and Freeway wanted to play with her. But he was kind of gawky and uncoordinated; sometimes he would misplace a paw or get too wild, and Leilani would yelp. So I gave Leilani an out: I put a folding chair in front of the door to the garage that she could run under when Freeway got too rough. Freeway was too big to follow her, so Leilani had her own sanctuary. Make sure that both puppy and existing resident, or just larger and smaller dog, can get out of the situation if it becomes too much.

Follow these same guidelines when you bring home the ultimate new pet: the new baby. Have the dog greet the new noisy little creature and allow her to get acquainted with all the new scents and sounds, and you'll start out on the right track. Once the baby arrives, try to maintain the dog's normal routine, and if he's a trustworthy guy, allow him to be present when you feed, change, rock, and walk the baby. Make sure that all interactions between dog and baby are carefully supervised, and always provide the dog with an escape route he can take whenever first baby, then toddler gets annoying or intent on grabbing fistfuls of hair.

If your dog has had little or no experience with babies and kids, you might help prepare him for the new arrival by taking him to playgrounds and parks where he can get acquainted with the sounds and mannerisms of little humans. Kids move differently than adults, so this will help your dog see that a baby is not some weird alien, just different from what he's been used to. If you have any doubts about how your dog will react to the addition of a baby or child to the family, seek advice from a good trainer or behaviorist to determine if your dog will be safe with children. You might even do some test runs to see how your dog will react should a child decide to grab his tail or a pull on his hair. If your dog is prone to snap, you'll have to make the necessary arrangements—either keep child and dog permanently separated, as I have had to do with certain dogs, or find a new home for the dog. You have no choice.

Whether you're bringing home a new puppy, kitten, rabbit, or baby, you have to plan ahead and stay on your guard so you don't accidentally start ignoring the existing dog or dogs or in any way foster resentment, jealousy, and messy altercations. If you take the necessary time and do everything you can to make this change in the routine a cause for celebration, you will find yourself the head of a happy family.

TWELVE

THE CANINE ATHLETE

As an athlete, one of the most exciting things for me about the middle years of a dog's life is the physical potential of the dog. After the two of you wait patiently through puppyhood, your dog reaches his middle years, ready to roll, ready to run, ready to pull a sled, ready to round up ducks, ready to tackle an agility course.

The important thing to remember is that different dogs, because of breeding or even just personality, have different tastes, talents, and pre-dispositions. I have learned the hard way that what seems right for a dog—and what you may have dreamed of for that dog—is not necessarily what that dog is interested in or capable of doing. There are always exceptions, of course, but you're not likely to see Great Danes taking top honors in Frisbee championships, or a Chow Chow being named therapy dog of the year, or a pack of Samoyeds winning medals in national obedience competitions.

Even if you strike out at one activity, there's bound to be another one that both you and your dog will enjoy. A vast athletic world awaits the dog in his prime.

EVERY DOG AN ATHLETE

Take a look at service dogs—guide dogs, wheelchair assistance dogs, and such—for inspiration. At the age of two going on three, when these incredible animals usually begin their careers, their training has clicked into the hard-wiring of their brains and they go out in the world and help the disabled. This is the stage you may have dreamed about when you were dreaming about a dog in the first place. If you're like me, you visualized what it could be like, cycling along a mountain trail with a dog by your side, competing in agility with a little terrier who loves the challenge of the course, or swimming in the ocean with a big, water-loving dog.

Every dog needs something athletic and energy-expending to do every day. The extent of this activity will depend on the dog's breed or mix of breeds. A Border Collie, for example, will go crazy if he isn't offered a physical challenge every day that expends both his physical and mental energies. A tiny Maltese or Yorkie, on the other hand, may do fine with just a short walk around the block every morning and evening—as long as he's allowed to spend every waking moment indoors with you in the meantime, of course.

Large, medium, or small, dogs all need something to do, and you should consider what this something may be before you choose a new canine companion. If you're not up to meeting a particular dog's rigorous exercise needs, be honest about it before you take the plunge and choose a more appropriate dog. You can't get a dog expecting, "Oh, once the dog is here, then I'll start exercising." You probably won't. The shelters are filled with big, friendly Retriever- and Shepherd-mixes whose original owners realized they wouldn't be fulfilling that resolution once that cute little puppy blossomed into a large, energetic—and now very destructive—dog.

It's exciting to think about all the activities that are now open to all kinds of dogs, both purebreds and mixed breeds. So many fun things are available, from formal showing to obedience to agility to Frisbee competition to water rescue trials to search-and-rescue practice to therapy work.

With my background as an athlete, a dog's exercise program is a subject near and dear to my heart. I want to approach any athletic activity in the right way, with proper attention to all the details. First, it's best to get the dog's health checked out before you dive into any new physical activity, just as a human should. You need to make sure that the dog's heart and lungs are up to the job. You need to make sure he's structurally sound and that his joints are going to work properly and not be damaged by the type of activity you'll be participating in. The veterinarian's blessing will give you some peace of mind as you start your new exercise program or activity.

Once the veterinarian gives you the go-ahead, you have to think about conditioning in a commonsense way. You can't decide one day that you'll start jogging with your dog and then expect him to run a marathon the next. You have to build up gradually, just as you would for yourself, even if this means starting out by walking, then walking longer and longer distances, until you finally break into a jog.

Diet is part of conditioning, too. High-energy foods are now available for active dogs, but in my opinion, these are only necessary if your dog is a heavy-duty athlete, such as a sled dog that runs races every

Freeway tends to suffer from stage fright in any kind of formal event— conformation showing or obedience trials—but make it light and informal, like this Pedigree agility event, and he's happy to join in the fun.

weekend. Even then those foods may be necessary only during racing season. Most regular high-quality maintenance foods will be all the fuel the typical active dog needs.

Diet also plays a role when you are trying to help a dog with a weight problem lose some of those extra pounds. You have to be careful not to demand too much activity from a dog with a weight problem. An exercise program can help slim down a dog whose owner has been a little bit too generous with the treats and table scraps, but be patient, and commit to helping your dog with a sound, healthy diet. Let the weight come off gradually, with proper diet and moderate exercise, and don't stress your dog by pursuing the weight-loss fast track.

Where exercise is concerned, you also have to pay attention to the weather. *When* you exercise is just as important as *how* you exercise. During the warm summer months, you may have to restrict your dog's outdoor exercising to the early mornings or early evenings—never the high heat of the day. Go out at midday and you're just asking for a potentially fatal case of heatstroke. If your dog's skin is sensitive to sunlight, the way my Ryan's skin was, you might try fitting him with an oversize T-shirt that he can wear when he's outside that can help protect him from the ultraviolet rays. Ryan's T-shirt became his trademark.

REMEMBER THE SUNSCREEN

If you plan to be out in the sun with your dog, don't forget the sunscreen (minimum 15 SPF)—for both you and the dog. The bridge of the dog's nose and his groin are the areas most vulnerable to ultraviolet light.

Cold weather, too, can be a challenge. Most dogs can tolerate the cold pretty well, but some breeds, such as Greyhounds and even my Danes, don't do well when it's freezing. Don't laugh at those little doggie booties and sweaters and coats you see displayed at the pet supply stores. Those can actually help a dog with a low tolerance for cold stay warm. If you're too embarrassed to go into a store and buy a coat for your dog, try converting a sweatshirt or ordering from one of the many mail-order catalogs that specialize in pet products. If it's really cold and your dog isn't a Nordic sled-dog-type breed, you might have to think up some indoor games to play to satisfy the bulk of your dog's exercise needs. In the meantime, your dog's winter wardrobe can help keep him warm enough to run outside and do his business.

In cold weather or hot, every dog has to have access to fresh water all the time. It's easy for a dog to become dehydrated without his knowing it. Having so much fun, he may just keep on running, hiking, or catching a Frisbee, not taking time to drink, not knowing what terrible damage he might be doing to his health. It's your job to protect him from this. Keep water with you whenever you're out running around with your dog, and make sure he drinks some periodically. Some dogs can even learn to drink out of sports bottles, and all dogs will swallow from a spray bottle. The important thing is to maintain hydration. At home, always make sure his water dish stays full, cool, and accessible, too.

THE IMPORTANCE OF WALKING THE DOG

When we talk about the dog as athlete, we don't necessarily mean that the dog needs to be running the Iditarod in Alaska or herding sheep in the outback of Australia. Your dog may enjoy these activities if she's a northern sled-dog breed or has herding blood in her veins, but you don't have to go to such extremes. Probably the most classic activity you can do as a dog owner is walking your dog. If this is the primary exercise activity that you offer your pet, you have nothing to be ashamed of. You're giving your dog exactly what she needs and what she wants.

It sounds like such a simple activity, and really, it is, but the importance of walking the dog can't be overemphasized. Getting out there and seeing the world—dogs love that, and the daily walk ends up being good for both of you in so many ways.

Dog walking actually provides a dog with the two types of exercise she needs to stay healthy and well-adjusted. It exercises her body—her muscles, joints, organs, and circulatory system—and it also exercises her mind by exposing her to all the exciting, new surprises she'll encounter along the way. A lot of people don't think about the importance of stimulating the dog's mind, keeping her thinking and making life interesting with a change of scenery. Throwing a dog out in the backyard and call-ing that exercise won't satisfy any of these requirements.

You have to get your dog out where she can walk and run and explore all the different sights and smells and sensations that wait there. Even if you walk the same route or go to the same park every day, it's different every day to a dog, whose senses are so much keener than ours.

CLEANUP PATROL

When you're out walking your dog, bring along your pooper-scooper or cleanup bags so you can set a good example of dog ownership while you're exercising your pet. You may even want to bring some extra bags, which you can politely offer to other dog walkers who have con-veniently "forgotten" cleanup materials of their own.

If you're out walking the dog, then walk the dog. So often you run into somebody who's not paying any attention to the animal on the other end of the leash. Simply having a leash on a dog does not constitute your having control of your pet. Pay attention, for everyone's benefit.

Walking will be pleasurable only if your dog is trained not to drag you down the sidewalk and threaten every other person and dog she sees. Walking is a great opportunity for training and socialization exer-cises, and a mannerly dog is a lot more fun to spend time with—and less of a liability. The dog doesn't have to stay in a perfect heel the whole time, or even any of the time, because that's not much fun for the dog and it doesn't give her much physical exercise or mental stimulation. But you shouldn't have to have shoulder surgery because the dog pulled your arm out of the socket during your evening walk.

Dog walking is also a valuable supplementary activity for dogs who are out in public all the time and have to mind their manners as part of other activities, such as conformation showing. When I was showing two of my dogs, Great Dane Murphy and Pembroke Welsh Corgi Trev'r, I'd take them to this big outdoor shopping area and walk them by the shops and through the crowds. They'd see lots and lots of other people and dogs and be bombarded by the stimuli. It was a great socialization exercise. In this setting, it was fun and it was safe.

Well, usually safe. Once with Murphy I was crossing the street, and a woman walking next to us was talking and flailing her arms. All of a sudden Murphy jumped, and I realized that the woman had been holding a cigarette in her flailing hand, and it had touched Murphy's head! She actually burned my dog. I am always trying to look around and be aware and anticipate potential problems, but I could never have anticipated this. The woman realized what had happened and stopped and said she was sorry. Then she suddenly switched gears and said, "Oh, what a pretty dog," and reached down to pet her. I yelled, "Don't touch my dog! You burned her head!" First of all, Murphy might have reacted defensively to this woman who had hurt her, and second—no one hurts my dogs.

FORMAL ACTIVITIES

The dog world is pretty amazing. You can find every kind of person and every kind of dog involved in every kind of activity. Some of these are informal, such as hiking and cycling, but a network of formal activities is growing more and more active all the time. These include conformation showing, obedience competitions, herding trials, and agility, which is one of the fastest growing activities of all.

Getting involved in some of these activities can be intimidating to a newcomer. You can't just walk in and show a dog in the conformation show ring without knowing a lot about it ahead of time: handling, grooming, pedigrees, classes—there's much to learn. Before you can even think of setting foot in the show ring, you'll have to learn about the grooming requirements of your breed. (For some breeds, such as Poodles, they've become pretty sophisticated through the years.) Ideally, you should take handling classes to learn how to present your dog to the judges.

The best way to get involved, and to start your education, is to get in touch with the local dog network. You can start with your dog's breeder (if you're lucky, you originally found a breeder who knows you're interested in showing and is willing to be a mentor) and your local kennel club. Both can be valuable resources. You should also attend

Lambchop and I had a special chemistry when it came to showing. She hadn't been doing real well in the ring, but I started handling her and I incorporated play into it. That really clicked for her. Ironically, we didn't win when we were together, but when she moved on to another handler, she started winning, and that handler told me that it was because I had put Lambchop on the right track and made showing fun for her.

dog shows, including puppy matches, which are great training grounds.

Conformation shows are often called the beauty pageants of the dog world, and a definite aura surrounds them: lots of money behind some of the show dogs, lots of pressure to win. But you'll also find lots of wonderful people, from breeders to handlers to judges, who love talking about their dogs and are happy to welcome new people into the fold.

It's easiest to approach these people at smaller shows where the pressure isn't too great. I have taken a dog to Westminster, not as a handler, but as kennel help for a stunning little Corgi named Texas, whom I co-owned, and I can attest that you probably shouldn't go to Westminster or Cruft's, the English equivalent, and expect to find a mentor. You're likely to get your head bitten off if you ask for advice and assistance, and I don't mean by a dog. These shows are essentially the Olympics of the dog world. I certainly wouldn't have wanted my focus interrupted when I was competing in diving at that level.

When you find the right advisers and mentors, and you find a nicely made dog who may not be Best-in-Show material but who likes strutting his stuff in the show ring, then you're ready to get your feet wet. When you finally gather up your courage, I would advise starting with fun puppy matches, where you and your pup can learn, enjoy yourselves, and get some experience. It's a really positive, relatively low-pressure way to make your entrance into the show world. That's what I should have done more of when I was starting out with Freeway, and what I would do differently if I were just starting out today.

PUPPY MATCHES

When you're just starting out in the show world, puppy matches offer you the opportunity to get a judge's evaluation of your dog's strengths and faults—faults to which your breeder may be kennel blind. Don't take personally any negative feedback a judge may give you; it's all part of your ongoing quest to learn as much as you can.

If you're inspired by one of the more active showing disciplines—say, obedience, agility, flyball, tracking, or herding—contact local trainers and find out if there is an obedience-training club in your area. Contact the American Kennel Club and the United Kennel Club, too, for information on events they sponsor around the country and the requirements for participation. Some events allow mixed-breed dogs as well as purebreds, plus some organizations now sponsor events especially for mixed-breeds. Whatever you choose, these are all wonderful opportunities to socialize your dog, to get him out meeting people and other dogs and other breeds.

Attend many of these events as a noncompetitor and you'll be amazed at what you can learn—and how inspired you can get—especially with agility. Agility is becoming so popular because getting through the agility obstacle course with the coaching of an owner is something almost every dog can do. It's fun to watch, and the dogs love it. As Freeway can testify, you can't always say that the dogs that are prancing around in the conformation or obedience ring love it.

No matter what you do, please don't take yourself, your dog, or your involvement in formal dog activities too seriously. These activities are supposed to be fun. Lose sight of that, and you could end up alienating your dog and seeing him as something other than a companion and member of your family. I started out because I thought that showing, conformation, and obedience, would be something fun to do with my dogs on the weekends. I didn't go in assuming that I would soon take Best-in-Show honors at Westminster, the Olympics of dog shows. I would have been in for a big disappointment if that was my expectation. My role as kennel help at "the Garden" was demanding enough for me, thank you very much.

My involvement with showing, though, actually came as kind of an unexpected surprise. When I got Freeway, showing was the last thing I was thinking about. But he was a show-marked harlequin Dane, so with his breeder's encouragement, I decided to give showing a try. I started going to handling classes and shows and matches. We made the rounds, and I would ask different judges to point out his faults (every dog has faults) and his assets. Most of them were very honest with me, and I started to understand what a judge looks for in the breed. It was a gradual education. I've seen too many people barge in, deciding that they are going to take the show world by storm and theirs is the dog to do it. For me, it was just an activity for us to share, and we both enjoyed it more because I wasn't putting such terrible pressures on me or my dog.

You have to maintain a healthy attitude toward showing, which means keeping your sense of humor about it. The dogs need that. Everyone has stories of how his dog chose the most inappropriate time to become a clown in the show ring. One time when I was showing two of my Danes, Donna and Lambchop, we had been on the road for a while, and we were now nearing the end of the circuit. They were both a little antsy. They looked at me and I could see what they were thinking: "Let's play with Greg!" They decided to do everything wrong they could think of, the exact opposite of what I asked them to do or what they knew they should be doing. They would jump up on me and smother my face with kisses. They'd suddenly plop down when the judge wanted to evaluate their movement or take a look at their teeth. They were so wild that I couldn't gait them across the ring—this after weeks of good behavior. The judge didn't dismiss me, but he could have. This will happen from time to time, and you can't let it get to you.

By nature I'm a competitive person, but I have always been able to keep my attitude toward showing in perspective because it's not just me involved—it's my dogs, too. I don't want to put them through the kind of stress I went through when I was competing as a diver. Basically, some dogs like showing and some dogs don't.

When I could see that Freeway wasn't having fun, we tried obedi-ence, an equally humbling experience. I actually had him in the obedience ring sooner than I should have. Freeway convinced me pretty quickly that we were in over our heads, that he was never going to be an obedi-ence champion, and I certainly wasn't going to force him. Freeway was and is a champion where it counts—ever the gentleman, always doing everything I ask of him outside the show ring, always a pleasure both at home and in public. You need to keep focused on what is really impor-tant. Family is much more important than trophies and blue ribbons.

All too often in the show world you see a disregard for what the dog does or doesn't want to do. Some dogs are born show dogs and love the spotlight, others tolerate it, and some can't stand it but are forced, because of their breeding and conformation, to make a career of it. This occurs more in the conformation show world than in the other, more active disciplines.

Obedience trainers, on the other hand, at least the ones who repeat-edly take high-in-trial honors and obedience championships, make sure particular dogs are up to the demands of the job before they even choose them as students. They do temperament testing to make sure this is really something the dogs want to do. The same goes for search-and-res-cue and herding. You want a dog who is excited by the activity. You'll just be hitting your head against a wall if you try to force an uninterested dog to participate in something that requires thought and action.

Talent alone won't cut it. Even if the dog has the talent and instincts, he may not have the interest. Listen to your dog. I finally listened to Freeway and figured out, first, that he wasn't enjoying conformation showing, and then that obedience really wasn't something he wanted to do, either. He was doing it just because he wanted to be with me.

But our show ring experience was good for both of us. We both

*Give your dog a break. Yes, I spend lots of time training my dogs, but I make
sure they receive their fair share of play too. Here I am heading off for a hike
with Brutus and Donna, sharing an activity that's just as good for me as it is
for my dogs.*

learned a lot. Everyone was shocked at first to see a Great Dane in the
obedience ring, and he actually inspired some other Dane people to get
involved and try obedience themselves. One guy who did really well,
whose dog really enjoyed it, told me that he would never have even
thought of trying it if he hadn't seen Freeway and me out there.

INFORMAL FUN

The dog world is not restricted to activities that involve judges,
strict protocols, perfect grooming, and big egos. There is a world of
informal activities you can participate in with your dog. You're limited
only by your imagination, your creativity, and your dog's training and
physical conditioning. I've even been known to take my dogs to the park
and play with them on the swings, on the slides, in the sandbox, and on
the fancy jungle-gym sets—after all the kids have gone home, of course.

I remember when I first started in-line skating with my dogs. The sensation of powerlessness can be pretty scary at first. You're on wheels, of all ridiculous things, and your dog has the power, well, to kill you if he wants to. In my case, my worst fall resulted in my being sprawled in a bed of ice plant. I had been working on the skill of skating with a dog in tow and decided to try it with *two* dogs: Donna and Brutus—big dogs, big mistake. Another dog happened to cross our path, and that was it. I probably looked like something out of a bad slapstick comedy, trying to get my wheeled self in a safe place while at the same time trying to control almost 300 pounds of uncontrollable Great Dane muscle, and ending up in the ice plant. At least it was soft, but I could swear the dogs were laughing at me.

That event was a big lesson for me. That was when I started working on teaching my dogs the "no dogs" command, to be used in just such situations to keep their attention on me and the activity at hand, even if another dog wanders by. I also started working on setting some new rules on just how activities such as this would be handled. People joke around and think that when you skate or ride a bike with a dog, the dog

I like to make sure that my dogs keep up with their civic and charitable duties. Here's a shot of Freeway and me when we were asked to help grant a wish for the Make-A-Wish Foundation. I was a diving coach for a day, and Freeway was a great supervisor.

is doing all the work. If that is really how you're doing it, you're asking for trouble—and a potentially bone-crushing accident. Only well-trained dogs should be invited to participate in activities like this. You have to be in control, and the dog has to respect your authority. That means doing the groundwork with the obedience before you go up on wheels.

Of course, not every informal dog activity is so potentially life-threatening. Take search-and-rescue, for example. It starts as a game of hide-and-seek: hide the toy, find the toy, reward and praise the dog. Eventually it becomes find the hidden person, then find the lost person. There's nothing more rewarding for the search-and-rescue dog than finding that lost soul—and saving a life.

Another rewarding activity for dogs and their owners is pet-therapy work. When you see dogs that visit hospitals, nursing homes, children's centers, hospices, and places like that, you're seeing therapy dogs in action. These dogs, the ultimate examples of what socialization can do, can work wonders with the patients they're assigned to help. More and more facilities now honor their power to help and heal and allow them in to work their magic, but it wasn't always that way.

Obviously, not every dog is cut out to be a therapy dog. These dogs have to be totally reliable, gentle, friendly, and healthy. There are organizations that certify dogs as therapy dogs, and that certification is only given to dogs that pass rigorous health and temperament tests such as the AKC's Canine Good Citizen test. Certification helps ease the fears of facility administrators, who worry about having dogs on the premises, and the more dogs are accepted in this niche, the better it is for the patients, who benefit from dogs being there. The value of the human/animal bond has been proven again and again in situations like this—and I've seen it in my own life, as well.

Even if your dog isn't cut out for therapy work—which can be kind of traumatizing for a dog that isn't naturally in love with the entire human race—just working on the Canine Good Citizen test is a good activity. Trainers often offer classes that work only on the various elements of the CGC test, such as basic obedience, mannerly walking on the leash, and tolerance of strangers. It's great practice, and great training. The test tells you where you are with your dog. It's a good indicator of what you need to work on, what you have to look out for, and just what you need to do to be a more thoughtful owner and more responsive to your dog's needs.

If yours is a herding dog, you can participate in formal herding trials or just have fun watching those instincts at work around the house. Border Collies are always trying to herd kids on bicycles or gather the neighbor kids into a single yard. My Corgi, Trev'r, used to play a game that we called Herd the Danes. I'd say, "Go get the kids!" and with a big smile on his face, this squatty, little guy would round up these hundred-plus-pound dogs. He'd herd them up and bring them in. It wasn't the Danes' favorite game, but for some reason they couldn't resist obeying their smaller, very bossy, housemate.

Even the informal activities you pursue with your dog depend on individual likes and dislikes—both yours and your dog's. Some dogs, for example, such as Labs and Springers and Newfoundlands, are natural water dogs. They were bred for water and naturally enjoy a good swim. Now, my dogs have not been traditional water dogs, but because I have a pool, I have tried to make them water-safe, even if that means just getting them in and encouraging them to just paddle around a little and learn where the steps are if they fall in.

I did have one Great Dane, though, who was a water dog—an ocean dog, actually. I'd go out swimming in the ocean, and Brutus would follow me in and bodysurf. He'd be swimming, and then when I'd catch a wave, he'd catch it, too, and ride it in. While most Danes would just run back and forth along the shore not even wanting to get their paws wet, he would just dive right in simply because he wanted to be with me. He was able to master a pretty amazing skill because of it. Now Nipper is carrying on the tradition, proving to be a strong swimmer at home, but I think we'll forget the bodysurfing bit.

Teaching a dog an activity and making that activity something you share is one of the greatest joys for a dog owner—and for a dog. These shared experiences build health in both dog and owner and foster well-being, but they also create a bond that will enrich your life forever.

THIRTEEN

MIDLIFE HEALTH AND
WELL-BEING

There are moments in a dog's life that you never forget. One of those occurred for me when Freeway was four years old. He had always been in perfect health, his movement really good. Incredible, really. Then, one day, he started stumbling, wobbling in the rear. "Oh my God," I thought, "he's dysplastic." But that wasn't possible. His hips were perfect—rated OFA Excellent. It didn't make sense. But here he was, unstable on his feet, insecure, his rear beginning to atrophy. I was scared, but I can only imagine how scared, how confused he must have been. Finally, the diagnosis: cervical vertebrae impairment (CVI) or wobblers syndrome, a malformation of the neck vertebrae that occurs commonly in Dobermans and Great Danes. In time he would be paralyzed.

I decided that we would fight this. I found a specialist, just as I did for Ryan's cancer, and Freeway had surgery. No one knew how it would turn out. It was a long, grueling process—terrifying for me, painful for Freeway—but $5,000 later, he wasn't perfect, but he no longer wobbled. He was, and would always be, a little unsteady in the rear, which was frustrating for me until I realized that my expectations were unrealistic. What the surgery did was restore Freeway's quality of life and double his life expectancy—that's what mattered. If I hadn't done anything, I would have lost him. I can't imagine what all the years since the surgery would have been like without him. For us, the surgery was the right thing to do.

Dog owners are faced with tough health decisions like this all the time. I have probably experienced more than my share of this because I have been involved with a giant breed that can be affected by some pretty serious problems. But every dog owner has to realize that health-care decisions for every dog are tough. Sometimes treatment is just too expensive. Sometimes the prognosis is too iffy and the treatment will be too intense and painful for the dog. We can never feel guilty about that. The only reason to feel guilty is if you fail to offer the dog the best care you can until you are faced with that tough decision. In the meantime, there are things we can do to protect and promote our pets' health, and it is our responsibility to do them.

PREVENTIVE MEDICINE

When dogs reach their middle years, many owners decide they don't have to pay as much attention to their pets' health. Puppies are always getting into trouble, and their developing immune systems aren't up to the demands of protecting them, but once the dog reaches his prime, there are still routine veterinary exams, vaccines, dental care, and blood tests that must be kept up.

If you wait until it's broken, as many of us do, it may be a lot harder to fix. It may even be impossible. A better plan is to build a solid health foundation during the puppy years and continue that tradition throughout the dog's adult years. Keep paying attention to preventive care: vaccines, annual veterinary checkups, daily observation, and keep on the lookout for internal parasites. Have the veterinarian examine fecal samples from your dog every six months to check for worms, and keep your dog on a heartworm prevention program—one pill or wafer each month—for this deadly parasite that is transmitted by mosquitoes. Plenty of things can go wrong during a dog's middle years: some of them are due to infection and parasites, some are genetic, and some are caused by injury.

What many people don't realize is that a dog presents an important health barometer to his owners each and every day: his feces. Yes, yes, I know it sounds disgusting, and it's something you might prefer not to discuss, but the consistency and color—and even the odor—of your dog's daily calling cards are directly affected by what is going on in your dog's

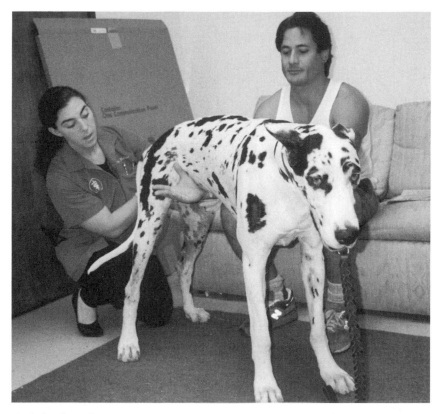

Only bitches of top-notch health and quality should be bred. The mother-to-be should x-ray OFA Good or Excellent for hip dysplasia, her eyes should be clear of genetic problems, and she should be free of any other genetic conditions that affect her breed. Before the breeding, take her to the veterinarian for a thorough physical examination, and make sure she is current on her vaccines, free of parasites, and built for whelping.

system. Know what they look like when the dog is healthy, and you'll know instantly that something isn't quite right when they suddenly change. It doesn't have to be something serious. It could just be a temporary reaction to something the dog ate or a minor parasite infestation, but if you notice blood or mucus in the feces, it could be a severe, life-threatening infection such as canine parvovirus, which requires immediate care.

As a responsible owner who cleans up after your dog every day, you will be in the absolute best position to detect problems as soon as possible. If your dog usually defecates twice a day, constipation will be pretty obvious when he goes a whole day without doing it even once. It's the same with urinary habits: if you notice that your dog strains to urinate but produces little or nothing for his efforts—lifts his leg for an unusually long time and nothing happens, kidney problems or a bladder infection could be to blame. Get to the veterinarian right away. Kidney problems can kill.

This same philosophy applies to your evaluations of your dog's general health. Spend the time when your dog is healthy to commit to memory what is normal for the dog: Get to know the smell of his ears, the color of his eyes, and any normal markings or lumps or bumps on his skin. That way you'll recognize right away when something changes— such as the development of a tumor on the dog's shoulder or a foul odor from his ears. The earlier dogs are treated for conditions like this, the better chance they have of a smooth recovery and survival.

Preventive observation is no great challenge. Just feed him a healthy, high-quality diet, stick to a sound grooming and bathing and parasite-control program, and exercise your pet regularly. I also pay attention to news of disease outbreaks. A few years ago I heard of a parvovirus outbreak in a part of Los Angeles where I was going with my dogs. While I was there, I wouldn't allow the dogs to walk on the grass. If they got out of the car, they had to stay on the cement sidewalks, and we avoided the feces that other dogs had left behind. I do this as a matter of course anyway. I wasn't taking any chances with parvo.

GARAGE WARNING

Pay attention to garages. They are filled with things like antifreeze and rat poison, which can be tasty treats to a curious dog. Keep the number of your local poison-control center near the phone for this and any other potential poisoning emergencies.

As part of your prevention program, check your dog from head to toe when you come in from outdoors, too. Look for foxtails between the toes (or salt or ice balls if you've been out in the snow), cuts on the feet, ticks on the skin, and sudden discharges from the nose or eyes. On a few occasions I had to pull foxtails and even tacks out of Donna's paw pads. Imagine how those situations could have escalated if I hadn't bothered to examine her feet after our time outdoors.

You have a responsibility to your dog and to all dogs. That's why I believe it's important, if you get a dog from a breeder, to let that breeder know if your dog experiences any health problems. As a breeder I would want to know if one of the dogs I bred was dysplastic or bloated or developed heart murmurs or cataracts—it's in the breeder's, the line's, and the breed's best interest.

The breeders I've worked with have always been responsive to my feedback, and I've always been responsive to the feedback from my own puppy buyers. Some others out there don't want to hear it, but that attitude has to change if we're ever going to get rid of some of the terrible genetic problems we're dealing with. The same goes for temperament problems. If one dog in the litter has a temperament that isn't typical of the breed—as with one of my Danes, who was uncharacteristically skittish and wary of people—the breeder should know about it and want to know about it.

Another important part of preventive canine health care is preparing yourself for an emergency. This is especially true if you're out playing with your dog a lot, especially in areas where there might not be a veterinary hospital on every corner. Hiking in the hills, playing at the beach, cross-country skiing in the mountains: these are the most likely places where injuries can occur, and where if you don't bring along a first-aid kit, you won't have any emergency supplies if an accident happens.

Once I was out with Donna and she was running in an open field. Suddenly she stopped and came limping back to me. She had cut her paw, actually torn the palm pad. It was bleeding heavily. Fortunately, I had my trusty first-aid kit with me. I cleaned the wound, medicated it, put gauze on it, and then put a sock on her foot that I taped in place to her leg. If I hadn't had the supplies on hand, I would have been in trouble. Stopping the bleeding might have been impossible, and without antibacterial medication along, it might have become infected.

TICK REMOVAL

When you venture into wooded areas with your dog, keep on the lookout for ticks, which can cause Lyme disease and other serious illnesses. Examine your pet thoroughly after you venture into the great potentially tick-infested outdoors, and if you find a tick on your dog's skin, remove it as follows:

- Grasp the tick's head and body firmly with tweezers or between your thumb and forefinger, and pull it out with a smooth, steady motion.

- Apply antibiotic cream or ointment to the site.

- Watch your dog for the next few weeks for signs of joint stiffness, lethargy, and respiratory problems, which could indicate a tick-related illness.

Prevent these consequences by keeping a first-aid kit handy—the same kit can double for both you and your dog. Keep it well stocked with supplies, including various sizes of gauze pads and bandaging materials, strong tape, antibacterial cream, tweezers, snakebite kit, Benadryl (for bee stings), towels, rubbing alcohol or hydrogen peroxide, and yes, even some old socks.

WHEN A DOG IS SICK

You can't be squeamish when you live with dogs. Health care isn't always pretty. I've been through it all with my dogs: I've sat in on some of my dogs' surgeries—including the castrations of Ryan and Freeway, I've dealt with pyometra (a frightening and messy infection of the uterus), I've had to give my dogs injections, I've delivered my dogs' puppies (another messy, potentially frightening job), and I've washed out more bleeding wounds than I can count. That doesn't count the normal responsibilities such as cleaning up bodily fluids of all kinds and dealing with diarrhea, gooey ear infections, and internal parasites. This is all part of what we agree to take on when we live with dogs, so make sure you're prepared for it ahead of time. Sometimes it can make you feel kind of woozy, but you get through it—you have to. If you plan on having children someday, just consider it good training.

Despite these sometimes gruesome details, there's something very satisfying about caring for a sick dog. I've been through a lot with my dogs, from back surgeries to open wounds to every kind of infection to Ryan's battle with cancer. Even though I wish my dogs had never had to go through all this, I'm glad I was there for them when they did. When they were weak, vulnerable, and under the weather, they needed me in a different way, and they knew they could depend on me. These can be special times when you realize that your dog needs you as much as you need her.

I've probably been through enough health crises with my dogs to have earned an honorary veterinary degree, but I'm no doctor. I do

The best thing you can do for your dog's health is to get to know your dog. Get to know his behavior, his bathroom habits, his appetite, the contours of his skin and structure, the texture of his coat, and even his smell. That way you'll know instantly when something isn't right and you can get him to the veterinarian for treatment as soon as possible.

know, though, how to tell when a dog is sick, and how we need to go about making him well again—if we can.

One good thing about dogs is that they aren't nearly as secretive as cats are when they're sick. Most dogs will let you know that they're not feeling well—many will be incredibly big babies about it. Even though your dog might be a royal wimp when he's sick, you should still get to know the basic signs of canine illness. No matter what the dog may be suffering from, the symptoms will probably include any or all of the following:

- loss of appetite

- a change in normal behavior, such as when a really cheerful, friendly, active dog suddenly becomes sullen, lethargic, or aggressive

- blood in the feces or urine

- limping

- hiding

- an uncharacteristic clinginess

- a refusal to go up or down stairs

- vomiting

- diarrhea

- a discharge from the eyes or nose

- a sudden disregard for housetraining protocols

These symptoms can indicate any number of conditions, some of which require immediate veterinary attention. Others aren't quite so acute but still require attention. If you notice blood in your dog's feces, for example, get the dog to the veterinarian ASAP, especially if this is combined with other symptoms such as lethargy and a loss of appetite. Don't hesitate for a minute. The cause could be canine parvovirus, or the less critical coronavirus. Without supportive treatment to keep the dog hydrated and to fortify the immune system so the dog can fight off the virus on his own, the dog could die of dehydration.

It's pretty obvious what the signs of a structural problem would be. As Freeway's battle with CVI illustrated, a sudden change in movement, pain, or an outright inability to walk can be signs of pretty serious conditions such as a herniated disk in the back, genetic skeletal malformation or joint degeneration, or even the onset of hip dysplasia. Treatment can include anything from pain management to surgery, which may or may not be effective.

Also serious are urinary problems, including kidney disease and bladder infections. Blood in the urine, excessive urination and/or unproductive urination, and an unquenchable thirst are the warning signs of urinary tract problems. They should send you running to the veterinarian immediately. These conditions can sometimes be treated with medication and special prescription diets; some can result in chronic pain and sudden death. You need the veterinarian's expertise to deal with them.

You may also need the veterinarian's help to deal with respiratory ailments. The dog's respiratory system can be infected by viruses, bacteria, or fungi, and some can be pretty serious. You'll notice that something isn't right when your dog starts coughing, wheezing, sniffling, sneezing, and/or having trouble breathing. There will also probably be a discharge from the eyes and nose. In other words, the symptoms are identical to the symptoms that appear in people with a respiratory illness. You may decide not to see a doctor for your own minor cold, but it's a good idea to get the dog to the veterinarian for his. It could be something annoying but relatively minor such as kennel, or canine, cough—or something as life-threatening as pneumonia.

Probably one of my greatest canine health fears is of canine bloat, or gastric dilatation-volvulus. This is probably because Great Danes are always named first or almost first when someone is naming the large, deep-chested breeds that are most commonly affected by this condition. It usually happens after a dog has eaten—especially if he has eaten right before or after an exercise session. If the dog tries to lie down but can't get comfortable and keeps getting up, and lying down again and so on and so on; if her stomach swells; if she tries to vomit but can't—these are the classic signs of bloat. That's exactly how it happened with my Leilani.

At the first suspicion that a dog might be bloating, you need to get her to the veterinarian. If you're quick enough, the veterinarian may be able to pass a stomach tube down and release the air that has become trapped and caused the bloating. I've always been ready to do this myself if I have to. But if you let it go too long, the stomach twists, which is called torsion, and you can lose the dog quickly. Emergency surgery may save her, but there are no guarantees. If the stomach twists and that oxygen gets cut off from the gut, the dog will die. It's that quick. I was fortunate with Leilani. She had the surgery and she came through it, but after that I had to watch her during and after mealtimes even more closely than I did before. I've been even more paranoid about bloat ever since with all my dogs. Big dogs may be the prime candidates for bloat, but it can happen to any dog.

Another life-threatening condition that can affect a dog in midlife, especially an active dog that spends lots of time out running around in warm weather, is heatstroke. A dog suffering from heatstroke—which can have an incredibly quick onset—will exhibit excessive panting, shallow breathing, restlessness, pale mucous membranes, and maybe vomiting. Finally the dog will collapse, and if you don't get her cooled down with shade, air-conditioning and cool, not cold, water, she could be dead within minutes. Of course this can all be prevented by leaving your dog home where it's cool during the warm hours of spring and summer, and by planning the dog's exercise for the cooler parts of the day.

These are all serious illnesses and conditions. It's important to educate yourself, especially once your dog is diagnosed with something specific. But it's also important to get a second opinion if you think one is warranted. Any good vet, or any good doctor, is going to encourage you to talk to someone else and get as much information as you can. The good ones know they're not perfect and that they might have missed something that could be obvious when viewed through fresh eyes. Take advantage of the technology and advancements available these days, and take advantage of specialists. Just like doctors in human medicine, veterinarians are specializing these days, and I know that my dogs have benefited quite a bit from the care of veterinary specialists.

It all boils down to communication with the veterinarian and work-ing together for the well-being of your dog. If you have any question or suspicion at all, don't be afraid or embarrassed to call the veterinarian. It's best to be cautious, and that's what a good veterinarian is there for.

GROOMING BASICS

Grooming is more than just something we do to keep our dogs beau-tiful. It's another aspect of your dog's preventive health care. Assuming you have introduced the various grooming procedures positively to a puppy, grooming the middle-aged dog shouldn't be much of a problem.

The basis of a good grooming program is daily or almost daily brushing and/or combing. Whether a dog has long hair or short hair, the coat needs to be groomed, the oils of the skin distributed through-out the skin and hair. Otherwise, you're asking for skin problems and, in the case of the long-haired dog, matting that will have to be cut out or shaved off. There's an art to brushing and combing. You have to brush or comb down to the skin, from the top of the head to the tip of the tail. This can be a great bonding activity and something you both look forward to.

As for bathing, I probably bathe my dogs more than I need to, but they love the attention and it gives me an opportunity to check for lumps, bumps, ticks, fleas, anything like that. I usually wash my dogs in the shower. I've gone the bathtub route, but that's tough with a Great Dane or a Bouvier. What I do instead now is use a hand held shower-head. That way I can saturate the dog with water, suds him up, and get him rinsed, all without struggling or having to do any heavy lifting. A kitchen sink might be fine for a toy dog, or the outdoor hose for a dog of any size on a hot day.

With practice, you'll figure out the best bathing procedure for your dog. Just make sure that when you rinse the dog, you rinse all the sham-poo off thoroughly. Shampoo residue can result in dry skin. Also, make sure you give your dog a sense of security, maybe by placing a rubber mat on the floor of the shower, bathtub, or sink. Remember that as soon as the dog gets out of the bath, he will instinctively want to shake off the water. So that I don't have to do a full-scale bathroom cleaning after bathtime, I try to get my dogs outside as quickly as possible to shake— on a leash, or else they might run and roll around in the dirt and grass, and we'll be back at square one. After the bath, allow the dog's coat to dry thoroughly in a warm place. Bathtime is also a good time to clean the dog's ears—only the flaps of the dog's ears—which you can do best with some mineral oil on a cotton ball.

By some miracle, I haven't had too much of a flea problem. But for some people, fleas can be an incredibly frustrating and ongoing fight. When you find either a flea or flea dirt (tiny specks of black flea excrement) on your dog or in your house, you need to treat the dog, the house, the carpet, the furniture, the outdoor environment, everything. You can't just put a little flea collar on your dog and say, "Okay, that's it. My dog is protected."

FLEA FIGHTING MADE SIMPLE

* Regularly treat your dog, your house, and your yard simultaneously for a successful three-pronged attack.

* Use flea products that are compatible with each other.

* On puppies, use only products approved for a puppy's delicate system.

* If you notice a single flea or flea dirt on your dog or in your home, assume you have a flea problem.

The good thing is that great new products are always coming out to help you fight fleas, and many of them fight ticks as well. Many of these are available only by prescription from a veterinarian, who should actually be your first stop when you realize you have a flea problem. The veterinarian may be able to suggest and prescribe some effective products for your particular pet—some of the new internal medications, bombs, sprays, dips, carpet services—and give you advice on what products are compatible with each other, which is important if you're going to prevent poisoning or toxic reactions in your dog.

Your dog's teeth could also use regular attention. It wasn't always this way. The teeth would last about ten years or so, which was also the average canine life span. But now, those teeth have to last longer. Dogs can get gum disease and all those horrible things just as people can, and it's painful for them. To prevent this, canine toothbrushing has become quite the rage. I have to admit that I don't do this as much as I should (and I hear the same lament from many of my fellow dog owners). Ideally, toothbrushing should be done every day (and ideally you should introduce the dog to it as a puppy). Also ideally you should use a toothbrush and toothpaste especially made for dogs. People products will only make them sick. Brushing should be supplemented with professional cleanings done by the veterinarian once or even twice a year. The entire program will help your dog keep his teeth well into his later years.

Probably the most challenging grooming activity is nail clipping. Without it, a dog can become crippled. The nails just grow and grow and start curling around. They splay the toes, cause limping, and some may actually come back around and puncture the foot. Nail clipping can be a challenge, especially if you haven't trained the dog positively to tolerate it or even just to have his feet handled, or if you're not careful doing it. You have to be careful not to cut the nails too short—to "quick" the nails by cutting into the blood-rich base that is usually darker in color from the outer edge. That will result in bleeding and pain. After that, your dog may not be so cooperative the next time. Keep the treats handy for this one (remember, a dab of peanut butter can be an effective distraction). If necessary, don't insist on doing all the nails in one sitting.

TREE SAP REMOVAL

Remove tree sap from a dog's coat with rubbing alcohol on a cotton ball or cloth. Be gentle when doing so, because the alcohol can burn the dog's skin and the fumes can irritate his sensitive nose.

I also consider foot care an important part of dog care, especially when you've committed to an active lifestyle with a dog. They say that horses are only as sound as their feet, and that can apply to dogs, too. Many times I'll be out walking and I'll spot a limping dog. I'll go up the person walking the dog and say, "Excuse me. Do you realize your dog is limping?" Sometimes they care, sometimes they don't. Often it's because of the nails. Sometimes it's something even more serious, such as an abscessed foxtail or piece of glass. Either way, a veterinarian should look at it.

DESIGNING A DIET BASED ON LIFESTYLE AND ACTIVITY

Puppies are "cute," but the well-turned-out adult dog, gleaming with health, maturity, and dignity, is "stunning." It's a high compliment to me when someone comes up to me and says, "Wow, your dogs look great." I do that to other people, too. When I see a dog that is in great shape, with a great coat and a great attitude, I always stop and ask what the secret is. What do you do? What kind of exercise do you do? What kind of food do you feed? I get some great information this way, and good ideas, and it makes the other owner feel proud.

Much of the information you collect when you see an amazing dog will probably revolve around diet. Once the dog gets through puppyhood and her adult coat is in all its glory, the effects of the healthy diet will show on every inch of her body and in every aspect of her life. Her overall health, vitality, and even attitude will be affected, so this is one area where skimping just should not be tolerated.

A dog does better on a steady diet. Keep switching its food all the time, and you'll cause gastric upset, finicky eating, and an unhealthy fixation on food. It's okay to change your dog's diet if the food you're feeding doesn't agree with his system or if you are switching from puppy food to maintenance adult food or some other life-stage diet, but never switch for the sake of switching.

I have changed my dogs' food from time to time. Once it was because they just refused to eat the food I was giving them. Always honor their likes and dislikes. Another time I switched because I didn't think my dogs' coats looked as good as they should. Skin and coat are the best indicators of a dog's health and the quality of his diet. Switching ended up making a big difference. Whenever you change diets, do it gradually. Begin by adding just a little bit of the new food to the old, and increase the amount of new food in the diet each day. This prevents a shock to the dog's system. Eventually the entire meal will be the new food.

As far as exactly what you feed your dog, make it a high-quality product that is tested according to feeding trial protocols with real dogs, who also play a role in testing palatability. Proper canine nutrition involves a lot of different nutrients that must be present in a balanced formula. Most of us don't have the time or the know-how to provide that on our own. Keep the treats healthy, too, and remember that treats are food. If your dog has more treats than usual—or gets into the kibble bin as Ryan was known to do—then you have to reduce that day's normal ration to compensate. That's why the treats should be balanced.

I also advise that owners of middle-aged dogs continue to feed their pets in two meals a day rather than one large meal—stick to the schedule you kept for puppy feedings. As it does with puppies, this is a good way to keep the dog from feeling hungry or deprived during the day, and

I take grooming very seriously. It's more than just making a dog look pretty—it contributes to overall health. Trev'r, like all show dogs, learned to tolerate and even enjoy grooming at a young age. Grooming was always a positive, and routine, experience for him, as it should be for all dogs.

it can also serve an important preventive health function. Smaller meals that are offered neither directly before or after exercise can help prevent the dog from bloating.

Resist the urge to overfeed your dog. Too many dogs are overweight today. Obesity is the scourge of modern dogs, shortening their life span and detracting from their overall quality of life.

Weight problems usually make themselves known during a dog's middle years and then just continue to escalate as the dog ages. Now you might think that my own background as an athlete and a child performer makes me more sensitive to this, but I don't think so. For me it boils down to what's good for our dogs. Dogs don't know any better. They don't know that when we stuff them with table scraps and treats, we're hurting them. They don't understand that when they end up waddling around, huffing and puffing and struggling to move from one end of the room to the other, we're the ones who did that to them. It should be illegal to do that to a dog.

For many people, feeding endless treats to a dog is a way of showing love. It's the people who have to be trained to change their "treating" habits when it's time for a dog to take off some weight. They have to learn the better way to show their pets love. It's attention that the dog really wants, so spend time with him. When you feel the urge to treat, take the dog on a car ride or a walk. Or play a game of fetch. Anything rather than giving the dog a treat or feeding him from the table.

Living with several dogs at a time, you have to be really careful about managing mealtimes. You often need to feed the dogs separately, or you'll end up with some dogs that are overweight and some that are underweight. When I had Murphy, Ryan, and Freeway, Murphy wasn't much of an eater, so Ryan, who was always on the pendulum from chunky to thin and back again, would let himself into her area and eat whatever she left, which could be most of her meal. I had to really watch them, otherwise Ryan would have ended up the poster dog for Overeaters Anonymous.

There are several ways to tell if your dog is overweight: huffing, puffing, and a belly dragged across the floor are good signs, but sometimes an owner just isn't sure, especially with a long-coated dog whose coat hides the bulk. The classic test involves feeling the dog's rib cage with your hands. If you can't feel any ribs, the dog is obese. He may not live long, and certainly not comfortably. Feel the ribs too distinctly, and your pet could stand to gain a few pounds.

Some dogs are just naturally slim and trim or just aren't all that interested in food. You don't want an active dog to be deprived of the calories she needs to fuel her active lifestyle. You also don't want a dog to be too thin in case she happens to come down with an illness, when a little extra weight could help her get through the rough part. But never try to fatten up a skinny dog with junk food and empty calories. Stick to what is healthy, and that includes healthy treats. Supplements and treats of canned dog food, dog biscuits, sliced carrots, and zucchini are superior to carrot cake, leftover filet mignon, ice cream, pizza, or take-out Chinese food.

Your dog's ongoing health is your major responsibility as a dog owner. Someday your dog's health is going to fail, and you're going to have to make some tough decisions. So cherish the years you have together and make them last as long as possible.

PART FOUR

THE
GOLDEN
YEARS

FOURTEEN

A BOND LIKE NO OTHER

The time I spent as a volunteer with Pets are Wonderful Support (PAWS) was a really eye-opening experience for me. I remember one woman who had a Doberman, a really great dog. He was an older guy, and they really lived just for each other. They were like mirrors of each other, so perfectly matched, both with wonderful personalities, energetic and enthusiastic. What was probably most amazing about this couple was that they were both going blind. But that didn't matter. They were so bonded, so in tune with each other, that they refused to feel sorry for themselves. I didn't worry about them for a minute. I knew that that dog was in good hands—and the woman was in good paws.

I loved being a mobile groomer for PAWS, helping to make sure that people living with HIV could continue to keep and take care of their dogs. But there was more to it than that. Going into people's homes as I did, I witnessed special bonds between people and dogs that I don't think I've ever seen quite so vividly before. A lot of the dogs I groomed were older dogs, who had a wonderful aura of wisdom about them. They had been with their people for a long time and had struggled for years with them through some difficult situations. Because of this, they shared a bond that's hard even to describe.

You could see when you walked into these houses that the dogs were equals to the people they lived with. They had a unique interdependence and trust that is the direct result of experiencing a life-threatening condition with a companion dog. I would visit people who had been in and out of hospitals over and over again, and their dogs were sensitive to that and to everything that was going on. I'd come into the houses and I'd feel that the dogs were practically looking me up and down, checking me out, just to make sure that my intentions were honorable, to make sure I wouldn't be causing any trouble for the people they loved.

When you've built all those years of trust together, starting with puppyhood and on into the adult years, you arrive in the older years, the golden years, with a deep understanding of your dog. Some dog owners consider this time to be the very best time with a dog.

THE SPECIAL RELATIONSHIP BETWEEN OWNER AND OLDER DOG

Throughout this book we've tried to look at the various stages of a dog's life, and our role in those stages, through the eyes of the dog. Now if we are to look at the world through the dog's eyes—the old dog's eyes this time—we would likely see a picture that's a little different from the one we saw from the perspective of the puppy and the middle-aged dog. People who have never experienced life with an older dog usually think this is an unbearably sad time. Yes, it can be—I'm not denying that. But it can also be the most rewarding.

My PAWS experiences got me thinking about the bond that exists between a dog and the person that dog has lived with for years and years. An unspoken understanding develops between them, kind of like the understanding and loyalty that exist between people who have lived together for a long time. It's hard for me to contemplate that some people actually look at the older dog as disposable. Just go to the shelter sometime and see the older dogs there—ten, eleven years old. Well groomed, well fed, but the family had to move. How can people do that? What about loyalty? What about trust? How can you throw an animal away?

I like to think about that idealized scene where you're sitting in front of a fire reading a book with an old dog lying at your feet. That scene doesn't have to be an ideal. It can and should be reality. This can be the time when you pay your dog back for everything he has given you through the years—and a time when he will at last be willing to let his guard down a little bit and agree to depend on you. He trusts you

It can be sad when a dog enters his older years, when he slows down and can't go running marathons with you anymore, but it can also be a time of even deeper bonding in your relationship. (Photo copyright © Chris Strother)

because of the foundation you have built together, and now you can both reap the benefits of that trust.

Most of us spend the majority of our dogs' lives feeling protected by our pets. Even the smallest dogs can have a giant protection instinct. Now, you are the protector. You have to be even more alert to other people and dogs and potentially threatening situations, whether you're at home or out in public. Your dog can't protect himself the way he used to. He may not even be as capable of detecting threats. Now it's your turn to make your dog feel as safe as he has always made you feel.

All along, traveling from puppyhood throughout middle age, we have talked about how important it is to be sensitive to your dog and what he is going through at a given time. Think about it. The dog is aging. His senses dull, his joints get achy, he may become less tolerant to heat and cold, he can't exercise as vigorously as he wants to (or as vigorously as he knows you'd like him to), he may require more trips outdoors to relieve himself to accommodate the faltering bladder control of old age, and he may require more frequent trips to the veterinarian, which is probably not going to be his idea of fun. With all this going on, now is when you really need to be there for him.

This can be a challenging time because of the physical and emotional changes your dog can and probably will go through, but you can make it a rewarding time. You will probably have some tough decisions to make for your older dog, but if you have a good, close relationship with your pet, you will feel more confident in making those decisions. And you will probably be better equipped to make the decision that you think your dog would want you to make.

Basically, you need to offer the older dog a sense of security, now more than ever. If he feels more vulnerable because it's harder for him to get around and he's not as alert as he used to be, then you have to take

Outdoor charitable events can be great activities for dogs who aren't as young as they used to be but still crave attention and the electricity of being out in public. Ryan and Freeway always enjoyed going out and meeting their public in informal settings, evident here where I am introducing Ryan to Jeanie White-Grinder—the mother of my buddy Ryan White, for whom my Ryan was named.

up the slack. You have to do this emotionally for the dog, and you have to do it practically. Think first about security: the older dog, just like the young puppy—actually, just like every dog—needs a place that's all his own, a place he can retreat to when he feels nervous or tired or scared. For Freeway, that would be the closet in my bedroom. He knows that's always open to him. Another option is to keep a crate in a quiet corner where the dog can go if things get too hectic. Over time, you'll figure out the best system for your dog that will offer him comfort when he's old and gray. Or your dog will let you know what he prefers—the way Freeway did with the closet. Older dogs need a safe place.

It's kind of natural for owners of aging dogs to think that maybe now would be a good time to get a new puppy. I ask owners who talk to me about this to please rethink it. Trust me on this: in most cases, a new puppy will not make the old dog feel secure. Now I know this may sound as if I'm saying do as I say, not as I do, but my situation is a little bit different. I am always having dogs of all ages coming in and out of my house for a variety of reasons. It's never a big shock for my older dogs because this pattern has just been a part of their household routine since they were puppies. But in a single-dog household—a single-*aging*-dog household—a new puppy could be just the ticket to making his last years miserable. I really doubt that that's your intention.

When your dog begins to age, it's natural to start thinking about what life will be without him. It's natural, too, to think that a puppy will help make things easier for you when your old companion passes on. But be honest and admit that adding the new puppy is for you, not for your older dog. That's probably the last thing he wants to deal with as he begins to face the vulnerability and instability of aging. There are excep-tions, of course. I've seen it happen where a new puppy helps keep an older dog young and spry. The older dog thrives in the role as mentor to the pup. But more often, I think the opposite happens. The stress of the puppy accelerates the older dog's decline and erodes the quality of life that he should enjoy in his later years. So again, rethink this idea. Explore your motives and think about your older dog.

THE EFFECTS OF OLD AGE

In discussing older dogs, I think it's important to point out that what is old for one dog is the spring-chicken years for another one. I guess I'm extrasensitive to this because I have lived with Great Danes for so long. Eight years is the typical life expectancy for a Dane. For most other non-giant dogs, eight is usually considered just the beginning of a dog's older years. Nowadays some dogs live quite happily until fifteen, sixteen, even seventeen. That's why it's important not to think about "dog years" or the number of candles on your dog's imaginary birthday cake. Instead, just pay attention to your dog. He'll tell you all you need to know about his particular aging experience.

Once they reach the "golden years," dogs can age—and decline—quickly, even within weeks or months. Such health problems as kidney trouble, cataracts, or arthritis can develop and accelerate, even before you notice anything out of the ordinary. A more slow and steady change also occurs. You may notice this first in the subtle changes in the dog's daily rhythms—that's where I usually first see it. Most dogs are morning creatures. But as they get older, you may notice that they don't just bound out of bed, running into your room as if to say, "Okay, let's go!" at the crack of dawn the way they used to. You notice that they're willing to relax a little bit more in the morning—and maybe go to bed earlier at night, too. The older dog may just need more sleep now, during the day and at night. Allow him that privacy and quiet.

The older dog may need to go outside more frequently than he used to, too, because his control over his bladder may not be as reliable now. Or the problem may be something like what Leilani experienced. Her back grew so weak that she had no muscle control in her back end. When she went to the bathroom, she would fall back into the pile. This can obviously be frustrating for an owner who has gotten accustomed to a certain routine with a strong, robust, self-sufficient dog—imagine how it makes the dog feel.

Having an accident in the house because of a lack of bladder control can be devastating to a sensitive dog who has been perfectly house-trained and accident-free for years. In his mind, he knows what you expect and he knows he's failing you. You have to do your best to prevent this. First, get the dog to the veterinarian to make sure this isn't the sign of a beginning kidney or bladder problem. Certain prescription diets may help with urinary tract problems, but you need the veterinarian's expertise to figure that out.

Once you know what you're dealing with, commit to increasing the number of trips outdoors for bathroom duty. You might also try to devise a new system, say, with a doggie door, that will allow the dog to let himself out into a safely confined space when nature calls. That's what I did for my two old guys, Ryan and Freeway. When I had to be out of the house, I would leave them in my bedroom and leave the door open so they could go in and out freely as they needed to. It worked out great. There were never any accidents. They understood the reason for the change in our routine. But whatever you do, do not, and I repeat, *do not,* punish the dog for age-related accidents. Talk about devastation. He can't help it. And again, just as with housetraining a puppy, if your older

The older dog needs you in a new and different way. He starts to depend on you just as you have always depended on him and values more than ever spending time with the people he knows and loves. It's a good thing my coach Ron O'Brien has never minded sharing the sofa with 150 pounds of dog.

dog does have an accident, it's your fault. You weren't looking ahead and anticipating what he needs at this stage of his life. Scold yourself for this event, not the dog.

RESISTING PITY

It's natural to pity a dog as he ages and his senses dull, his joints stiffen, and his stamina wanes. But your dog doesn't want your pity. He wants your respect, your sensitivity, your companionship, and your assistance in helping him adapt to his new challenges.

Pay attention, too, to your dog's new physical constraints. Make sure at bathtime, for example, that the dog has a rubber mat to stand on in the tub or shower. I think owners should do this for a dog of any age, but it can be especially comforting to the older dog. Rubber matting will offer the older dog the stable footing that he needs now more than ever.

As I've said, I even choose my cars with my dogs in mind. This is probably most critical with the older dog, again because of physical constraints. Now if the dog is small or medium-sized, then the distance from the ground to the seat probably isn't all that important. Just lift the dog up. No problem. But with a 130-pound giant such as Freeway, who isn't as limber as he once was but still insists on riding in the car, lifting the dog up can be a problem. I have always found it upsetting to watch an older dog struggle to climb up and try to get comfortable when he's obviously stiff, unsteady, and maybe in pain.

The remedy? Certain minivans can be great for the older, stiffer, more arthritic big dogs because they sit lower to the ground and all the dog has to do is step up. If getting a new car or van isn't possible, then you might try devising a ramp or getting some portable steps that will make the dog's entrance a little more graceful and comfortable—and a lot less upsetting for you. Of course, even with these concessions, I have had to start leaving Freeway home more than I used to. It's just not fair to make him get in and out of the car all day like that. That's frustrating for him, because he knows it used to be so easy for him. I can see the

My house is always full of dogs of all ages, and my older dogs are accustomed to that. While the addition of a new puppy can bring life back into the eyes of some older dogs, in most cases, that annoying little critter is just an irritation that diminishes the quality of the older guy's lifestyle.

frustration in his eyes. "I used to be able to do this!" he seems to say. "What happened?"

Be aware of all the subtle changes that come with age. Be sensitive to your dog. Don't force her to do things that she's really not interested in. I mean, the dog still needs to mind you and everything, but it's not fair (or safe) to force an older dog (or any dog) to baby-sit the visiting three-year-old or to play social director to your poker buddies. I keep things pretty quiet in my house. If people are coming over, I give the dogs the option to be there or not. And usually, I find the older dogs in my bedroom. I'll go looking for them and find them all content and quiet by themselves—especially Freeway. So I'll turn on the TV—preferably animal shows—or a video. Freeway's favorite movie is *The Bear*. I know of other dogs who prefer *Never Cry Wolf* and even one who adores *The Age of Innocence*. You just have to pay attention to your dog.

You also have to be aware that your dog may not be as patient as when he was younger. Ryan would tolerate just about anything. When people came over, if they showed him a little attention, he'd just stay and keep soaking it all up—even when he wasn't feeling that great. He would somehow push his discomfort aside, and the attention seemed to make him feel better. But you can't assume this will be true of every older dog. Some dogs become mellower with age, but others develop a shorter fuse.

You have to think about this if you're bringing a new puppy or a new baby into the house—even if it's just for a visit. Don't assume your older dog will be thrilled about this. In fact, assume the opposite—and give him his space. Don't allow him to be harassed by either a young dog or a young human. Give him the freedom to get acquainted with the newcomer—and then to escape if he wants to. Ryan was always a great daddy to the puppies in the house, even in his older years when his health was really taking a toll on him. But Freeway was not. When Nipper came to live with us as a puppy, she was pretty energetic, and Freeway would get a little testy with her. He would just grumble—not strike or bite or anything like that. He just had to let her know where her place was—that her place wasn't bouncing around biting at his face as an invitation to play.

ACCOMMODATING THE DOG WHO HAS LOST HIS SIGHT OR HEARING

The most common, most obvious change that happens to an older dog—especially now that dogs are living as long as they are—is the loss of sight and/or hearing. I gained experience in this with my deaf Dane, Ryan, long before he ever approached old age. Ryan was born deaf, so dealing with his old age was easier because we were already working within the patterns that you establish with a deaf dog. But when your dog begins to lose his sight and hearing with age, you have to train your-self and your dog to work together.

What's amazing is that, for most dogs, this change isn't traumatic. It can be more traumatic for the dog's owner. The loss of sight or hearing usually happens gradually. The dog never even seems to realize that this drastic change has taken place, just as the dog that is born blind or deaf doesn't understand that anything about him is out of the ordinary. Dogs don't go into a deep depression, mourning their great loss or anything like that. They just start behaving a little differently and compensating for it. Dogs are incredibly resilient that way.

I used to be amazed at the reaction I'd get from people when I'd be out walking Ryan. People would stop and ask me what his name was. "His name is Ryan," I'd say, "but you can call him anything you want. He's deaf." I knew that the next words out of their mouth would be "Really? Oh, poor thing!" I would try to explain that there was no rea-son to pity him, but they'd think I was being insensitive. Ryan never felt sorry for himself, and that's the greatest lesson we can learn from an elderly or disabled dog. Ryan actually had a pretty incredible sense of humor about it. At times I'd be behind him waving my arms trying to get his attention. He obviously saw me quite clearly out of the corner of his eye, but he'd just ignore me. Being deaf was his situation and he dealt with it. It's the same with the older dog that loses his hearing or even his sight. He doesn't feel sorry for himself, and you shouldn't feel sorry for him either.

You may not even know right away that anything is different with your dog. Then, one day, you notice that he doesn't run barking to the front door when someone knocks. Or he doesn't hear you coming up behind him. Or he doesn't hear you call him from the other side of the park (and it's not because of adolescent rebellion). Or he seems to sleep a lot more soundly than he used to. Or he looks at you kind of sideways, kind of cockeyed sometimes. Or he doesn't seem to see the cat sitting up on the back fence, which has for years always sent him into a territo-rial frenzy. This is all just natural aging. Nothing to be sad about. Probably nothing serious. You'll just have to do some things now to accommodate him.

Age does not mean retirement from life. The older dog still wants to be included in the household activities, and you need to adjust the household routine and your dog-related activities, to accommodate him.

First of all, if your dog loses his sight, then it's probably not a good idea to rearrange the furniture. That wouldn't be nice. Dogs memorize the lie of the land in their homes, and if they can't see it, they rely on their memories to help them get around.

As for the deaf dog, I learned from Ryan that it's a good idea for all dog owners to prepare for deafness ahead of time—actually, when the dog is a puppy. I now train my dogs with voice commands *and* hand signals right from the start. Obviously, Ryan could only understand the hand signals, and from training him I learned how to use them. But train every dog this way, and if the dog does lose her hearing in her later years, you'll be ready. There will be a smooth transition, no major adjustment, because you have already learned how to communicate with hand signals. It's already natural for both of you.

Another important step when taking care of a dog who has lost her sight or hearing, or both, is to be even more alert when you're out in public with the dog. You have to protect her. Imagine how you'd feel if you couldn't see and suddenly a kid came screaming up to you and pounded you on the head awkwardly—his way of petting the "nice doggie." Or you couldn't hear and an aggressively barking dog runs up out of nowhere and jumps on you. All you have to do is imagine it from your dog's point of view. So keep your eyes and ears open, and remember that your older dog should always be on a leash when you're out in public. That's an important part of your job as your dog's protector during what can be the most vulnerable stage of her life.

It can also be the most rewarding stage of her life—and of your relationship. There will be trials along the way, and sadness at times, but keep these in perspective as you make the necessary decisions and maintain the proper level of sensitivity. View caring for the older dog as a privilege, and someday you'll look back at your dog's later years as the golden years they are meant to be.

FIFTEEN

GERIATRIC HEALTH AND WELL-BEING

I remember the moment when I first realized that Freeway had become an "older dog." He was seven at the time. We had gone out for a hike to a particular beach that was kind of secluded and not that easy to get to. We took a steep hill down to the water as we had done so many times before. We played and ran around, and then when it was time to go back up the hill, that's when it happened. Freeway just stopped. He stood looking at me, helpless and frustrated. "I can't do it, Dad," he seemed to say. "I just can't do it anymore." I've heard this happens to guide dogs, too. After so many years of service, one day they may just stop, lie down, and that's it. "I can't do it anymore, Dad."

It can be a sad day when you realize that your dog has entered this new stage of life. Sad, but not the end. It's just the message to you, loud and clear, that you'll have to be making some changes now. You've entered a new era, a new stage of your relationship as well as a new stage of your dog's life. I urge you to listen to the message your dog is sending you. I still feel guilty about what happened with Freeway at the beach that day, even though his aging had seemed to sneak up on me. I hadn't meant to, but I had put him in a position where he failed at something, and he ended up feeling as if he had let me down. I'll never forget the expression in his eyes. But actually, I was the one who had let him down. One event like that and you do whatever you can do to prevent it from happening again.

In a way, it's no different for humans. For me, as an athlete, I don't want to admit that I can't do a reverse three-and-a-half anymore. I want everybody to believe that I can, and I want to believe myself that I can. But the reality is, it's not going to happen. Thank God my coach doesn't ask me to try it. I just might try for him. Well, dogs go through the same thing. They just don't want to let anyone down.

Older dogs know perfectly well that they used to be able to do this or that. They're mature and fully formed, and they understand that things are happening beyond their control. They want to please us, but we have to help them through it. We have to do some thinking for them and keep them out of no-win situations. We have to do what's in their best interest, to gently tell them, "Okay, I understand. We're going to do *this* now, instead." After our fateful moment at the foot of that hill, Freeway can still go to the beach, but it has to be a beach that's flat. And even then I'm careful about how far we go. He still wins because I set it up so he can. I watch him, I watch our surroundings, I plan our activities carefully, and I keep focused on his health. For their health and well-being, that's what we have to do when our dogs start getting up there in age.

HEALTH, THE VETERINARIAN, AND THE OLDER DOG

When a dog ages, she can experience some dramatic changes in her health. It's all part of natural aging, but her owner needs to be aware of it and help her deal with it.

A lot of these changes are linked to the immune system. The older the dog gets, the more her immune system may naturally begin to break down, making her more susceptible to various conditions. These can range from gastrointestinal illness to allergies to urinary infections to gum disease. Skin problems can also be more common in older dogs, such as various lumps, bumps, and growths and even skin cancer or mange.

Arthritis and general joint achiness are common in older dogs, too. So are back problems, and if your dog's hips aren't OFA picture-perfect for hip dysplasia, then hip problems are, too. If your dog has spent her life jumping up onto high furniture and down again, especially if she is a smaller dog, she might be faced with back, shoulder, and/or knee problems as she gets older. The veterinarian may then tell you that you need to stop your pet from jumping like that from now on, or even to stop her from going down stairs. Good luck with that one. You'll have to catch her first.

KEEP OFF THE STAIRS

If your dog is diagnosed with joint or back problems when she gets older but refuses to stop running up and down the stairs, block both the foot and the top of the stairway with gates that are designed to restrict babies and kids. In time, your pet will learn that from now on you will be carrying her up and down the stairs, or if she's a big dog, she'll just have to stay off them altogether.

Older dogs are also more prone to cataracts, which can be corrected by surgery just as they are in humans. But surgery of any kind is always more of a risk for the older dog, primarily because of the risks of anesthesia. That's why a good veterinarian will do a blood panel on an elderly patient before performing surgery. This way he or she can make sure that the dog's system will be able to withstand the stress of surgery and the effects of anesthesia. If the veterinarian recommends surgery for your older dog but tells you that a blood test isn't necessary, I would get a second opinion on that one—and maybe a new veterinarian.

The same rule applies to teeth cleaning, which requires anesthesia if it's being done the right way. Anytime the older dog needs anesthesia, you should first decide how necessary the procedure is, and then, if it is necessary, make sure that a blood panel is done beforehand. Look at the bright side of this test. It's one more opportunity to find out what's going on in your dog's system—his organs, his blood, all of that. Older dogs age much more quickly than younger dogs do. Several months can actually translate to several human years of aging. Sometimes it seems that changes in an older dog's health can occur practically overnight, but if you catch a serious condition early on, early treatment might also produce practically overnight improvements.

Now I'm not trying to make you paranoid about your older dog's health. I'm just trying to stress how important it is to be aware of potential problems that can affect the older dog, and how quick their onset can be. It should be obvious that if you, the responsible owner, haven't already gotten to know your dog's veterinarian well by this time, you certainly will now. Trusting your dog's veterinarian and being comfortable with his or her abilities can make a dog's later years, and the decisions necessary to make them as comfortable as possible, much easier for everyone.

Most veterinarians recommend that when a dog reaches her senior years, the annual veterinary checkup should be increased to twice a year. And no, this isn't because this means more money for the doctor. It's because this is what's best for your dog's health. Now more than ever you need to stay on the lookout for subtle changes in behavior, skin and coat quality, movement, bathroom habits, appetite, all those canine vital signs. You need to give the veterinarian the opportunity to look for

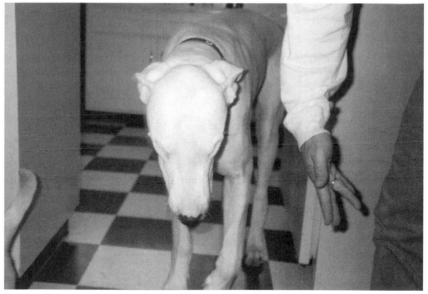

I started training Ryan with hand signals when he was a puppy because he was deaf, but it's wise for all owners to teach their dogs hand signals. As your pup approaches old age, he could lose his hearing, and it's nice to think that even if that happens, you'll still have a way of communicating clearly with him. That communication can be a great confidence builder for the older dog who's beginning to feel vulnerable.

these, too, from a more scientific perspective—and you need to report anything you find to the veterinarian as soon as possible.

If you're like me, you may find that you're going to the veterinarian even more than twice a year because you find a lump on your dog's shoulder or see blood in her urine or notice a sudden change in her gait. I certainly hope you will visit the veterinarian when you notice things like this. But even if your dog is healthy, the twice-a-year rule could save your pet's life. The geriatric veterinary visit usually includes a blood test; a urinalysis; a look at the teeth to see if any should be extracted; the typical look into the eyes, the ears, and the nose; the palpation of the abdomen—an overall evaluation. With these tests, the veterinarian could detect something that won't be obvious to you or even to your dog for months—and it may be a lot easier to treat it now than it would be months from now.

THE CHALLENGE OF FEEDING THE OLDER DOG

It's never smart to overfeed a dog, but when you overfeed, or inappropriately feed, an older dog, you can make his day-to-day life miserable. An overweight dog with, say, arthritis will suffer even more with his condition because the extra pounds put so much more stress and strain on his aching joints. Or if you decide to fill your dog up with gooey treats, his sensitive digestive tract is sure to rebel. Just say no to yourself when you feel this impulse. You're not doing your old friend any favors.

But a dog's older years are usually when well-meaning owners decide that they are doing their companions a great favor by tickling their taste buds with foods that used to be forbidden. Veterinarians can talk about this until they're blue in the face—and I've seen them do that—telling owners of older dogs that by feeding their dogs pound cake, baked potatoes with butter and sour cream, and sirloin steak, they're shortening their dogs' lives and making their remaining days uncomfortable. But many owners just figure, "Why not? He doesn't have that much time left anyway."

The thing is, you never know—he could have more time left than

The older dog wants to know that you still value his presence and his wisdom. Here Ryan checks out the taping job on Brutus's ears—and probably feels grateful that he never had to go through it himself. (Photo copyright © Lester Kowalsky)

you know. Ryan fooled me numerous times. Over and over again, he'd come out of surgery low in energy and listless or have a serious bout with his skin cancer, and I'd think, "Okay, this is it. I'm going to have to put him down," only to find that two days later he was acting like a puppy again. By assuming that the dog doesn't have much time left anyway and filling him up with junk food or table scraps, you may actually be the one who is assuring that his days are numbered. Diet can make a big difference in a dog's health and the kind of stress on his organs. Just remember: your dog didn't need the treats and table scraps and junk food when he was young, and he doesn't need them now.

What the older dog does need is a steady diet of high-quality commercial food, which will supply him with the balanced nutrition that he requires to keep his organs running smoothly and to fuel his energy needs, which are now less than they were when he was in his prime. Foods are available that are specifically designed for older dogs. Most of these are lower in calories and protein than regular maintenance adult diets. Some people have great success with these foods, they swear by them, but there is still debate over how necessary they are. It's best to consult your dog's veterinarian to determine what is most appropriate for your particular dog, given his current health, weight, and medical history. Your veterinarian may also recommend feeding a special prescription diet, maybe one formulated for allergies or urinary tract problems, that will help your dog deal with his specific age-related conditions.

Obesity is a serious problem that affects way too many older dogs these days, but it's not just overfeeding that you need to worry about with the older dog. Some dogs have the opposite problem. They're too thin. Maybe they've never had much of an interest in food, or maybe a loss of appetite has happened gradually with age. Either way, you can't allow the dog to starve herself, especially if she's dealing with a chronic health problem. You have to keep her weight on and keep it stable. Otherwise she has no protection from current health problems or from others that could take advantage of her weakened state.

Ryan was like that. He was why I started feeding canned food as well as dry to my dogs in the first place. For years Ryan had fought cancer, but it started becoming more of a battle when he got older. I saw him getting thinner and thinner, and he needed nutritional fuel to fight off his illness. With the advice of his veterinarian, I added canned food to his diet and for a while actually doubled his daily ration. I was a little hesitant about increasing his food, but he was looking so thin to me and his energy level was definitely lower. At the same time, his appetite was good and he was interested in eating more than I was giving him, so we tried it and it worked. We got his weight back to a healthy, steady state, and his energy levels increased. He needed that. And it probably prolonged his life.

THE THREE-MEATBALL METHOD

When it's time to give your dog medication, hide the meds in cheese or meatballs made from canned dog food. With Ryan, I would use the three-meatball method: the first meatball to let Ryan know what kind of treat he was getting, the second with the hidden meds, and the third to help encourage him to gulp down the all-important second one laced with the meds.

Canned food can be great for this kind of situation. It can also be a great treat food. It is usually more palatable than plain dry food, and I found that it was also helpful for Ryan with the medications he had to take. Canned food can be just the thing for hiding a dog's medications—and older dogs are often on medication for such things as thyroid imbalances, seizures, joint and back pain, and cancer. Hide the medication in a meatball made of canned dog food, and you might have an easier time getting the necessary medicine into your dog's system.

EXERCISING MIND AND BODY

Several years ago when I was taking care of my dad when he was ill, we used to go out walking with Freeway. One day we were out walking on a warm afternoon and we came across an Old English Sheepdog. He was just lying by himself by the side of the road. First, I checked to see if he had been hit by a car, but he had no injuries. He was just a big, friendly guy lying by himself by the side of the road.

I started petting the dog, and I could see that he was elderly. He enjoyed the attention and we became friends. Obviously, I wasn't going to just leave him there. Then a guy drove up in a car and said, "Oh, thanks so much for staying with my dog. We were out for a jog and he couldn't quite make it. He was just too tired. He's kind of old. Plus he's dysplastic, so you know how that is." I was horrified once again at the insensitivity. Here he had an old dog, covered with long hair, being asked to run on a warm afternoon—and with bad hips! I explained to the guy as nicely as I could about the pain the dog was in because of his hips, that the heat was endangering the dog's life, and that he was just too old to be out exercising at that level. Short walks in the cooler hours of the day were best for the dog now.

What's really upsetting is that so many owners do this to their older dogs—even nice, well-meaning owners such as the Sheepdog's owner. He didn't mean to put his dog in that situation. He just didn't understand, didn't know any better. I like to think that that day was his moment of truth, his turning point, just like my moment of truth with Freeway at the beach. Sometimes this moment and its message come out

Leilani recuperates from her back surgery at the animal hospital with fellow
patient Silver. Deciding on major surgery for a dog of any age is tough. I've
been through it more times than I care to think about, and I let my dogs be my
guides in deciding what's right for them.

of the blue, and we just have to listen to it. I hope that from that day on
the guy realized that he couldn't take his wonderful old dog—a dysplastic dog, at that—out jogging on a warm day anymore. I hope he realized
that short walks during the cooler hours of the day should be the new
exercise routine. I tried to help him realize this. I hope he took what I
had to say about age, hip dysplasia, and heat to heart.

Consider this stage of life as your dog's retirement. He retires from
the level of activity that he enjoyed during the prime of his life and now
participates in a mellower, less demanding way. Even human retirees still
play golf and swim and that kind of thing. Just be sensitive to what is
now appropriate for your dog. And don't try to force him into something that he can no longer participate in. The older dog will still try to
please you, even if physically he shouldn't be pulling a sled or hiking the
Rockies or running marathons. He could seriously hurt himself trying to
please you.

Freeway could still go to the beach after our turning point, but we
no longer go to beaches that are accessible only by steep hills. He still

rides in the car with me, only now not as frequently. We stay closer to home these days, too. We still practice our obedience commands, and I'll still ask him to walk at the heel sometimes, only now I don't expect him to do an automatic sit when we stop. It's too much of an effort for him to get up and down. When I take a walk with him or any other older dog from my house, I'll walk uphill first so that when we come home we'll be walking downhill. It's easier that way for an older dog that's getting tired. And no matter what we do—or what age dog I'm with—I always stay alert to my dog's heart rate and breathing. If an older dog starts breathing too heavily or seems to be overdoing it, I give him a graceful out. I say, "Come on, let's sit down awhile. I need to rest." Even if he knows I'm doing it for him, I have to be considerate.

Another thing I have had to be considerate about is my older dogs' arthritis. Arthritis affected both Ryan and Freeway—and even if it's not debilitating or crippling, it's still a stiffness that makes things uncomfortable, especially when the air is damp or rainy. You need to be sensitive to this in the older dog. Waking up and running right out to exercise at the crack of dawn when everything is cool and damp outside may not be the best thing for a dog who gets stiff in the joints in the morning. I have always tried to wait until things warm up a little bit—both the air outdoors and my dogs. I let my dogs get up and walk around first—to limber up and wait until the outdoor temperature is a little friendlier to their condition. Not too cold, not too hot. Most older dogs aren't tolerant of either extreme.

Sometimes the older dog just doesn't know her own limitations and will push those limitations just to please you. You have to protect her from hurting herself that way. I had my work cut out for me with Leilani in her last months of life. It was so hard for her. She was still sharp in the mind, still wanting to play, but her body just couldn't keep up with those desires.

It must have been so frustrating for her. I'd pack up the dogs to go to the park or the beach, and in her prime, Leilani would have been doing handsprings when she saw what we were getting ready to do. But after major back surgery and a weakening of her back end, she just stood there, wanting to play with the other dogs, but unable to. I'd lift her up into the truck, and even that, I knew, was an indignity for her. We'd get to the beach and I'd help her down into the sand, and again, she'd want to play. She would have tried to if I had let her, but even if she had been physically able to play with the other dogs, she wouldn't have been able to make it back to the truck. And she was a big girl—I certainly couldn't carry her. I might have ended up hurting her more than I hurt myself.

It's not that older dogs can't play. They should still be encouraged to exercise their play muscles, but within their new limits. You have to develop an instinct about this. Let's say you have an older dog who has had major back surgery. You can't just say, "Oh, look. She wants to play with the neighborhood Rottweiler twins. If she's up for it, it must be safe. Okay, doggie, there you go. Go on and play." Honor your instincts, and remember, you know best. Your dog doesn't. Your dog will want to play the way she used to. It's fine for the dog to play, just not as she did in her prime.

For instance, I'll throw the ball for an older dog to fetch, but I won't throw it as far, and I'll do it, say, five times instead of fifteen. Then when the dog brings it back to me, I praise her as if it's the most wonderful thing she's ever done. Whether she is a veteran of sled-dog racing or just in-line skating with her owner, she needs to continue to feel the victory.

Go ahead and set the dog up to succeed. Let her pull a wagon on level ground, ask her to herd the kids in for dinner, that type of thing. Keep her involved in the daily rhythm of things. Allow her to use her skills in a modified form. When she does the new task, praise her. It's the same philosophy that search-and-rescue teams use. In the midst of the serious disasters they're working, they'll arrange mock rescues of live people so the dogs won't get depressed when they find people who are dead. It's your responsibility to keep up your dog's morale—any little thing you can do to help her feel that she is still a winner.

Also, beware of senior-citizen laziness. As they start to slow down, some dogs may not be interested in much exercise at all. There is danger in this, too. You still have to get them out there. You don't want the muscles atrophying, the weight increasing, and the mind turning to mush. I had to work with Freeway on this. He got older and got a little bit lazy. He would have been happy just to lounge around all day, and I couldn't let that happen. In the face of that kind of laziness, I had to become motivator, cheerleader, and activity director.

The perfect activity for most older dogs, whether they are lazy or active seniors, is walking—in moderation and custom-tailored to the dog's abilities and stamina. Walking keeps their muscles toned, their joints in working order, and it's good for the organs—the heart, the digestive tract, and everything else. Walking also exercises the brain. An older dog's mind is just as much in need of stimulation as a young mind is. Dogs thrive when regularly exposed to sights, sounds, and scents that they don't find at home. Low-impact walking in a public place is the ideal activity for exercising the mind and the body of the older dog, as well as that of the older owner.

If you live with several dogs of all ages as I do, you'll need to tailor an exercise schedule to everyone's needs. Younger dogs will probably have to be exercised separately from older dogs so they can get their full quotient of energy-expending activity. But when you take all the dogs out together, the needs of the older dogs have to take precedence. For example, when Murphy lived with us, she was one that I could in-line skate and jog with and all that, but when we had the older set with us— Freeway and Ryan—we had to slow things down. Activity was limited to walking and we couldn't go as far as I could with Murphy alone. The same rule was in place when Nipper came along, and now with Speedo and Mikey, too. In our house, we respect and honor the elderly.

SIXTEEN

THE HARD GOOD-BYE

Sorry, but we can't avoid this chapter. We started out with the intention of following a dog's life from birth to old age, and our journey wouldn't be complete without looking at its end. As anyone who lives with dogs knows, there comes a time—a difficult time, a terrible time—but one that all of us have to face sooner or later, when you have to say good-bye to your best friend.

You've spent a lifetime looking at things through your companion's eyes. If you've been together since he was a puppy, you protected him from harm when he tried to chew on electrical cords or eat bathroom cleanser. During his adolescence, you understood his rebellious surge of independence but made sure he understood that rules were rules. In your pet's prime, you shared countless hours playing, traveling, training, running, and just hanging out together. As he got older, you offered him loving encouragement to slow down a little bit and gave him a shoulder to lean on in exchange for all the times he allowed you to depend on his sixth sense and protective instincts.

Now, your dog has reached the end of his journey. Again, he looks to you to make the right decisions, just as you always have. Your gift to him is to take one last glimpse through his eyes. From that perspective, you'll find that all he asks for now is his dignity.

This was what I wanted to make sure I offered Ryan at the end of his life. We had been through so much together, so many memories, so much mutual comfort. And there had been so many traumas with his health: cancer, thyroid problems, skin tumors, arthritis, surgery, chemotherapy. So many times I figured, "Okay, this is it." And so many times Ryan would march out of surgery with that old familiar twinkle in his eye and let me know that, nope, he wasn't ready yet. It wasn't his time.

Then, one day, the twinkle was gone. There had always been such incredible communication between us, and now I couldn't escape what he was telling me. It was his time, and he was asking me to help him get where he needed to go. Ryan was eight. That's up there for a Great Dane. I never even dreamed I'd have that many years with him. Even though I had a long time to prepare, I can't say the decision was easy—it never is—but I knew it was right. I knew it was time, and now when I think about it, I'm glad that it happened the way it did.

Ryan knew the veterinarian who came over to the house. He liked her and trusted her. He lay down in his favorite spot, and I lay down with him for a while. After we shared a few last moments, the doctor gave him his final injection, and he fell asleep in my lap. It wasn't on a cold, hard floor or a cold metal table. It was at home, his favorite place. It was peaceful, we said good-bye, and he just went to sleep. My last gift to him was a quiet, peaceful, dignified end, something we all hope for. I believe that we should all try to offer that to our dogs when they come to the end of their journey.

DIFFICULT DECISIONS

When you live with dogs, you will be asked during your companions' lives to make decisions that will determine their fates—life-and-death decisions. These are the most difficult decisions that can face a dog owner: Should you pursue heroic health treatments for your dog that could be painful and possibly unsuccessful? How much pain should you allow your dog to endure? Should you put your dog out of her misery? I've been there plenty of times, and it can be awful—believe me. I expect to be there plenty more times in the future. It's the toughest part of living with dogs, but I wouldn't trade the experience for anything. It's just another responsibility that I agree to take on when I invite dogs in as members of my family.

I always try to put myself in my dog's position: "If this were me, what would I want for myself?" The answer always boils down to one important element: quality of life. I used to have discussions about this with my dad when he was diagnosed with cancer. We both agreed that, for us, it was quality of life, not quantity of time. I know my dogs feel the same way.

When you give that kind of respect and consideration to the dog, it makes the tough decisions easier. That's how I stuck it out with Ryan. I told the veterinarian that just as long as he wasn't in pain and as long as his attitude was good, then we'd keep fighting. I knew that's what Ryan wanted me to do, and that's exactly what I want for myself. When the pain became too much for him, he let me know. If you have a deep bond with your dog, you just know. It may take a while to admit it to yourself because the realization can be devastating, but you just know. Once you know, your dog will depend on you to do what you have to do.

SECOND OPINIONS

Part of making the tough decisions is collecting all the information you can, and that means getting second opinions from veterinarians about your dog's health. This isn't always necessary, but if you have any doubts or are still unclear about what the first veterinarian is telling you, don't hesitate to get an opinion from another doctor.

It's not always an older dog that requires you to make difficult decisions—and it's not always the end of your dog's life that you're asked to make a decision about. Sometimes it's a question of medical treatment: Do you or don't you? A puppy, a middle-aged dog, or an older dog can all be the cause of sleepless nights, insane worry, and a guilty conscience. Freeway was pretty young when I spent those sleepless nights worrying about his CVI, trying to decide whether we should go ahead and do the surgery. Surgery on the vertebrae in his neck. I decided that, yes, we would. That doesn't mean that it was the right decision for every dog owner who is faced with this dilemma. It was just the right decision for Freeway and me.

Most people wouldn't spend $5,000 on a surgical procedure that you don't even know will be successful. Most dog owners couldn't

Throw sheets come in handy for dogs of all ages, as Murphy demonstrates here. In homes where dogs are allowed on the furniture (like mine), you can protect your furniture and make your dogs more comfortable at the same time, and cleanup involves nothing more than throwing the sheet into the washing machine.

afford to. In that case, the dog would have faced increasing muscle weakness and atrophy and finally, paralysis. Eventually he would have been put down. There would have been no other choice. It's sad, but just the reality. The kind of reality that dog owners have to face every day. Not everyone can afford the surgery, and not everyone wants to put a dog through it. No miracle awaits at the veterinarian's office, no matter how much money you spend. Saying no to extensive surgery and treatment is a legitimate decision. It takes a lot of courage to make that tough decision.

NO GUARANTEES, NO GUILT

No surgery, no treatment, is guaranteed. Part of being a responsible dog owner is realizing that you can't feel guilty when you make the hard decision not to go ahead with medical treatment.

When you are faced with a tough decision like this, you need to get as much information as possible. First, you have to learn all you can about the dog's condition, which means discussing it at length with the veterinarian. This is why it's important to work through the years with a veterinarian you can talk to, one who will answer your questions. You want to know that your veterinarian respects you enough to supply you with all the necessary information—even the technical information— and that he or she will support you if you want to get a second opinion. It's also smart to do your own research: read books and articles and do research on the Internet.

Once you're well informed, look at your individual pet and his possibility of recovery. That was a major factor in my decision to go ahead with Freeway's CVI surgery. He was young enough that I knew he would probably respond well to the surgery. Even if the dog is a strong candidate for treatment, you still need to ask what the dog's quality of

The older dog will need to go outdoors and relieve himself more often than he did in his prime, and he'll need more sleep, too. Give him a soft, private, quiet spot where he can nap. Ryan would always seek out the softest spot in the house.

life is going to be afterward. How is the treatment going to affect his temperament? How will it affect his energy levels? What's the worst-case scenario? What's the best-case scenario? How will the dog tolerate the discomfort of sutures and dressings? How will you? Can you deal with the trauma of the surgery and treatment, and the gory details of caring for the dog? Be honest with yourself, and don't beat yourself up if you decide you can't afford to deal with such treatment—or if you decide that you just don't want your dog going through it. It's your decision, based on the quality of life you and your dog will have.

While you're sitting there being honest with yourself about the realities of the whole thing, you have to remember that any surgery or invasive treatment, especially with anesthesia, is a risk. It's a risk for older dogs, sure, but for younger dogs, too. You have to have all the information if you're going to make the decision that's best for you and your dog. You have to be confident about deciding your dog's fate, because your dog trusts you to make the right decisions.

THE HEARTBREAK AND HEROISM OF EUTHANASIA

In a perfect world, when a dog's time came, he would just lie down on a soft pillow, drift off to sleep, and never wake up. It actually happens that way for some dogs. But in most cases, the owner has to take an active role in bringing the dog's life to a peaceful end. Dogs usually know when it's time long before their owners are willing to admit it, and dogs face it without fear. You can see it in a dog's eyes. It may take us a little while longer to gather up the courage to allow nature to take its course.

When you take a puppy into your home, there's no way of knowing how or when the end will come. It could be five years, it could be fifteen. It could be sudden and unexpected or the merciful end to a long and lingering illness. It could be the end of natural aging or the result of an accident or sudden illness. Regardless of the reason for the dog's declining health, deciding on euthanasia is never easy. Stay at this game long enough and live with enough dogs, and euthanasia becomes something you expect to face, and probably more than once.

I look at it as my responsibility to end a dog's pain. That pain doesn't just have to be physical—it can be emotional, too. When Leilani was almost five, she suffered a slipped disk in her lower back. As I did with Freeway, I elected to have the surgery. After that, I never really knew if she was in pain. She was weak, and for the next couple of years, she gradually lost muscle control, but physical pain? I'll never know.

I do know that Leilani was in unbearable emotional pain. She was depressed and weak. It was hard for her to get up. She couldn't play. She couldn't run. She couldn't go up and down steps—she actually started falling down the steps. She was falling back into her own feces, and she got more unsteady all the time. I knew that she felt that she was not only failing herself, but me as well. She knew she wasn't the dog she used to be—and she wasn't the dog she wanted to be. I looked at it from her perspective, thought about what I would want for myself, and I knew what I had to do.

Still I hesitated, waiting for a miracle. The moment of truth came one day when I was trying to take pictures of Leilani with Donna's pup-pies. Leilani was the ultimate mom, and she loved puppies. Here she was, surrounded by those little guys, and she couldn't even lift her head up. I was trying to get her to look up for the pictures when I realized that she couldn't, that she was trying to tell me something. That's when I knew. After that, I spent hours and hours thinking about it. I had terrible fears that I would be out of the house and she'd fall and break her hip or something, and no one would be there and she'd be left lying alone in excruciating pain for hours, suffering.

I knew that she was already suffering, and I made the appointment. When I took her into the vet clinic, until the very end I was still worried about the decision I was making: Was I doing it out of convenience for myself, just because it would be easier for my own schedule? Was I doing it so I wouldn't have to worry about her when I was traveling? Was I doing it just to get that terrible image of her falling out of my mind?

On the day that I decided to have her put down, several people were in the waiting room of the animal hospital. Leilani wouldn't sit or lie down because she knew it would be too difficult for her to get up again. Then a woman asked me how old she was. Six and a half, I said. "Wow," said the woman, "she's in such good shape!" That made it worse.

Here I am in the waiting room about to put my dog down and having all these concerns about whether I'm doing the right thing, and somebody tells me what good shape my dog is in. It wasn't until after I had Leilani put down that I had the film of her and the puppies developed. That's when I knew I had done the right thing. When I saw her deep, expressive eyes in the pictures, I saw such sadness. She *was* trying to tell me something that day.

Sometimes the guilt can be overwhelming, and you're left feeling that you've failed the dog. I felt that way with Donna. Her loss was definitely the toughest for me. I never saw it coming. With my other Danes—Ryan, Leilani, and Freeway—I've had time to prepare. But Donna's end came suddenly and unexpectedly. She was only five and I was on the road promoting my first book. Donna was my soul mate and my protector, and when she needed me, I wasn't there for her. I also wasn't ready for what happened, and it was probably the hardest dog situation I'll ever have to deal with—at least I hope so.

It began with a cough, a chronic cough. Each time I came home, Donna would be coughing. I would take her into the veterinarian's office and she'd be put on antibiotics again, with the same pattern continuing

I felt terrible guilt when I put Leilani down, questioning myself daily about whether I had made the right decision. But after she was gone, I had the pictures I had taken of her with Donna's puppies developed, and when I saw the depression and sadness in her eyes, I knew I had made the right decision.

My advice to people who live with dogs: Keep your camera ready and take lots of pictures throughout your dog's life. When your dog passes on, it's such a comfort to be able to look back at pictures of the happy times and the memories you shared—like this one, when Donna, Jasmine, and Freeway demonstrated how well they followed the house rule that everyone must get along.

for several months. When I was on the road, which was a lot at that time, I'd call home to check up on the dogs, and the first thing I'd do was ask how Donna's cough was. "Oh, she's not coughing anymore," they'd tell me. "Don't worry—she's fine." But I'd come home, and she'd still be coughing.

The veterinarian was perplexed, too, so we discussed it and decided to do a noninvasive diagnostic procedure that would allow the doctor to take a look at what was going on with Donna's trachea and larynx. She was anesthetized so that the doctor could do the procedure. When Donna was coming to afterward, her trachea collapsed. It had atrophied so badly from all the coughing that it just couldn't handle the stress anymore.

The veterinarian made sure I was sitting down before he told me that Donna had died. I couldn't believe it, and I had to go into the operating room to see her for myself. When Donna's trachea collapsed, she went first into respiratory failure and then into heart failure, and then she died.

I had to know what the cough was, and I asked them to do an

autopsy. They found out that her trachea had been malformed, that something was probably getting caught in there and was aggravating the situation. They said it might have been corrected early on with surgery. Whatever it was, we found out too late, and we could have done nothing more for her.

After I lost Donna, I blamed myself. If I'd pursued her condition more actively from the beginning, if I'd trusted my instincts, I told myself, maybe I could have saved her. Over time, my guilt has subsided, and I have learned to see that Donna would never blame me for what happened. She knew then and she still knows that I did everything I could, and that I always kept her quality of life foremost in my mind.

GRIEVING

It's sad to think that some people out there have lost a dog only to be told by insensitive people, "It's only a dog." I'm thankful I've never had to hear that. "Love me, love my dog" is something I've always applied to my life. The people I surround myself with are understanding and accepting of my bond with my dogs. They would never make a callous comment to me like that after the death of one of my dogs. They know better.

After you live with a dog for eight, ten, fifteen years, you come to know that animal well—and he knows you. When you lose an old friend, especially one that has been a member of your family, you have to grieve. It's nothing to be embarrassed about. You lose your friend, you grieve, whether that friend has two legs or four.

You have to move at your own pace with grieving. You have to allow yourself to be sad, devastated, depressed. For a time, you might even feel angry. You may react by saying "I'm never going to get another dog" or "I'm never going to get attached to another dog again." That's natural. If you love dogs, though, you'll probably change your mind about that once you start feeling better. You'll begin to remember how much your dogs enriched your life. In the meantime, you'll probably go through the same steps of grieving that Elisabeth Kübler-Ross outlined for human grief: denial, anger, bargaining, depression, and acceptance. It's okay to feel this way for a dog, too.

Sometimes the grieving actually begins before the dog passes on. Sometimes the dog is old and has some health problems. You know there isn't much time left, but you don't know just how much. That's how it was with Ryan and Freeway when they were both still around. They were getting up there in age. I started reflecting on our lives together and how things would be without them. It was a way of preparing myself. People would ask me, "Isn't it sad knowing that they might not be around much longer?" Well, sure, but you get past that. You learn to concentrate on the positive. You'll still miss them, you know that, but you learn to reflect on what wonderful lives you have given them and that they have given you. You look at the bigger picture of how they've enriched your life. You cry, you mourn, you let yourself feel sad while you can still comfort each other. Then you help your dog prepare for a dignified end.

As of this writing, Freeway is still with me, but I of course miss my old buddy Ryan. We had so many false alarms that I had already started saying good-bye to Ryan long before it actually happened. He'd go through another major surgery, I'd be preparing myself, and then there he'd be, coming out of it with that same "up" attitude that he always had. One day I knew that attitude would change. I discussed this with friends who also loved Ryan, and it was good getting their feedback and reassurance that when it was time for me to make the decision, I would be doing it for the right reason: for Ryan. Each time I would feel that I was given some extra time with him, and I appreciated every extra minute of it. But no matter how much preparation you do, it's always hard to make the decision, and harder still to let go. You're never ready for the moment you realize that, no, he's not on his pillow at bedtime. He's not at the front door asking to go for a ride in the car. He's not lying at your feet under the table, and he never will be again, at least not in the physical, flesh-and-blood sense.

It's been several years since I lost Donna, but I still sometimes feel that I see her out of the corner of my eye around the house. Now that my home is filled with a whole new pack of dogs that Donna never knew—dogs that are learning the house rules and the ins and outs of being well-trained canine citizens—I still catch myself thinking about her when I'm around my other guys—comparing them, actually: "Oh,

Donna, my protector, was taken so suddenly from me that I still sometimes can't believe that she's gone. But I have plenty of wonderful memories of our time together, and I wouldn't trade those for anything. The benefits of living with dogs always outweigh the pain and the sadness. (Photo copyright © Kitten Rodwell)

Donna could do *that.*" "Well, if Donna were here, she'd be doing this." "Donna was more athletic." Some dogs never leave you. Actually, considering all the dogs I have met through the years who have left their permanent pawprints in my memory, I think that none of them have ever left me. That's just how dogs are.

Nevertheless, I felt alone when Donna died—more alone than I have with the passing of any of my other dogs. Donna was a kind of extension of me. I felt complete with her around, and she would always do whatever she could to be with me. She would even contort her body into unbelievable positions and make her way up to the top bunk of the RV we used to travel in, just so she could snuggle in with me. It seemed to mean everything to her to be with me, and the feeling was mutual. She was taken away from me too soon, and so suddenly. Maybe that's why her loss has been so profound.

If you live with more than one dog, you have to be aware that the other dogs in your house will go through their own grief when one of the family passes on. I definitely noticed this when I put Leilani down. The other guys knew that I had left with Leilani, but I didn't come back with her. I walked into the house, obviously upset, and there were Ryan and Freeway. They looked at me, and they could tell. They seemed to ask, "Hey, aren't you forgetting something?" But they knew. They were depressed for a few days after that—we all were. You have to let dogs grieve, too.

Dog lovers are lucky to be living in this day and age. Owners have always grieved for the loss of their dogs, but it used to be something they had to keep a secret. You don't have to do that anymore. We are evolving and learning that it's okay to grieve for a dog—and that we shouldn't minimize the grief of people who lose their pets. Books and support groups are available for people who are dealing with the loss of their pets. There are counselors who specialize in pet loss and even cards you can send to people whose pets have died. Plenty of people now openly discuss their grief about losing a pet (including me). Just look on the Internet sometime. You'll find pages and pages of tributes to dogs who have passed on—and lots of opportunities to talk about your own dogs. I have even done this on my own Web site, including a letter to my Donna about how much I miss her and how much she meant to me.

That's actually something I've done to help me get through the grief of losing one of my dogs. I write letters and I think about all the good times we had. I think of the good life and the value we gave each other. I focus on how this dog enriched my life, and how I wouldn't be the same person today if he or she hadn't been part of my family. That helps me get through it and convinces me that as sad as losing a dog can be, the joys of living with these animals make it all worthwhile. It makes me realize that I cannot live without dogs, and I never will. There will always be dogs in my life.

Dear Donna,

My baby. I'm so sorry. I feel so lost. I walk into a room looking around, wondering, "What am I doing? Why did I come in here?" My thoughts are flooded with the feel of your paw on my lap, remembering when you lifted my arm with your nose to give you pats and lovin'. My little girl, I can't believe you're gone. I expect someone to smack me on the back and say, "April Fools!"

You touched so many lives in your short four years of life. Like a comet, you imprinted on everyone's mind what a wonderful spirit you had. Your funny little games, your protective nature, your compassion and love. I miss you. I'm lost right now without you. I'm scared without you. You and Freeway have always been my protectors. I always felt safe by your side. I'll never forget when we were in Canada and you and Ryan Luke went chasing after the largest jackrabbit I've ever seen. You were only seven months old and I suddenly felt in my heart that you and Ryan Luke were gone. Fear rushed over me like an icy waterfall when I heard a train passing in the distance, in the direction you two went. But you brought our deaf father, Ryan Luke, back—out of breath, panting but with that devilish smile on your face in appreciation of the chase.

I'm angry at myself, the doctor, you for leaving me so soon. I wasn't ready for this, honey. I know you'll see your mommy (Leilani) soon, and you and Ryan White will be my guardian angels. You'll love him as I did and do. I love you and selfishly want you back. You're a very special spirit that will always be with me. So many lonely nights you kept me company, safe and warm. I already miss that because you know what a bed-hog your father Ryan Luke is.

You were so patient with your puppies, and any puppy who came into our house. Thank you. You were patient with me, too. I love you, Donna, and I'm missing you, but I look for you in the stars at night, my little comet, my little girl. My little Donna Doo.

Love, Daddy
April 1996

SEVENTEEN

THE CIRCLE OF LIFE

Now we come full circle, and a circle is really what it is. There is no true beginning and end to living with dogs. It is a continuing thread that carries us from one dog to the next. It connects every member of the family of dogs and all the people who love them. When you look at it this way, you see that things don't end with the death of a single dog. Death is just the end of one era and the beginning of the next. Once living with dogs is in your blood, you won't be able to live without one. For most of us, when one dog passes on, another will be waiting for us. Maybe not today, maybe not next month, maybe not even next year, but somewhere down the line, there will be another wonderful dog.

I guess that's why I love the sweet and sentimental movie *Old Yeller* so much. My approach to having dogs in my life is inspired by its focus on the circle. Although it's pretty brutal as far as the emotions it plays with, it ends with hope. Yeller sacrifices himself for his family, but he fathered a litter, so the circle keeps going. One incredible dog has enriched a family's life and is gone, and that family will now give its love to another dog who will carry on the canine tradition of enrichment. That's how we have to look at it in our own lives.

ANOTHER DOG?

When you lose your dog, your best friend, it's natural to believe that you will never again invest your love in another dog. It seems too painful. I have had that feeling myself in the past, and I got through it. It's all part of the grieving, which is a very personal process. But people have to make the "next dog" decision for themselves—first whether they are going to get another dog, and then when they might do it.

For some people the answer is to go out and begin the quest for a new dog or a new puppy right away. I can understand that need: you get used to having a dog around the house, and it just doesn't feel right without one. But I also understand the other viewpoint—that you have to wait a while to mourn and reflect on what your next step will be, and who your next dog will be. We all have to move at our own pace.

Probably the most important thing to understand when you start toying with the idea of the next dog is that you must move cautiously. Your grief may not help you to see things straight. A sudden-impulse buy is always dangerous. Remember what we have discussed in this book. We are back at the beginning of the circle, back to doing the homework, doing research, evaluating lifestyle, choosing wisely, and not rushing into anything. Once you've gotten through that maze, you're back again with the training, the socializing, the consistency, the getting acquainted—the incredible time commitment. Are you ready to go back to square one again?

Now is not the time to make any rash decisions. You have to realize that you're not going to replace your dog. Each dog has his or her own unique spirit, even when they are the same breed, even from the same litter. But when you lose one dog, you may feel that you have to get a new one exactly like the one you just lost. That's a natural reaction. That's what a lot of people look for. They've spent all this time and energy raising and training the animal, doing all these fun things with him, taking care of him in his old age, and then suddenly, he's gone. Just like that. So they run out and get a puppy, not even thinking about whether they have time right now to give the puppy all the attention and the endless training he needs. It ends up sad and confusing for everyone—especially the puppy, who does not have the same personality, the same temperament, the same habits and quirks. It's not fair to expect him to be somebody he's not. The new puppy is an individual, and he deserves to be treated that way.

AN EASIER TRANSITION

To emotionally ease your new puppy or dog into your home:

1. Don't compare him to or expect him to be a clone of the dog who came before.

2. Make a thoughtful, well-planned choice—no grief-driven impulses, please.

3. Enter the relationship with as few expectations as possible about your new pet's personality.

4. Respect your new pet for who he is.

5. Start obedience training as soon as possible to build your bond.

Expectations play an important role. The best thing to do when you're starting all over again, no matter what breed or mix of breeds you're starting over with, is to go into it with as few expectations as possible. You should have expectations about your behavior—you'll behave consistently and affectionately and attentively—but try not to have any expectations of who your new dog will be.

You should expect that you'll be having to change your entire household routine to accommodate the needs and patterns and maybe even the age of the new addition. The dog will have to learn the floor plan of your house, the house rules, and what you expect of his behavior—including where he should go to the bathroom and where he shouldn't, and his basic obedience commands. You also need to help him understand how you intend to communicate with him (consistent commands, immediate responses, and hand signals)—and be clear about it. Expect some rocky and even uncomfortable times in the beginning. It's not always going to be fun, and you're in big trouble if you think it will be.

You're naturally going to make some comparisons to your old friend, just as I still compare my dogs to Donna, but you'll have to resist that. In time, you'll start to appreciate the differences as well as the unique habits and personality of your new addition. Open yourself up to this, and give your new dog a chance to be who she is.

MY OWN NEXT DOGS

Throughout the writing of this book, over a year's time, I have experienced just about everything we've covered here with my own dogs: from choosing a puppy to raising a puppy to old age to euthanasia. Of course that's not unusual when you have a house full of dogs. A single year in the life of a household like mine always holds a variety of surprises from every stage of canine life.

My situation is different because there are always other dogs to comfort me when one is no longer there. But that doesn't mean I don't feel the loss or that I don't feel the gap that our lost family member has left behind, and I don't recommend that people fill their homes with dogs to dull the pain of pet loss. A multidog household can be a major challenge to manage, with unique responsibilities and rhythms. My situation is pretty successful, but it has been years in the making. It has evolved gradually, and so have my skills in making it a success. It's not something you can just jump into overnight.

I've known people with older dogs who tell me they want to get a puppy now so it won't be as hard for them when the older dog passes on. It really doesn't work that way, though. Bringing a new puppy in might make the older guy's remaining days a lot more stressful than they would be without an annoying little newcomer in the house. A puppy doesn't make it easier when the old guy does pass on. The puppy might even make you feel sadder.

Although my older dogs were used to young puppies coming into and going out of the house for years, it wasn't always successful, as our experience with Murphy illustrated. Nipper was nothing new or shocking to the boys—even though she was to me. Ryan and Freeway supported me through the tough times. Because of their own experiences with puppies, they taught me a thing or two, but not all older dogs have had their experience.

As I was thinking for this book about the many responsibilities of raising a new puppy, I was living with them every day, first with Nipper, then with Speedo and Mikey. I had to start with the challenge of choosing wisely, then work through all the problems and frustrations that come with a new puppy. At the same time, I was dealing with the failing health of my Ryan and the uncertain health of Freeway. And then one day, I was faced with the inevitable decision, and Ryan was gone. And then we were three: Freeway, Nipper, and me. And then we were four. And then we were five.

Freeway has tolerated this drastic demographic change as gracefully as my old gentleman has tolerated all the other changes in his life. Sure, he'd love to be an only dog, but he dealt with remarkable ease with his sudden transition from one old dog living with another old dog to one old dog living with three young dogs. Everyone respects Freeway—everyone always has—he just has that way about him. Speedo can be a little energetic at times, but she's never too hard on him and he lets her know when enough is enough. The two little terriers have sort of a hero-worship thing going with Freeway. They kind of look up to him as if he were Buddha. I think he likes that. Who wouldn't? As long as I still have plenty of attention for him, Freeway will be happy until the end. I'll see to that.

As for the newcomers, well, knock on wood, I consider them poster puppies of what this book is all about. We survived adolescence; everybody is following the all-important house rules that are the core of our household; and all three of them are thriving with the consistency, the attention, and the new routine we have established together. They also know that they can depend on me, the top dog, to be consistent and fair.

My three newcomers are anything but three peas in a pod. Each one is very different—even the two terriers. Nipper, of course, is the driven, little type-A powerhouse who thinks that even though she weighs only twelve pounds she can take on the world. The obedience training keeps her distracted and focused—and out of trouble. She's doing so well that she goes with me everywhere, and I'm a proud dad.

As for Border Terrier Mikey, I describe him as the marshmallow of the group. When you approach him, his head goes down and he just melts into the ground. He acts as if he's been beaten, but I know he hasn't. He's just a little actor who does "pathetic" very well. His personality is definitely living up to his breed's reputation as one of the mellower terriers. You pick him up and he buries his head in your chest and

Respect the older dog if you decide to introduce a new puppy to the family. Allow him his privacy and don't force him to be companion and mentor to the newcomers—it's up to him. At the same time, make sure the puppy has an out, too. She should be able to escape if the play gets too rough or aggressive for her.

just cuddles—very un-terrier-like. He plays great with the other dogs and has adjusted smoothly. He has even stood up for himself with Nipper, but he'll never be outgoing, which is fine with me. I have other dogs who fill that niche. They can't all be the centers of attention.

Speedo is the clown of the group, especially when we play fetch and she retrieves a long rope toy that happens to have a growling little Nipper hanging on to the other end. Speedo is sweet and clings to my side. She's sweet with the other dogs, too—even with Nipper. Speedo doesn't back down when Nipper, all twelve pounds of her, tries to push her around. Sixty-pound-plus Speedo stands up to her little terrier sister in a very gentle way, and Nipper backs down, which is good. Nipper

Once a dog house, always a dog house. I can't imagine living without a pack of dogs in my home—for me, they make a house a home. Deciding when and how to get a new dog, though, is a very personal decision, and you should take the leap only when you're good and ready.

needs to be put in her place—regularly. I've already seen how Speedo is destined to be the new family protector. Clown and protector: a nice combination.

Actually, it's a nice combination all around—a nice mix of personalities and a nice mix of breeds. They helped me to heal after the loss of Ryan, partly because they're all so different from him. I didn't want to compare my new guys with Ryan, which is one reason I decided to try out some new breeds. Another reason is that after all my years with my Danes, a breed I love, I needed a breather from some of the health problems that can affect the giant breeds. Because of this, I'm experiencing a dramatic change of atmosphere in my household that can happen when you bring breeds of different temperaments into your home. A single dog can change a household. It's a testament to the richness of personality that every dog is blessed with.

This is one way to avoid thinking you're going to replace an old friend with a new puppy or adult dog. If the new dog is of a different breed, you'll be less likely to expect that your new dog will be a clone of your old one. But after as many years as I have spent with Great Danes, I understand the desire to stick with the same breed. You have a positive experience, you love the breed, you can't imagine your house with anything but that breed. When you make a change, you have to do the necessary research and accept the differences.

For the first time I'm experiencing terrier terrorism, and it has brought a new spark into my house. Taking care of Nipper and Mikey has been a whole new experience for me, and given my success, these guys have really broadened my dog expertise. They have made me a more valuable spokesperson for responsible ownership, and I thank them for that. I travel all over the country with a Jack Russell Terrier, and people say she's an angel. But it didn't start out that way, and it's taken lots of time and effort to get beyond our troubles. First I had to take a crash course on terrier behavior and terrier parenting.

Ryan helped me with that. Through the years I've gotten accustomed to the fact that the dogs are the best teachers when I'm trying to understand them—and even myself sometimes. I was used to the steady temperaments of my working dogs and the attentive personalities of my herding dogs. When Nipper came along, there was a period of frustration, but then I agreed to look at it as a new adventure. I learned how terriers express emotions and how they, too, can be trained. I learned to work with their energy levels, their territoriality, and their feistiness. At times, I wasn't sure I was up to the task because it wasn't going the way I thought it should have. I was often guilty of comparing Nipper to my other dogs, but we got beyond that. Now I realize that this tiny dog has enriched my life more than I ever imagined she would in such a short time. I look forward to the new adventures that await us in the future.

All my dogs hold the potential for new adventures. Speedo is the one that may be destined for the show ring, aside from Nipper's obedience and agility aspirations, of course. I'm willing to learn from my past mistakes, and I don't intend to allow negative history to repeat itself. I pushed Freeway into the show ring long before he was ready—and then realized that if it had been left up to him, he would never have been ready. That's why I'm taking my time with Speedo. I decided that if I was going to get a Bouvier, I was going to do it right, and I spent a year researching her breed and the grooming requirements.

Part of doing it right means that I'll be paying close attention to see if Speedo even wants to be a show dog. If she does, we'll approach it slowly, and always with the sense of humor you have to have if you're going to enjoy anything together. In the meantime, I'm enjoying her sense of humor and her protective nature, and I'm enjoying training her. Sometimes she reminds me of a big, beautiful Great Dane I used to know named Donna—not that I'm making any comparisons or anything!

If Speedo does shine as a show dog, if she blossoms into a great example of her breed in health, temperament, and conformation, then my future might include playing assistant mom to a litter of tiny black Bouviers. But circumstances would have to be pretty extraordinary before I'd be willing to take that potentially heartbreaking step again. If it does happen, I've learned from my past mistakes. When I say playing mom, I mean playing mom. I would be there for Speedo and her pups every minute, every step of the way: no traveling, no entrusting any-one's well-being to someone else. When it comes to breeding, you have to be there. That's how it is with family.

THE CIRCLE, THE BOND

So here we are. As you can see, things change quickly when you live with dogs. It's never boring, and if you are bored, you're doing some-thing wrong. We influence our dogs, and they influence us. Every day they bring new surprises into our lives. Every day they're there for us, ready for adventure, ready to make new memories, and ready to give us new insights into ourselves. In the meantime, we're all works in progress. I look at my dogs that way because I've learned to look at myself that way, too.

Dogs keep us young.

Dogs keep us healthy.

Dogs keep us moving forward.

Dogs make us better people.

Think about it: we are the most important figures in our dogs' lives, which is a heavy responsibility. We must try every day to live up to that responsibility. When I'm out in public, dogs are what I notice first. Like most dog people, I have a radar that instantly detects any canine in my vicinity. I automatically spot the dogs, evaluate their situations, and often, I intervene. I worry about them, just as I worry about my own dogs. I'm encouraged when I see people playing with their dogs, enjoying their dogs, hugging them and kissing them. It's like watching great parents playing with their kids. You can see the wonderful bond between them, and it just makes you happy. It warms your heart.

I get that feeling when I see people playing with their dogs, treating their dogs as members of their family, with the confidence that they can be out in public playing, going places together, sharing experiences, honoring each other with open affection. Those people and those dogs trust each other, and they love being in each other's company. They are family. They are the circle. You can see it in the bond they share, the bond that made me want to write this book, the bond I wish for every human and every dog, from birth to old age, and everywhere in between.

Losing your old friend is sad, but when you go to meet a litter of puppies in search of a new companion, your faith can be renewed by the invigorating circle of life that is at the heart of the great family of dogs.

These are only some of my favorite books and videos, which I'd like to share with you. Many other books and videos are out there. Don't limit yourself!

DOG TRAINING

These books and tapes all feature positive training, which is the direction I'm going in:

Karen Pryor, *Don't Shoot the Dog: The New Art of Teaching and Training.* (Bantam Books, 1995.) This is on the top of my list for a reason: it will help in training your four-legged canine friends as well as your two-legged human friends.

Terry Ryan, *The Tool Box for Remodeling Your Problem Dog.* (Howell Book House, 1998.) Wonderful basics, even if you started out on the wrong foot, and ways to start out on the right feet.

Gary Wilkes, *Click and Treat Training.* This kind of training is great fun for you and your dog, and the results are only as limited as your imagination.

Karen Pryor, *Clicker Magic.* (J&K Publications, 1998.) This is a great introduction to clicker training.

Ian Dunbar, *Sirius Puppy Training.* Good basics.

Ted Turner (not Jane Fonda's husband), Patty Ruzzo, Leslie Nelson, *The Proof Positive Series.* This is a five-tape series, expensive and rather advanced, but rock solid in training theories and methods to challenge the brave at heart. A must for the true trainer.

THE CANINE ATHLETE

Joan Payne, *Flying High: The Complete Book of Flyball.* (KDB Publishing, 1996.)

Jacqueline Parkin, *Flyball Training Start to Finish.* (Alpine Publications, 1996.)

Ruth Hobday, *Agility Fun the Hobday Way.*

HEALTH CARE

Carlson and Griffin, *The Dog Owner's Home Veterinary Handbook.* (Howell Book House, 1992.) Good to keep around when things don't seem quite right for your four-legged buddy.

Linda Tellington-Jones, *The Tellington T-Touch.* The famous T-touch; this will help you and your dog relieve stress in both of your lives. Give it a chance—it works!

CONFORMATION

The AKC's *Complete Dog Book.* (Macmillan, 1998.) Read and study the breed standards. That and attending dog shows will help you choose your purebred dog in a smart manner.

BREEDING

Holst, *Canine Reproduction: A Breeder's Guide.* (Alpine Publications, 1985.) From conception to whelping, all your questions will be answered. Read it first and you may have a change of heart about breeding your dog and opt for spaying or neutering instead.

Herbert Richards, *Dog Breeding for Professionals.* (TFH Publications, 1989.) Good photo references for what to expect. Read this and you really *will* change your mind . . . possibly.

GRIEVING

Herbert A. Neiburg, *Pet Loss.*

Martin Scott Kosins, *Maya's First Rose: Diary of a Very Special Love.* (Berkley Publishing Group, 1996.) This last one is a bit extreme but very heartfelt.

ACKNOWLEDGMENTS

Eric Marcus, co-author of *Breaking the Surface*, introduced me to Jed Mattes, my literary agent, who got us together with an incredible editor, Mitchell Ivers, who in turn introduced me to Betsy Siino, whose knowledge of animals has made this book what it is.

The catalyst was a Wire Fox Terrier, Finnegan, who's dad happens to be Mitchell Ivers. Because of Mitchell's love for his little boy, always wanting the best for him, and knowing my passion for canine care, the seed for this book was planted.

I have learned so much from a group of friends who share my feelings and concerns for the well-being of our four-legged families: San Dee Slagle and Maryann Wilson, from whom I got my first harlequin Great Dane, Jill Ferrera, who shared her extensive knowledge of the breed with me, Kathleen Mallery, an expert on Corgis and Labs; and Greg Castillo and David Bueno, my Rhodesian Ridgeback's extended family.

And my deepest gratitude to the many trainers I've worked with and will continue to learn from.

Greg Louganis

This book could not have been completed without the support of some very dedicated souls. First—and always—thank you, thank you, thank you to my ever-inspiring home team: my Michael, my Christopher, and my little, old dog Rebel. Thanks, too, to oh-so patient agent, Jed Mattes, who regardless of the challenge, never ceases to amaze with his sense of humor and his focus on the bright side. Mitchell Ivers, I salute you for your profound editorial instincts, your genuine passion for dogs, and the respect you showed this project. I thank you, Mordecai Siegal, for that first introduction and your faith in me, and you Audrey Pavia, for being cheerleader/confidante as I juggled my work with deadlines and a 3,000-mile move. I am indebted, as well, to my darling Jacie for the peace of mind she afforded me during those treacherous journeys through El Niño's fury. And finally: thanks Greg, for the love you show your dogs and your desire to share that love for the good of dogs everywhere. It's been a pleasure.

Betsy Sikora Siino

GREG LOUGANIS is a four-time Olympic gold-medal diving champion. He lives in Malibu, California, and he raises and trains harlequin Great Danes, a champion Jack Russell Terrier, a Bouvier des Flandres, a Border Terrier, and a best-in-breed Rhodesian Ridgeback.

BETSY SIKORA SIINO, a director of the Dog Writers Association of America, and an award-winning author, has written articles for *Dog Fancy, Dogs USA, Horse Illustrated, The AKC Gazette, The Los Angeles Times,* and *Pet Health News,* as well as fifteen books. She lives in Orchard Park, New York.